Relocating to San Francisco
and the Bay Area

Relocating to San Francisco

and the Bay Area

Everything You Need to Know
Before You Go—and Once You Get There!

Cristina Guinot

PRIMA PUBLISHING

© 1996 by Cristina Guinot

PRIMA PUBLISHING and colophon are registered trademarks of Prima Communications, Inc.

Maps © 1996 by Nathaniel Levine

LIBRARY OF CONGRESS CATALOGING-IN-PUBLICATION DATA

Guinot, Cristina.
    Relocating to San Francisco and the Bay Area: everything you need to know before you go—and once you get there! / by Cristina Guinot.
        p. cm.
    Includes index.
    ISBN 0-7615-0249-1
    1. San Francisco (Calif.)—Guidebooks. 2. San Francisco Bay Area (Calif.)—Guidebooks. 3. Moving, Household—California—San Francisco—Handbooks, manuals, etc. 4. Moving, Household—California—San Francisco Bay Area—Handbooks, manuals, etc. I. Title.
    F869.S33G85 1996
    917.94'610453—dc20   96-11825
                                                                                                  CIP

        97 98 99 00 AA 10 9 8 7 6 5 4
    Printed in the United States of America

HOW TO ORDER:
Single copies may be ordered from Prima Publishing, P.O. Box 1260BK, Rocklin, CA 95677; telephone (916) 632-4400. Quantity discounts are also available. On your letterhead, include information concerning the intended use of the books and the number of books you wish to purchase.

VISIT US ONLINE AT **http://www.primapublishing.com**

Writing this book and seeing it published are great milestones in my life.
I'd like to thank the following:

My agent, Karen Nazor, for her support and friendship;
Laurie Parres for all her positive words of encouragement;
Stuart Lerner for his helpful assistance while I researched the book;
my mother for her support throughout my writing program and this project;
and God for making this book part of the plan.

CONTENTS

Maps   IX–XIII
Introduction   XV

•••••▶ **PART 1**
Making the Move
Chapter 1   *The Cost of Moving*   3
Chapter 2   *Planning the Move*   9
Chapter 3   *Where to Stay When You Arrive*   17

•••••▶ **PART 2**
Finding a Place to Call Home
Chapter 4   *How to Find a Place to Live*   41
Chapter 5   *Where to Find a Place to Live*   51

•••••▶ **PART 3**
Job Hunting
Chapter 6   *Temporary and Permanent Job Placement*   125
Chapter 7   *More Job-Finding Ideas*   135

•••••▶ **PART 4**
Settling In
Chapter 8   *Getting Involved in the City*   151
Chapter 9   *Something for Nothing*   177
Chapter 10   *Things to Do on the Weekends*   185

Appendix 1   *Year-Round Calendar of Events*   195
Appendix 2   *Numbers to Know*   199
Appendix 3   *Local Government*   205
Appendix 4   *Schools*   211

INDEX   217

CALIFORNIA

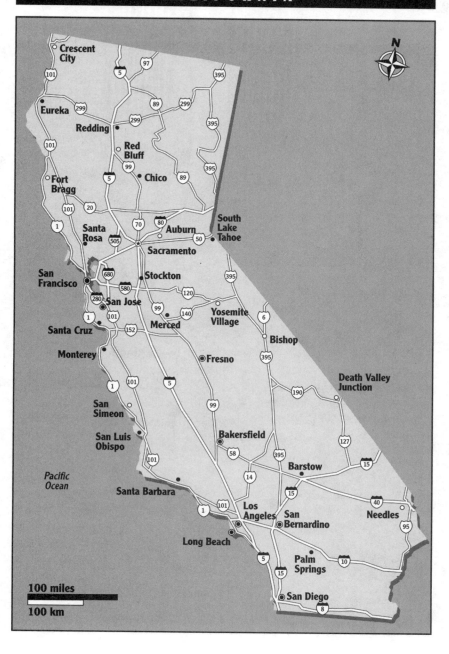

N

Crescent
City

Eureka
299
299
89
299
Redding
299
97
5
395
395
395

101

Red
Bluff
99
Chico
89
395

Fort
Bragg
5

101
20
101

1
Santa
Rosa
505
70
80
Auburn
50
South
Lake
Tahoe

Sacramento

San
Francisco
680
Stockton
395

580
120

280
San Jose
99
140
Yosemite
Village
6

1
101
152
Merced
Bishop
Santa Cruz

Monterey
395

Fresno

Death Valley
Junction
San
Simeon
5
190

San Luis
Obispo
99
127

101
Bakersfield
58
395
Barstow
15

Pacific
Ocean
14
15

Santa Barbara
101
40
Needles

1
Los
Angeles
San
Bernardino
95

Long Beach

5
15
Palm
Springs
10

100 miles

100 km

San Diego
8

BAY AREA

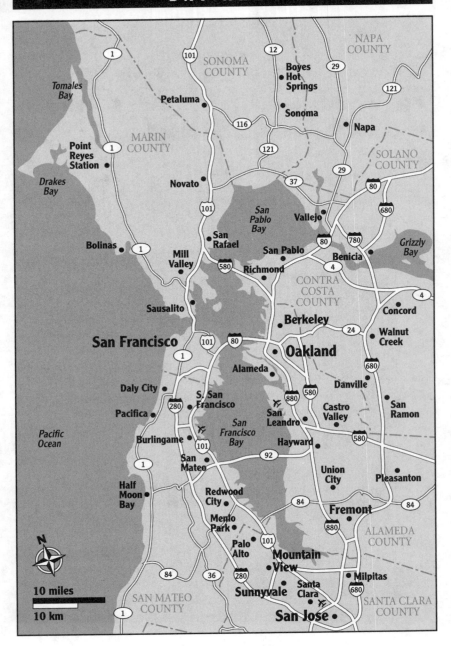

BAY AREA REGIONAL TRANSIT MAP

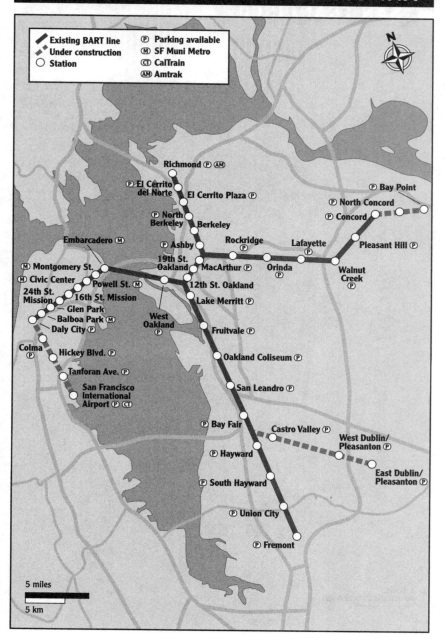

Legend:
- Existing BART line
- Under construction
- ○ Station
- Ⓟ Parking available
- Ⓜ SF Muni Metro
- Ⓒ CalTrain
- Ⓐ Amtrak

N

Richmond Ⓟ Ⓐ

Ⓟ El Cerrito del Norte

El Cerrito Plaza Ⓟ

Ⓟ Bay Point

Ⓟ North Concord

Ⓟ North Berkeley

Ⓟ Concord

Berkeley

Embarcadero Ⓜ

Ⓟ Ashby

Rockridge Ⓟ

Lafayette

Pleasant Hill Ⓟ

Ⓜ Montgomery St.

19th St. Oakland

MacArthur Ⓟ

Orinda Ⓟ

Ⓜ Civic Center

Powell St. Ⓜ

12th St. Oakland

Walnut Creek Ⓟ

24th St. Mission

16th St. Mission

Lake Merritt Ⓟ

Glen Park

West Oakland Ⓟ

Balboa Park Ⓜ

Daly City Ⓟ

Fruitvale Ⓟ

Colma Ⓟ

Hickey Blvd. Ⓟ

Oakland Coliseum Ⓟ

Tanforan Ave. Ⓟ

San Leandro Ⓟ

San Francisco International Airport Ⓟ Ⓒ

Ⓟ Bay Fair

Castro Valley Ⓟ

West Dublin/ Pleasanton Ⓟ

Ⓟ Hayward

East Dublin/ Pleasanton Ⓟ

Ⓟ South Hayward

Ⓟ Union City

Ⓟ Fremont

5 miles

5 km

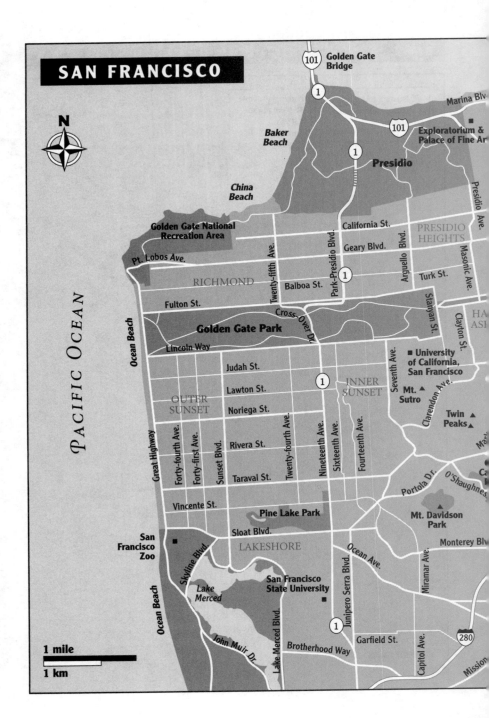

SAN FRANCISCO

101 Golden Gate Bridge

1

Marina Blv

Baker Beach

101

Exploratorium & Palace of Fine Ar

1

Presidio

China Beach

Golden Gate National Recreation Area

California St.

PRESIDIO HEIGHTS

Pt. Lobos Ave.

Geary Blvd.

Presidio Ave.

RICHMOND

Twenty-fifth Ave.

Balboa St.

Park-Presidio Blvd.

1

Arguello Blvd.

Turk St.

Masonic Ave.

Fulton St.

Cross-Over Dr.

Stanyan St.

Ocean Beach

Golden Gate Park

Clayton St.

HA ASI

Lincoln Way

University of California, San Francisco

Judah St.

Seventh Ave.

Mt. ▲ Sutro

Lawton St.

1

INNER SUNSET

Clarendon Ave.

OUTER SUNSET

Noriega St.

Twin ▲ Peaks ▲

Great Highway

Forty-fourth Ave.

Forty-first Ave.

Sunset Blvd.

Rivera St.

Twenty-fourth Ave.

Nineteenth Ave.

Sixteenth Ave.

Fourteenth Ave.

Ma

Taraval St.

Portola Dr.

O'Shaughnes

Ca

Vincente St.

Pine Lake Park

Mt. Davidson Park

San Francisco Zoo

Skyline Blvd.

Sloat Blvd.

LAKESHORE

Ocean Ave.

Monterey Blv

Lake Merced

San Francisco State University

Junipero Serra Blvd.

Miramar Ave.

Ocean Beach

Lake Merced Blvd.

John Muir Dr.

Brotherhood Way

1

Garfield St.

Capitol Ave.

280

Mission

PACIFIC OCEAN

1 mile
1 km

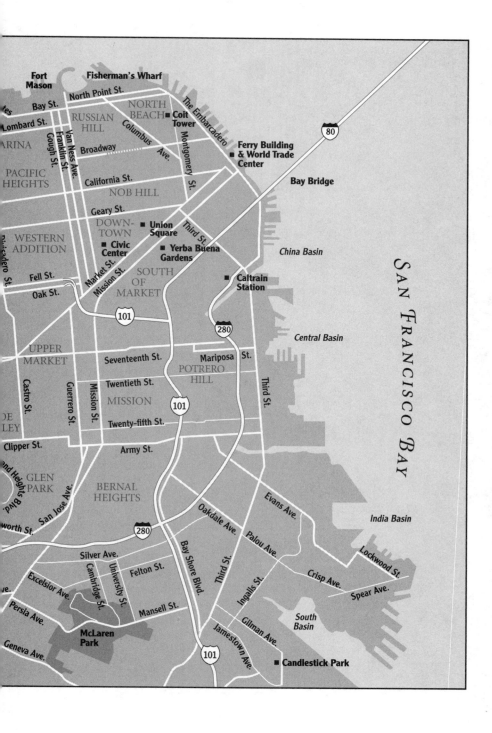

Fort Mason

Fisherman's Wharf

North Point St.

NORTH BEACH

Bay St.

Lombard St.

RUSSIAN HILL

Columbus Ave.

Coit Tower

The Embarcadero

80

Ferry Building & World Trade Center

Bay Bridge

Van Ness Ave.

Franklin St.

Gough St.

Broadway

MARINA

PACIFIC HEIGHTS

California St.

NOB HILL

Montgomery St.

Geary St.

DOWN-TOWN

Union Square

Third St.

WESTERN ADDITION

Civic Center

Yerba Buena Gardens

China Basin

Fell St.

Market St.

Mission St.

SOUTH OF MARKET

Caltrain Station

Oak St.

101

280

Central Basin

UPPER MARKET

Seventeenth St.

Mariposa St.

POTRERO HILL

SAN FRANCISCO BAY

Castro St.

Guerrero St.

Mission St.

Twentieth St.

MISSION

101

Third St.

Twenty-fifth St.

Clipper St.

Army St.

DE LEY

GLEN PARK

San Jose Ave.

BERNAL HEIGHTS

Evans Ave.

India Basin

Heights Blvd.

worth St.

280

Oakdale Ave.

Palou Ave.

Lockwood St.

Silver Ave.

Bay Shore Blvd.

Third St.

Ingalls St.

Crisp Ave.

Spear Ave.

Excelsior Ave.

Cambridge St.

University St.

Felton St.

Persia Ave.

Mansell St.

Gilman Ave.

South Basin

ve.

McLaren Park

Jamestown Ave.

Geneva Ave.

101

Candlestick Park

S A N   F R A N C I S C O   is a great place to call home. It's physically beautiful, culturally and historically stimulating, and full of individuality and diversity, making it an interesting and exciting place to live. The time is better than ever to be a part of the San Francisco community. Since the 1989 Loma Prieta earthquake, the city has gone through a renaissance that includes development of the South of Market area and Embarcadero waterfront, conversion of the Presidio military base into a national park, and improvements of neighborhoods and historic buildings that were near collapse.

South of Market has experienced tremendous positive growth with the opening of the new Museum of Modern Art as well as Yerba Buena Gardens. Along the Embarcadero waterfront, where the freeway used to block magnificent views of the bay, now stands a double row of 65 Canary Island date palms running from the Ferry Building down to China Basin. This section also has a street car system under construction that will travel two and a half miles along the bay from China Basin to Fisherman's Wharf. The 200-year-old Presidio military base has turned over its 1,480 acres to the management of the National Park System. Now this open space is enjoyed by residents and tourists alike. Besides outdoor recreation such as hiking and biking, there are more than 500 historically significant buildings to visit that represent every major period of U.S. military history since 1853.

CITY TIMELINE

1769   San Francisco Bay is discovered by Sergeant Jose Ortega of the Portola Serra Exhibition.

1772   San Francisco Bay shores are explored by land by Captain Pedro Fages and Father Juan Crespi.

1776   Presidio of San Francisco and Mission Dolores are founded.

1833   The Pueblo of San Francisco is duly erected and constituted a municipal corporation.

1834   Elections are held to elect municipal officers.
        Boundaries are assigned to the Pueblo of San Francisco by Governor Figueroa.

1835   First building is erected at 823-37 Grant Avenue.

1840   Monterey becomes the capital of California.

1845   Mary Elizabeth Davis is the first Anglo-Saxon child born in San Francisco.

1846   Entrance to the San Francisco Bay is named *Golden Gate*.
        First public school is opened.

The most convincing reason for being part of the San Francisco community is a certain pride residents have about their city and a standard of excellence maintained and enjoyed by both residents and tourists. For example, San Francisco voters are more likely to approve a measure that will upgrade and retrofit its more-than-century-old Steinhart Aquarium than balk at the costs and have it closed forever. Other improvements in the works include upgrading city hall and the opera house, opening a new main library, and redesigning the old library's historic building to accommodate the city's world-renowned Asian Art Museum. These are all big improvement projects going on in the city, but what's really neat are the neighborhood improvements. Communities that were once teetering on decay have been brought back life by ambitious San Franciscans who weren't afraid to move in and improve the area with home renovations and small businesses. This is all proof that the people of San Francisco care for and take care of their city. While we hear of other metropolitan centers across the U.S. wasting away, constant improvement seems to be going on in "The City."

The San Francisco Bay Area refers to nine counties: Alameda, Contra Costa, Marin, Napa, San Francisco, San Mateo, Santa Clara, Solano, and Sonoma. San Francisco County is the smallest county not only in the Bay Area, but also in California, measuring 128.76 square miles. San Francisco city is 46.4 square miles laid out over 40 hills reaching heights of almost 1,000 feet, lending to some amazing views. It also has some very comfortable and consistent weather with temperatures averaging about 60°F. Of course, the type of weather conditions you experience depends on where you are in the city. The hilly terrain is the reason for the different microclimates one will find. When it's sunny and warm in the Mission neighborhood, it could also be cold and foggy in the Sunset district.

1847	San Francisco's first newspaper, the *California Star*, publishes its first issue. San Francisco is renamed from Yerba Buena.
1848	First Commercial Bank is established in San Francisco. Gold is discovered in Coloma, California. First shipload of Chinese immigrants arrives in San Francisco. First post office opens at Clay and Pike Streets.
1850	California Exchange opens. Legislature creates bay region counties: San Francisco, Contra Costa, Marin, Santa Clara, Sonoma, Solano, and Napa. San Francisco County government established. City of San Francisco charter goes into effect. First San Francisco city directory is published.
1851	Fire destroys entire city except for submerged hulk of ship. Chamber of Commerce organized. State capital moves from Monterey to Vallejo.
1852	First legal execution, a hanging, takes place on Russian Hill.

Following are some interesting statistics about San Francisco:

Size	46.4 square miles
Population	739,600 (as of 1993)
Tallest building	Transamerica Pyramid (853 feet, 48 stories)
Oldest street	Grant Avenue
Steepest street	Filbert Street from Hyde to Leavenworth Streets (31.5% grade), and Parnassus Avenue to Arguello Boulevard (31.5% grade)
Longest street	Mission Street (7.29 miles)
Widest street	Van Ness Avenue (125 feet)
Narrowest street	DeForest Way (4.5 feet)
Geographical center	East side of Grandview Avenue, between Alvarado and 23rd Streets
Highest hill	Mount Davidson (938 feet)
Crookedest street	Lombard Street, between Hyde and Leavenworth Streets, (eight turns)
City colors	Black and gold
City flower	Dahlia
City tree	Monterey cypress, located in front of McLaren Lodge at Kennedy Drive near Fell Street in Golden Gate Park
San Franciscan's most common fear	Gephydrophobia (fear of crossing bridges)

1853	California Academy of Science is organized. The first city street signs go up. State capital moves from Vallejo to Benicia.
1854	Principal streets are lighted with coal gas for the first time. First U.S. Mint opens. Lighthouse on Alcatraz is established. Old St. Mary's Church is dedicated. State capital moves from Benicia to its current home of Sacramento.
1856	San Francisco city and county are consolidated.
1858	San Francisco Water Works Company begins operation.
1859	Present seal of the City of San Francisco adopted.
1860	First Pony Express rider arrives in San Francisco from St. Joseph, Missouri. Service begins on the city's first street railway from the foot of Market Street to the Mission.
1863	The famous Cliff House opens.
1866	Equal rights to all men without distinction as to color is adopted as a resolution.

San Francisco is a highly cultural city with world-renowned and respected opera, symphony, and ballet companies, a new modern art museum and main library, and the remodeled Palace of the Legion of Honor. Because of the city's open attitude and support for the arts, there is fine art, theater, and performances available here that are not found anywhere else.

For all its magnificence, San Francisco had a humble beginning. It was discovered by accident in 1769 by an overland expedition of Spanish soldiers from Mexico trying to reach Monterey. This discovery occurred more than 200 years after the founding of California. It is believed the thick fog obscured the narrow entrance to the bay, making its appearance nonexistent. At first San Francisco was mostly inhabited by Christian missionaries, until 1846, when the Gold Rush brought some 40,000 people from all backgrounds and walks of life to the city. Most of these people stayed on and even today the city has a strong multicultural population.

The greatest feature about living in San Francisco is the sense of community one feels, a feature almost unheard of in big city living. This sense of community is evident in the over 30 neighborhoods that make up the city, many of them with their own neighborhood newspaper and neighborhood groups. There is also a very active nonprofit network that helps and supports the poor, homeless, and disenfranchised. If there is a need in the city, there is most likely an organization to fill it. San Francisco is an easy city to move to because of all the support networks already in place. This support includes many apartment- and job-finding agencies as well as countless social and professional organizations. Even if you don't know a soul, there are numerous resources to help you get settled and start your new life.

This book is divided into four parts that will further ease your transition to the Bay Area. The first part guides you through all stages of the move with tips on

1868	SPCA is formed.
1869	Free postal delivery formally inaugurated.
1870	Legislation to create Golden Gate Park is approved.
1873	Postcards sold for the first time in San Francisco. Ground broken for world's first cable street railroad.
1875	Pacific Stock Exchange formally opens. Native Sons of the Golden West is organized. Palace Hotel opens.
1878	Hastings Law School is founded. San Francisco's first telephone book is issued.
1879	Public library opens in rented quarters.
1880	The New State Constitution of California goes into full effect.
1887	Snow covers San Francisco.
1891	Stanford University is chartered.

planning, packing, and finding a place to stay when you first arrive. 1
part provides detailed information on apartment-searching technique
vices. Also included is a detailed guide to the services of various neighоогпоoos.
The third part gears you up for the job search with information about job lines,
temp services, and more. Once you've settled in, the fourth part lists a wide variety
of activities and organizations that will get you involved in your new city.

As you read more about San Francisco and the Bay Area, you'll soon agree it is a
wonderful place to move; many job opportunities, attractive neighborhoods, and
social and cultural activities await. Enjoy!

· ·

WORLD WIDE WEB RESOURCES

Bay Area Network Companion
(http://www.milk.com:80/bay-guide/)
is a comprehensive guide to Web resources in the San Francisco Bay Area.

BayNet World, Inc.
(http://www.baynet.com)
contains Bay Area information such as employment, demographics, real estate,
associations, and more.

Best of San Francisco
(http://www.creativegroup.com/bestofsf/)
This home page is titled Best of San Francisco, though the ratings system is not
revealed. The impression is of a school home page recognizing businesses that
provided financial support.

1892	John Muir establishes Sierra Club and becomes lifetime president. First buffalo born in Golden Gate Park.
1896	Sutro Baths open.
1897	Ferry Building opens.
1898	New city charter approved authorizing municipal acquisition and ownership of public utilities.
1899	New city hall opens after 29 years of construction.
1900	Bubonic plague hits San Francisco.
1904	End of bubonic plague epidemic.
1906	Great earthquake of 1906. Fire destroys large part of city. First prisoners moved from city jail to Alcatraz.
1907	A. P. Giannini, Bank of America founder, introduces branch banking.
1910	Angel Island opens West Coast immigration station.
1911	San Francisco Symphony Orchestra is formed.

San Francisco Bay Area and Beyond
(http://www.hyperion.com/ba/)
Established in 1994, this home page lists Bay Area information on attractions, employment, sports, and out-of-town activities, to name a few.

San Francisco City Link
(http:/banzai.neosoft.com/citylink/san-francisco/default.html)
has information on what to see, what to do, where to stay, where to eat, and where to shop.

San Francisco City Span
(http://www.ci.sf.ca.us/)
is subtitled "Bridging Government and Citizens through Technology." This site has city government department information such as Recreation and Parks and the Arts Commission.

San Francisco Gay
(http://www.coming-n-going.com/)
is the city's gay home page, with such categories as cruising, activities, and AIDS.

San FranZiskGo! Presents: The Ultimate Resource for San Francisco
(http://www.mediaband.com/sf.html)
is a good resource for San Francisco information on art, bookstores, businesses, events, and more.

Z San Francisco
(http://www.zpub.com/sf/)
lists many San Francisco resources and information about neighborhoods, jobs, history, weather, and more.

• •

1912	Women vote for the first time in San Francisco.
1914	Stockton Street Tunnel is completed.
1915	Civic Auditorium is dedicated. Alexander Graham Bell speaks from New York to Thomas Watson in San Francisco, making it the first transcontinental conversation by phone.
1917	Nonstop distance flight record set by Katherine Stinson, who flew 610 miles from San Diego to San Francisco in 9 hours and 10 minutes.
1918	Ferry Building siren sounded for the first time.
1921	The De Young Museum in Golden Gate Park opens.
1923	President Warren Harding dies at Palace Hotel. Steinhart Aquarium in Golden Gate Park opens.
1924	Palace of the Legion of Honor is dedicated.

1925	Kezar Stadium in Golden Gate Park opens.
	Embarcadero subway opens.
	Harding Memorial Park opens.
1929	New pedestrian traffic signal system is inaugurated.
1932	Dedication of Stern Grove.
	Opera House dedicated with performance of *La Tosca*.
1933	Coit Tower is dedicated.
	Alcatraz Island becomes a federal prison.
	San Francisco Ballet debuts.
1936	Bay Bridge opens to traffic.
1937	Golden Gate Bridge is dedicated.
	San Francisco Chronicle newspaper begins publishing Herb Caen column.
1939	Aquatic Park is dedicated.
1941	Cow Palace opens.
1954	Joe DiMaggio and Marilyn Monroe marry at city hall.
	San Francisco International Airport opens.
1964	Cable cars are declared a national landmark.
1967	Summer of Love in Haight-Ashbury.
1971	McDonald's opens first restaurant in city.
1974	Muni's "Fast Pass" is initiated.
1978	Dianne Feinstein elected as the first female mayor of San Francisco.
	Moscone/Milk assassinations.
1980	Last day of home milk delivery in San Francisco.
	Davies Symphony Hall opens.
1989	7.1 earthquake hits Bay Area.
1991	Oakland Hills fire is the largest urban wildland fire in U.S. history.
	Former Police Chief Frank Jordan is elected mayor.
1992	Rodney King verdict riots occur in downtown San Francisco.
1996	Willie Brown, San Francisco's first black mayor, is elected.

PART 1

MAKING THE MOVE

SAN FRANCISCO CONVENTION & VISITORS BUREAU PHOTO BY SANDOR BALANTONI

CHAPTER ONE

The Cost of Moving

MOVING ISN'T CHEAP, but that shouldn't prevent you from looking for adventure, expanding your horizons, seeking your fortune, or whatever is motivating you to make the move. I could lecture you on accumulating six months of savings and having a job lined up before you go, but let's face it—life for most of us doesn't work that way. This chapter will help you take a realistic look at the costs of moving. It is possible to move with $500 in your pocket, but that means you will need to start working right away. It also means you're not going to have enough money to get your own apartment. But that's okay. Living with roommates is like having instant friends in a new city. You'll also have to put fun things that cost money, like going out to dinner, on the back burner until you can catch up financially. It should be no surprise that the more money you have, the easier your move. But don't let a little thing like money prevent you from moving on to greener pastures.

So what are the costs of moving? I've divided them up into three categories: big costs, setting-up costs, and daily living costs.

BIG COSTS

Big costs are just what they mean—costs that can really deplete your savings. These include the following:

- **Movers** These are the guys that pull up in the big truck and do all the grunt work. You may be in a financial position to hire professional movers to pack and move your stuff to San Francisco.

- **Moving van rental** For do-it-yourself movers, moving van rentals aren't cheap but are a considerable savings over hiring professional movers.

- **Short-term accommodations** Chapter 3, "Where to Stay When You Arrive," discusses short-term accommodations that may seem pricey but cost less than staying at a basic hotel. Many also have kitchenettes or meal service, which can help justify the cost.

- **UPS/mail delivery of boxes**   If you don't feel like renting a moving van, you can cram as many of your belongings in your car or suitcase (depending on how you will be traveling) and pack the rest away for UPS delivery. Besides UPS and U.S. Postal Service charges, you may have to buy packing materials like boxes, tape, and bubble wrap.

- **Transportation to your destination**   If you're driving, you'll have to pay for gas, tolls, car inspections, and any unexpected mechanical problems that arise. If you're flying, consider the price of an airplane ticket. If you're taking the train, it will probably cost you as much as flying.

- **Monthly storage fees**   If you need to store your furniture and boxes until you find an apartment, take into account monthly storage fees.

You'll have to do your own research on these big costs (except for the estimated costs of short-term accommodations, which are provided in Chapter 3), because they will depend on your personal circumstances.

SETTING-UP COSTS
Setting-up costs are the expenses to set up your new life in San Francisco. The following are necessary financial considerations when moving:

- **Apartment deposits**   Most landlords or apartment managers will charge an application/credit check fee, the last month's rent, and a security deposit. Review Chapter 5, "Where to Find a Place to Live," to get an idea of rental costs in different areas of the city.

- **Apartment broker fees**   If you join an apartment- or roommate-finding agency, a fee will be involved. Review Chapter 4, "How to Find a Place to Live," to get an idea of agency fee amounts.

- **Necessary furniture**   If you have no furniture, you'll need to buy a bed and some other necessary pieces.

- **Services deposits**   Once you find your apartment, you'll need to set up electric, phone, and gas services, which all require deposits.

- **Auto registration/insurance**   You'll have to register your car in the state of California, which involves a safety check and smog inspection. If your car doesn't pass, then getting it up to standards could cost several hundred dollars. Also, when you notify your insurance company of your new address, your rates may change.

- **Memberships**   This could include professional organizations you join to help you find work, a health club membership, or a social organization to get you involved in the city.

DAILY LIVING COSTS

Day-to-day living costs are those costs that make you say "Where did all my money go?" It's that two-dollar latte and the one-dollar diet cola. As you may have experienced, these daily living costs can really add up. If you buy your lunch every day, for example, plan on spending around $6 for a sandwich; multiply that by five days, and that's $30 a week.

- **Food**   This includes trips to the grocery store, your morning coffee at a café, the afternoon snack at McDonald's when you're job hunting, and whatever your eating habits necessitate.

- **Transportation**   Think about your transportation needs. These could include bus fares, monthly bus passes, cab fares, BART (Bay Area Rapid Transit) fares out to the East Bay, ferry service to Marin or Oakland, and car rentals. Remember that San Francisco is a city that you can walk and bike in, and those modes of transportation are free.

- **Laundry**   As much as you'd like to overlook laundry, it must be done. Many neighborhood laundromats and wash-and-fold services are available. If you're looking for a job that requires a professional look, take into account dry cleaning charges.

- **Photocopies/computer rental**   Part of your daily expenses may include services to help you with your job search. You might need to make copies of resumes and letters of recommendation for prospective employers. If you don't have a computer, you may have to visit a Krishna Copy Center or Kinko's to lease a computer by the hour. These charges will pay off in the long run because they are an investment toward getting a good job.

There are so many other details that will be specific to your situation. To get a clearer idea of your spending habits, keep an expense diary for a week or two to track where your money goes. This will help you figure out how to save money by making some temporary lifestyle changes. You might find a few surprises, like that the café mocha you drink every morning adds up to $50 a month.

MONEY-MAKING VENTURES/BUDGET PLAN

If the words "savings account" aren't in your vocabulary, the following are some ideas on how to come up with quick cash or save some cash for your move.

Stop dining out. Eating out can eat away your money. Eat at home and shop more conservatively at the supermarket. The sacrifice will pay off.

Cut out entertainment. It's only for a short while, but avoid pricey movies (discount matinees and video rentals can be a replacement treat). Entertainment also includes travel, weekend getaways, expensive sports like skiing and golf, and anything fun that costs money. Instead of being bummed out about this, think about all the fun and entertainment that awaits you in San Francisco once you get a job and have fewer financial worries. Chapter 9, "Something for Nothing," lists free activities in San Francisco.

Hold a garage/yard sale. The less material possessions you take with you on your move, the easier and cheaper your move will be. Remember, just because you have a dining room (and a dining room set) now doesn't mean you'll find an apartment with a dining room in San Francisco. That dining room table could fetch some good money for your move. Other items you could sell are clothes, tapes and CDs, kitchen items, books, barbecue equipment, jewelry you never wear, bikes and sports equipment, and more. This is also a good time to return to your parents' home and clean out your childhood room. If you can bear to part with childhood trinkets and memorabilia, then sell them to finance your move.

Remember deposits for which you'll be reimbursed. Make sure you know what money you're entitled to or what bills you've prepaid for the last month's services. Most services you currently use, such as phone, gas, and cable, required a deposit at the time they were set up. Your landlord probably collected a hefty sum of money from you for the last month's rent and deposits. Make sure you don't double-pay your rent and that you get your deposit back with interest (some states require landlords to pay tenants interest on any deposits they hold). Ask about partial refunds for cancellation of a health club or other club membership.

Get paid for vacation time not taken. Most companies will pay you cash for vacation time not taken.

Collect outstanding debts from friends. If you've been hesitating to ask friends and acquaintances for money they've borrowed in the past, hesitate no longer. Moving is a great excuse for collecting old debts.

Sell big-ticket items. Do you really need your car? San Francisco is a small city with good public transportation and a bad parking situation. A car sale could give you several thousand dollars instantly. What about that jet ski you hardly ever use? Or the extra television in the bedroom? Do you really need two TVs? Take inventory of your durable goods and sell or pawn them for the money to move.

CHECKLIST OF ITEMS TO BUDGET FOR

- Apartment deposits
- Services setup
- Movers
- Moving van rental

- Short-term accommodations
- Mail delivery of boxes
- Transportation to your destination
- Monthly storage fees

WORLD WIDE WEB RESOURCES

The Gate
(http://www.sfgate.com)
The *San Francisco Chronicle* and *Examiner* newspapers' Web sites have classified listings that include garage/storage and transportation/carpool sections. Browsing these can help you budget for storage, parking, and transportation, if necessary.

The Move Estimate
(http://mfginfo.com/mover/estimate/estimate.htm)
contains details on pricing your move. It has the elements of costs to consider, such as determining the weight of your project, distance of transit, packaging, labor, special items, storage, and insurance.

Share a Load
(http://www.synapse.net/~tall/move/sharefrm.htm)
helps people moving long distances to find others who may be able to share costs by sharing trucks and equipment.

The Virtual Mover
(http://mfginfo.com/mover.htm)
has a mission to create, develop, and maintain a medium on the Internet for the moving and storage industry that will catalog and deliver resource information about and for the industry. Some useful categories are classified bulletin boards, storage, and destination information.

WWW of Moving and Storage
(http://www.synapse.net/~tall/)
lists many sources of information that deal with moving, such as newsgroups and couriers.

CHAPTER TWO

⋮····▶ Planning the Move

A N ORGANIZED MOVE is a successful move. It doesn't take much effort
to organize and plan your move, but it does save you from possible head-
aches and frustrations. This chapter is structured as a timeline for your move,
with suggestions of things you could be doing from three months prior to your
move up to the day you move. These suggestions are intended to be a starting
point so you're not overwhelmed or unsure how to proceed.

THREE MONTHS BEFORE THE MOVE

• Get acquainted with San Francisco by reading the local *San Francisco Chronicle*
and *Examiner* newspapers. The Sunday edition will give you an idea of apartment rentals, job opportunities, local activities, and local news. For a subscription, call (415) 777-5700; if you have access to the World Wide Web, the address
is **http://www.sfgate.com**.

• Start saving some money for the move.

• If possible, try to visit San Francisco and explore it from a resident's point of view.

• Order and review your credit reports. These will be necessary when you look for
an apartment. The three major credit reporting agencies are Equifax at 800-
685-1111, TRW at 800-392-1122, and Trans Union at (216) 779-2378. Credit
bureaus charge a fee between $8 and $20 unless you have been denied credit
within the previous 60 days. In that case, you're legally entitled to a free copy.

ONE MONTH BEFORE THE MOVE

• Make moving van rental reservations or arrangements with a moving company.

• Make travel reservations if you are getting to San Francisco by means other
than a car.

• If you're driving, it's time to get that tune-up you've been putting off.

• Start collecting boxes, tape, and any other packing supplies. Instead of recycling
your newspaper, use it to wrap dishes and other breakables.

- Save moving receipts, because many of them are tax deductible.

- Start tying up loose ends at your job. Ask around for job leads in San Francisco.

- If you don't have a place to stay when you move, then make a reservation at a short-term housing facility (see Chapter 3, "Where to Stay When You Arrive").

- Give your one-month notice to vacate your apartment. Work out how security deposits and other refunds will be handled.

- If you need to store your furniture someplace, start making arrangements with friends, relatives, or a storage facility (see list of Bay Area storage companies later in this chapter).

- Gather your unwanted belongings for a yard sale.

- If you want to set up a post office box at your new destination ahead of time so you can forward your mail, now is the time. Visit your local post office and complete Form #1093 P.O. Box application. The postal clerk will verify your ID and send the application to any post office in the San Francisco Bay Area where you want a box. It takes two to three weeks to process this request.

- Cancel memberships to places like your health club or other organizations.

- Cancel, forward, or put on hold magazine and newspaper subscriptions.

TWO WEEKS BEFORE THE MOVE

- Start packing.

- Notify gas, electric, water, cable, and phone companies of your move.

- Arrange to close or move your bank accounts.

- Call temporary employment agencies in San Francisco to make registration appointments.

- Update your resume and have many copies on hand.

- Contact the California Department of Food and Agriculture at (916) 654-0312 for current information about what types of plants California allows into the state. Find new homes for your plants if they are restricted.

- Hold a yard sale.

- Clean your apartment.

- Give notice at your job.

- Get letters of recommendation from employers and professional acquaintances.

- Pull together a job-finding packet that includes resumes, letters of recommendation, a passport, portfolio of work accomplishments, and nice stationery for cover letters and thank-you notes.

- Pick up clothes from the dry cleaner.

- Return library books.

- Ask a veterinarian for advice about moving with your pet.

ONE DAY BEFORE THE MOVE

- Pick up the rental van.

- Check oil and gas in your car.

- Make sure you have any important or necessary items with you, such as medication or valuables.

- Make your final inspection of your apartment or house.

- Call to confirm housing and any other reservations you made in San Francisco.

- Tell loved ones how they can reach you while you are in transition.

- Review your travel itinerary and plans for when you reach your destination.

- Eat well and rest before the big day.

THINGS TO DO ONCE YOU MOVE

- Start looking for an apartment or living situation.

- Start looking for work, either temporary, permanent, or both.

- Register your car (this will include a car inspection).

- Register to vote.

- Get a new driver's license.

- Get to know the city by taking a walking tour or spending time in different neighborhoods.

PACKING TIPS

The following are some basic packing tips for your move. Moving van companies, such as Ryder and U-Haul, have free moving booklets with more information on how to pack and plan your move. Call your local moving business directly for details.

- Pack small appliances in their original container if possible or a carton cushioned with wadded newspaper or bubble wrap. Do not use shredded paper, because it can get into the machinery and cause damage.

- If you're moving dressers, you can leave clothing folded in the drawers. Trash bags are good for casual clothes, while suits and more expensive clothes can be folded in suitcases or placed in garment bags.

- Individually wrap each dish first in plastic bags (to save dishwashing later) and then with newspaper. *Do not stack flat.* Instead, place saucers, plates, and platters on their edge. Cups and bowls may be placed inside each other.

- Wrap glasses separately in bubble wrap and use newspaper for cushioning.

- Pots and pans can be stacked with some paper between them.

- If you are restricted from bringing certain plants into California, either sell them at your garage sale or give them away as gifts.

- Pack a personal suitcase with necessities like toiletries, medicines, toothbrush, a change of clothes, a book, your pillow, and whatever else will keep you comfortable for a day or two if you can't unpack or get settled.

- Label every box with the address of your destination and contents. If you're mailing boxes, number them (1 of 12, 2 of 12, etc.) and keep an inventory list in your possession.

- Don't pack jewels or other valuables. Keep them on your person.

- If you're overwhelmed, pack one room at a time.

- Pack everything that can't walk on its own.

- Pack heavy items such as books in small boxes so they'll be easier to handle.

- Wrap towels and sheets around fragile items like lamps and ornaments.

MATERIALS NEEDED FOR PACKING

Packing paper such as newspaper

Boxes of assorted sizes

Tape

Markers

BAY AREA STORAGE COMPANIES

There are so many storage companies in the Bay Area that choosing the right one is a personal decision. You can pick one by how accessible it is to you or what features it has or how much it costs. The following are some things to ask a storage company that will help you select the right one:

- When are you open? What are your hours?

- Can I drive up to the storage area?
- Who holds on to the key?
- Do you offer short-term and long-term rentals?
- What size storage space do you have?
- Do you offer insurance?
- Do you have any discounts or specials?
- What type of security do you have in place?
- Does the storage space have an alarm?
- Does the storage space have a sprinkler system?
- Are storage units at ground level? If not, are elevators available?
- Is a deposit required?
- Do you have a resident manager?

The following is a list of some San Francisco and Bay Area storage companies:

AAAAA Rent-A-Space
1221 East Hillsdale Boulevard
Foster City, CA 94404
(415) 341-2964

American Self Storage
1985 East Bayshore Road
Palo Alto, CA 94303
(415) 325-8609

American Storage Unlimited
1355 6th Street (China Basin)
San Francisco, CA 94107
800-863-5820

Attic Self Storage
2440 16th Street
San Francisco, CA 94103
(415) 626-0800

Bellam Self-Storage
24 Bellam Boulevard
San Rafael, CA 94901
(415) 454-1983

City Storage Loc-N-Stor
144 Townsend Street
(between 2nd and 3rd Streets)
San Francisco, CA 94107
(415) 495-2300

Concord Self Storage
1597 Market Street
(corner of Meadow Lane)
Concord, CA 94520
(510) 827-4141

Crocker's Lockers
1400 Folsom Street (at 10th Street)
San Francisco, CA 94103
(415) 626-6665

Economy Self Storage
2450 Mandela Parkway
Oakland, CA 94607
(510) 465-2450

Fort Knox
370 Turk Street (between Hyde and
Leavenworth Streets)
San Francisco, CA 94102
(415) 775-1195

Larkspur Storage
2160 Redwood Highway
Greenbrae, CA 94904
(415) 925-0138

Lock It Up
38491 Fremont Boulevard
Fremont, CA 94536
(510) 790-0330

7315 Johnson Drive
Pleasanton, CA 94588
(510) 463-0777

Mini Storage
Companies of Marin
415 Coloma Street
Sausalito, CA 94965
(415) 332-6520 (Main Office)

Locations in Mill Valley, San Rafael, San
Anselmo, Corte Madera, and Novato.

Pay Less Self Storage
321 Canal Boulevard
San Rafael, CA 94901
(415) 456-2300

Public Storage
2690 Geary Boulevard
(by Masonic Avenue)
San Francisco, CA 94118
(415) 923-0280

611 2nd Street
San Francisco, CA 94107
(415) 495-2760

Saf Keep Storage
655 Marina Boulevard
San Leandro, CA 94577
(510) 614-1300

Jack London Square
Oakland, CA 94607
(510) 839-4100

1650 West Winton Avenue
Hayward, CA 94545
(510) 293-8870

2480 Middlefield Road
Redwood City, CA 94063
(415) 322-2222

40543 Albrae Street
Fremont, CA 94538
(510) 252-1444

San Francisco Mini Storage
1000 7th Street
San Francisco, CA 94107
(415) 252-0300

Shattuck Avenue Self Storage
2721 Shattuck Avenue
Berkeley, CA 94705
(510) 841-3241

U-Haul Storage
1575 Bayshore Boulevard
San Francisco, CA 94124
(415) 467-3830

Walnut Creek Self Storage
2690 North Main Street
Walnut Creek, CA 94596
(510) 932-5088

The local phone company has a free tips line called *Local Talk* to give you information on storage companies. The main number is (415) 837-5050, and the choices are:

2230 Insurance and self storage units

2235 Leases and contracts

2240 Defining your storage needs

2245 How to ensure maximum security for your stored items

- -

WORLD WIDE WEB RESOURCE

Moving and Storage
(**http://www.sfgate.com**)
The *San Francisco Chronicle* and *Examiner* Web site classified section has a category for moving and storage.

- -

CHAPTER THREE

▶ Where to Stay When You Arrive

HANCES ARE WHEN YOU MOVE to San Francisco you won't have an apartment already rented. How could you? How would you check out the different places there are to rent? How do you know if you like the neighborhood? What about meeting the landlord or completing application paperwork? You can't really find a place to live until you move, but when you move you'll need a place to live.

Short-term housing is an ideal solution to this apparently no-win situation. Whether a furnished apartment or shared room, temporary housing offers a home base for newcomers to the city. It serves not only as a place to stay but as an address for mail and as a point of contact for job and apartment leads. There is no need to rush into a less-than-ideal living situation when you have short-term housing to fall back on. It gives you the chance to determine your housing needs and get acquainted with the city. Reservations for temporary housing can be made in advance so a place to stay will be available upon your arrival to the city.

San Francisco has several types of short-term housing available. In this chapter, I will discuss furnished apartments, residence hotels, and budget-minded options such as youth hostels, the YMCA, and a college dorm. Accessing the Internet will also be a part of the budget section, since it is a way to arrange for an inexpensive apartment sublease or house-sitting situation. Please note that the prices and amenities of housing listed in this chapter are subject to change.

FURNISHED APARTMENTS

Furnished apartments try to feel like home by including everything a typical household would have. Items such as sheets, towels, kitchen utensils, microwave, television, and VCR are provided to make you feel like you're living at home until you find a place of your own. The goal of furnished apartments is for a tenant to move in with only a suitcase of clothes and function like a resident. Short-term leases normally require a minimum one-week stay. The following are some short-term furnished apartment options:

The American Property Exchange
170 Page Street
San Francisco, CA 94102
(415) 863-8484 or 800-747-7784

The American Property Exchange is a real estate brokerage company that specializes in daily, weekly, and monthly apartment rentals. Their database has over 2,000 furnished units all over the city. Competitive rates start at $85 nightly, $350 weekly, and $650 monthly.

The company can locate available units that meet individual needs, handle all paperwork, and arrange cleaning, parking, phones, and other requested services. A $300 deposit will hold advance reservations. A $300 cash security deposit is required on all units as well as a signed, valid credit card slip. All moneys are refundable 45 days after vacating. There is also a one-time move-out cleaning fee charged when the reservation is made, and it ranges between $65 and $110 per unit depending on size. Note that there are no refunds for early checkout. Personal checks and Visa, MasterCard, and American Express are accepted.

TYPES OF APARTMENTS

Studios: $650 to $1,600 per month

One-bedroom:
$1,250 to $2,400 per month

Two-Bedroom:
$1,800 to $3,000 per month

PARKING
If requested, only apartments with parking will be searched and compiled. Depending on the property, the cost of parking may be included in the rent or as an extra charge.

HOUSEWARES AND LINENS
All linens and housewares are included.

TV/CABLE
Available if requested.

TELEPHONE
Telephones are installed in all units. Telephone calls will be charged immediately to credit cards and the receipts forwarded to the occupant. There is a 15 percent charge for telephone billing.

KITCHEN
All units have kitchens; select units have gourmet kitchens.

HOUSEKEEPING
Maid service is available daily, weekly, or monthly for an extra charge. In some complexes it is included in the rental charge.

LAUNDRY
Laundry facilities are available depending on the building and apartment.

Ashlee Suites
1029 Geary Street (at Van Ness Avenue)
San Francisco, CA 94109
(415) 771-7396

The Ashlee Suites are located in a culturally diverse neighborhood near movie theaters, shops, and many ethnic restaurants. Several bus lines in the area go to places such as Fisherman's Wharf, the Financial District, Union Square, and South of Market. The building is clean but could use new paint and carpeting. The apartments are cute, clean, and tidy, and a manager lives on the premises.

An application needs to be completed, and a credit check is processed. Reservations are suggested three weeks to one month in advance. A $300 deposit and $25 key deposit are required, both of which are refundable. A 30-day minimum stay and 30-day written notice to vacate is required. Visa, MasterCard, American Express, and Diner's Club are accepted.

TYPES OF APARTMENTS

Studios: $750 per month (they have a high occupancy rate and are usually not available)

One-bedroom:
$825 to $1,200 per month

Two-bedroom: $1,300 per month

PARKING

There is no parking on the premises. Local lots cost between $110 to $135 per month. The Ashlee can provide you with names of local lots, but you make your own arrangements.

HOUSEWARES AND LINENS

Towels, dishes, and kitchen items are provided and are included in monthly rent.

TV/CABLE

A color television and basic cable are included in the rent.

TELEPHONE

A phone is provided, but tenants are responsible for setting up and paying for service. The front office has a fax machine.

KITCHEN

Each unit has a fully stocked electric kitchen with microwave.

HOUSEKEEPING

An additional $100 per month will provide you with once-a-week maid service, which includes vacuuming and changing the linens.

LAUNDRY

Coin-operated machines are located in the building.

Mayflower Hotel

975 Bush Street (at Jones Street)
San Francisco, CA 94109
(415) 673-7010

The Mayflower Hotel is located in the downtown area known as lower Nob Hill. The hotel is actually 104 studio rooms with Pullman kitchenettes (these usually consist of a counter with a small sink and a couple of hot plates). The rooms can be reserved up to a week in advance with a $100 money order deposit that is then applied toward the rent. A refundable $50 phone deposit is also required on move-in if your stay is a month or longer. Be careful when estimating your length of stay, because if you move out early, you are not refunded for unused days. One week's notice is required to vacate the premises; the minimum length of stay is one day. Credit cards are not accepted. Buses and cable cars run nearby.

TYPES OF APARTMENTS

Studios: $300 per week with tax or $695 per month with no tax

PARKING

A garage is located in the building. The cost is $9 per day or $125 per month.

HOUSEWARES AND LINENS

Towels, sheets, and dishes are provided and are included in monthly rent. Residents need to bring their own kitchen items.

TV/CABLE

Each unit has a 13-inch color television.

TELEPHONE

The Mayflower will supply the telephones, but phone service is extra. Local calls are seventy-five cents; direct-dial long-distance has a one-dollar usage fee plus any phone company charges.

KITCHEN

Each unit has a Pullman kitchenette with a hot plate and dishes.

HOUSEKEEPING

Daily maid service for weekly rentals and weekly maid service for monthly rentals are included in the rent.

LAUNDRY

There are no laundry facilities on the premises, but you'll find a laundromat next door.

Nob Hill Place

1155 Jones Street (at Sacramento Street)
San Francisco, CA 94108
(415) 928-2051

Nob Hill Place is located at the top of Nob Hill overlooking historic Grace Cathedral, an ominous, Gothic-style stone church. The building has a very elegant and formal look that fits in nicely with the character of the neighborhood. Nob Hill Place is situated in a predominantly residential area except for a few upscale hotels like the Fairmount and Mark Hopkins. It is conveniently located near the Financial District and the Union Square shopping district. The California Street cable car and 1 California bus are the closest transportation lines.

Reservations are recommended at least a month in advance. An application needs to be completed, and a deposit is required. Deposits range from $300 to $600 and include a nonrefundable cleaning fee of $50 to $100 depending on the type of apartment. The premises may be vacated at any time without prior notice. Credit cards are not accepted.

TYPES OF APARTMENTS

Efficiency studio, kitchen not separate: $900 per month

Studio, separate kitchen: $1,300 per month

Junior one-bedroom: $1,300 to $1,650 per month

One-bedroom: $1,650 to $2,250 per month

Two-bedroom, fireplace: $3,500 per month

PARKING

The building has very limited parking (18 spaces). You'll find three garages in the neighborhood: Fairmont Hotel, Crocker, and Masonic Temple. Neighborhood street parking is scarce and by city permit only (see Appendix 2, "Numbers to Know" for parking information). Nob Hill Place and local garage parking costs around $200 to $240 per month.

HOUSEWARES AND LINENS
Towels, dishes, and kitchen items are provided and are included in monthly rent.

TV/CABLE
Basic cable and a color television are provided and are included in monthly rent.

TELEPHONE
Telephones are furnished by the management, but tenants are responsible for hooking them up and paying for service.

KITCHEN
The kitchen has all gas appliances and a microwave.

HOUSEKEEPING
There is maid service twice a month, including changing beds, cleaning the bathroom, and mopping the kitchen. This service is included in the price of the rent.

LAUNDRY
Coin-operated laundry machines are in the building. Two-bedroom units have their own washer and dryer.

Northpoint Executive Suites
2211 Stockton Street (at Bay Street)
San Francisco, CA 94133
(415) 989-6563

The Northpoint Executive Suites in North Beach offer full-service and economy units for rent. Both types are fully furnished apartments whose only differences are cost and amenities. Full-service units include in the rental cost many perks, such as parking and cable. Economy units offer only the basics but cost less and save money.

The property has nicely landscaped gardens, two heated swimming pools, and a full-service health club for residents. These apartments are conveniently located near a Safeway supermarket, Walgreen's drugstore, movie theater, Fisherman's Wharf, and North Beach with its abundance of Italian eateries. The Financial District is in walking distance. Four different bus lines and a cable-car line run in the neighborhood.

A two-week minimum stay is required, and a 14-day notice must be given to vacate the premises. This means the leasing office only knows of upcoming vacancies two weeks in advance. You can try to book your stay earlier than 14 days in advance, but due to the popularity of these apartments, occupancy rates are high. The Diner's Club credit card is accepted; you can use personal checks once you move in.

TYPES OF APARTMENTS

Full-service studio:
$1,300 to $1,600 per month

Full-service one-bedroom:
$1,500 to $2,000 per month

Economy studio:
$950 to $1,250 per month

Economy one-bedroom:
$1,100 to $1,500 per month

PARKING

Abundant parking is available in the building. Full-service units include the cost of parking in the rent. Economy units include parking for an additional $75 per month.

HOUSEWARES AND LINENS

Towels, dishes, and kitchen items are provided and are included in monthly rent.

TV/CABLE

A cable-ready color television is furnished in each unit. Full-service units receive cable as part of their monthly rent. Tenants in the economy units are responsible for hooking up and paying for their own cable.

TELEPHONE

A telephone is included in each unit, but the tenant is responsible for setting up and paying for the service.

KITCHEN

Units have electric kitchens equipped with a microwave.

HOUSEKEEPING

Full-service units include once-a-week housekeeping as part of the rent.

LAUNDRY

Coin-operated machines are located in the building.

The Olympic Hotel

140 Mason Street
(between Eddy and Ellis Streets)
San Francisco, CA 94102
(415) 982-5010

It calls itself a hotel and it looks like a hotel, but it leases studio apartments on a short-term basis. The Chez Paree XXX house across the street may not be the ideal neighbor, but it's outnumbered and outclassed by the exclusive San Francisco Hilton and Nikko hotels down the street. The location is right in the heart of the Union Square shopping district and near several bus lines and underground metro lines. You'll see many tourists as well as homeless people in this crowded part of town.

Reservations are suggested two weeks in advance. An application needs to be completed, and a credit check is involved. Monthly renters are required to pay a first- and last-month deposit; weekly renters pay a $100 deposit. These deposits are waived when a credit card is used. Visa, MasterCard, and American Express are accepted. Monthly renters must give a 30-day notice to vacate.

TYPES OF APARTMENTS

Studios: $240 per week or
$600 per month ($500 per month
for two months or more)

PARKING

There is no parking in the building, but a parking lot is located across the street with rates of $110 to $120 per month. Guests make their own arrangements with the garage.

HOUSEWARES AND LINENS

Towels and sheets are provided.

TV/CABLE

A color television is included in the rent. Cable costs include a $60 installation fee and a $25-per-month service charge.

TELEPHONE
Residents bring their own phone and are responsible for hooking it up.

KITCHEN
Units have a no-frills kitchen with a stove, sink, and refrigerator. The kitchens include no kitchen items, so bring your own pots and dishes.

HOUSEKEEPING
No housekeeping service or cleaning supplies are available.

LAUNDRY
Coin-operated machines are located in the building.

Pierre Crest
755 Bush Street (at Powell Street)
San Francisco, CA 94104
(415) 255-0252

Located in a bustling part of town right by Union Square, the Pierre Crest is a lovely, cream-colored, European-style building. Inside is an elegant marble corridor that leads to a sunny garden. The bright, medium-size studio apartments are fully furnished and include local phone, TV, VCR, cable, and laundry in the price of the rent. These apartments are open for viewing several times a week. Call the apartment manager for details. Several bus and cable-car routes run nearby.

An application needs to be completed and returned with a $25 processing fee for the credit check. A security deposit equal to one-and-a-half month's rent reserves an apartment. A 30-day written notice to vacate is required. The American Express card and personal checks are accepted.

TYPES OF APARTMENTS
Furnished studios: $850 to $1,245 per month (price reduces with stays longer than a month)

PARKING
There is no parking in the building, but parking is available across the street for about $175 per month.

HOUSEWARES AND LINENS
Towels and sheets are provided.

TV/CABLE
A color television with cable and VCR is included in the cost of the rent.

TELEPHONE
A telephone and local calls are included in the rent. Long-distance calls are the tenant's responsibility.

KITCHEN
Units have fully equipped kitchens with items like a coffeemaker (but no microwave).

HOUSEKEEPING
Maid service costs an additional $50 each time it's used.

LAUNDRY
Free laundry machines are located in the basement.

RESIDENCE HOTELS
Residence hotels have a more temporary and less private feel than furnished apartments. There is a definite social atmosphere in many of these places because of shared rooms, group dining, and recreation areas. Residence hotels rent single and shared rooms with or without a bathroom. Rates are

reasonable and may include meals and maid service as part of the package. The more private the accommodations (for example, a single room with private bath), the higher the cost. Sharing a room and bath can save considerable money. The length of stay can be one week to indefinite.

Abigail

246 McAllister Street
(between Larkin and Hyde Streets)
San Francisco, CA 94102
(415) 861-9728

This is a beautiful, Art Deco-style hotel located in the Civic Center neighborhood, where the city government and many poor and homeless reside. The hotel lobby has a marble checkerboard-patterned floor and stained-glass detailing on the windows that look out onto the domed city hall. The rooms are furnished in antiques and are very clean and well kept. An organic restaurant is featured on the premises, but if you want to save some money, a microwave and small refrigerator can be requested for your room as well as a TV. If your stay is longer than one week, an application must be completed for a credit check and a $250 deposit is required. Visa, MasterCard, American Express, Discover, Diner's Club, and checks are accepted.

TYPES OF ROOMS

Single: $79 a night or $275 per week

BATHROOM

All rooms have private baths.

PARKING

Parking arrangement with a garage a block away is available for $7.50 per day.

HOUSEWARES AND LINENS

Towels and sheets are provided.

TV/CABLE

Each room has a color TV with cable.

TELEPHONE

The rooms have phones. Incoming calls can be received, and outgoing calls are billed directly to the room.

MEALS

Continental breakfast is served. No kitchens are available.

HOUSEKEEPING

Maid service once a week is included in the price of the room.

LAUNDRY

No laundry facilities are located in the building, but management will send out your laundry.

Ansonia

711 Post Street (between Jones and Taylor Streets)
San Francisco, CA 94109
(415) 673-2670

The Ansonia Hotel has an old-fashioned feel with its decor of floral wallpaper, lace curtains, and red velvet covered furniture in the lobby area. The facilities are clean but a little worn. The stairs give a tired creak under step, and the carpet is balding in spots. The hotel is well located near Union Square and can serve as a quiet, peaceful, and affordable respite after a day of apartment and job hunting. Visa, MasterCard, and American Express are accepted, and stays over a week need to be approved by the manager. There is no application, credit check, or deposit.

TYPES OF ROOMS

Shared room with hall bath: $170 per week

Single with hall bath: $235 per week

Shared room with semiprivate bath: $180 per week

Shared room with private bath: $210 per week

Single with single bath: $310 per week

BATHROOM
Private and shared baths are available depending on the room rate.

PARKING
No parking is available on the premises. Neighborhood garages range from $80 to $120 per week.

HOUSEWARES AND LINENS
Towels and sheets are provided.

TV/CABLE
Each room has a TV without cable.

TELEPHONE
The rooms have phones. Incoming calls can be received, and outgoing calls are billed directly to the room.

MEALS
Breakfast and dinner are served daily (except no dinner on Sundays). Meals are included in the price of the room.

HOUSEKEEPING
Daily maid service is included in the price of the room.

LAUNDRY
Laundry facilities are located in the building.

Brady Acres

649 Jones Street
(between Post and Geary Streets)
San Francisco, CA 94102
(415) 929-8033

Brady Acres is located downtown near the Union Square shopping district. It's a small, comfortable hotel that has 25 clean studio rooms with newly tiled bathrooms. Rooms also have fully accessorized wet bars with a refrigerator, microwave, coffeemaker, and toaster. The management is very friendly and helpful and provides residents with cleaning supplies and even laundry detergent. Brady Acres is near three bus stops that service multiple bus lines. Several convenience stores are located in the neighborhood.

Brady Acres will hold a reservation with a $100 deposit. An application must be completed, and the length of stay (a check-in and checkout date) must be given when making a reservation. The minimum one-week stay can be extended if a room is available. If you shorten your stay, your money will be refunded for unused days. MasterCard and Visa are accepted.

TYPES OF ROOMS

Single: $300 to $330 per week for the first four weeks; after four weeks, you are eligible for monthly rates of $650 to $750

BATHROOM
All rooms have newly tiled private baths and hair dryers.

PARKING
No parking is available on the premises. Universal Parking at 644 Geary Street has $10 daily rates and weekly rates at around $60.

HOUSEWARES AND LINENS
Towels and sheets are provided.

TV/CABLE
Each room has a color television without cable and a radio/cassette player.

TELEPHONE
Each room has a telephone with a private number and answering machine. Local calls are included in the price of the room. Either calling cards or pay phones must be used for long-distance calls. A fax machine is on the premises, and incoming faxes are free (outgoing faxes are $1 per page).

MEALS
The rooms have a wet bar with a microwave, toaster oven, refrigerator, coffeemaker, dishes, and silverware.

HOUSEKEEPING
Guests using Brady Acres as a hotel and not taking advantage of the weekly specials receive daily maid service. Long-term guests can use the cleaning equipment available or pay an additional $25 per week for daily maid service.

LAUNDRY
Coin-operated machines are located in the building, and laundry soap is free.

Cornell Club
715 Bush Street (at Powell Street)
San Francisco, CA 94108
(415) 421-3154

The Cornell Club is a charming European-style hotel located between Nob Hill and Union Square. This is a non-smoking facility with 60 clean, individually decorated rooms with private and shared baths. Weekly rentals are $495 for a single, which includes breakfast and dinner. Dinner is prepared by a French chef and served in the Cornell Club restaurant, Jeanne d'Arc. Stays are limited to 28 days. Visa, MasterCard, American Express, and cash are accepted. There is no application process or credit check.

TYPES OF ROOMS

Single with private bath:
$1,450 per month
Single with shared bath:
$1,100 per month

BATHROOM
Private and shared baths are available, depending on the room rate.

PARKING
You can make arrangements with the garage across the street for $12 per day.

HOUSEWARES AND LINENS
Towels and sheets are provided.

TV/CABLE
Each room has a color TV with cable.

TELEPHONE

The rooms have phones. Incoming calls can be received, and outgoing calls are billed directly to the room.

MEALS

Breakfast is served seven days a week, and dinner is served Monday through Friday. Meals are included in the price of the room.

HOUSEKEEPING

Daily maid service is included in the price of the room.

LAUNDRY

No laundry facilities are located in the building. There are laundromats down the street.

Green Tortoise

490 Broadway (at Kearny Street)
San Francisco, CA 94108
(415) 834-1000

This is a hostel that operates as part of the Green Tortoise Adventure Travel Company. This travel company offers self-service, no-frills vacations oriented toward hiking and swimming in remote natural spots. The hostel is an active, bustling guest house in San Francisco's North Beach neighborhood. You get what you pay for, such as partially carpeted hallways, noisy lounges, a messy looking communal kitchen and eating area, and the company of a variety of guests that range from grunge rockers and hippies to Euro-travelers with their kids. Cash and traveler's checks are accepted, and stays are limited to 21 days. After 21 days, you are required to check out for a day and then you can check back in and stay another 21 days. There is no application, deposit, or credit check.

TYPES OF ROOMS

Single: $19.95 per day

Private double: $35 per day

Dormitory-style (usually single-sex unless there is a spillover): $15 per day

BATHROOM

There are no private baths. Most rooms have a sink.

PARKING

No parking is available on the premises. Neighborhood parking is difficult and by permit only.

HOUSEWARES AND LINENS

Towels and sheets are provided.

TV/CABLE

There is a TV/smoking lounge.

TELEPHONE

The hotel will take messages, but guests must use pay phones for outgoing calls.

MEALS

Free daily breakfast is served. You can prepare your own meals in a communal kitchen.

HOUSEKEEPING

Daily cleaning service cleans the building.

LAUNDRY

Coin-operated machines are located in the building.

The Harcourt

1105 Larkin Street (at Polk Street)
San Francisco, CA 94109
(415) 673-7720

The Harcourt is a residence club that offers room and board to its short-term and long-term guests. It is located near the downtown San Francisco business and shopping districts and is convenient to several citywide bus lines. The Harcourt is clean, decorated with functional furniture of the seventies, and is serviced by a helpful staff that includes a switchboard operator and manager. Guests can enjoy a television lounge as well as a sun deck. The clientele is screened by the management and includes foreign students and newcomers to the city.

Making reservations two weeks in advance is recommended. Room reservations require a $25 deposit, and rent can be paid either weekly, biweekly, or monthly. No application paperwork is required, and MasterCard and Visa are accepted.

TYPES OF ROOMS

Private room with private bath:
$720 per month

Private room with hall bath:
$600 per month

Shared room with private bath:
$500 per month

Shared room with hall bath:
$440 per month

BATHROOM

Rooms are available with either private or shared baths.

PARKING

No parking is available on the premises. Neighborhood parking lots cost around $110 to $115 per month. You can park on the street with a permit.

HOUSEWARES AND LINENS

Towels and sheets are supplied.

TV/CABLE

A giant-screen TV is located in the community room, but it doesn't have cable.

TELEPHONE

You can use phones in the rooms to make outgoing calls. All incoming messages are routed through the switchboard.

MEALS

Breakfast and dinner are included in the price of the room.

HOUSEKEEPING

Daily maid service is included in the price of the room.

LAUNDRY

No laundry facilities are located on the site, but laundromats are in the neighborhood.

The Kenmore

1570 Sutter Street
(between Gough and Octavia Streets)
San Francisco, CA 94109
(415) 776-5815

The Kenmore Residence Club is located on a quiet, tree-lined street two blocks from bustling Van Ness Avenue and several citywide bus lines. It offers its guests decent meals, clean and comfortable rooms, housekeeping, and a

24-hour message service. Guests can also enjoy a TV room, game room, small library, and reading room.

Reservations can be made two weeks in advance. A $25 deposit holds a room and can be applied toward rent. A refundable $20 key deposit is also required. No application paperwork is necessary, and the minimum stay is one week. MasterCard and Visa are accepted.

TYPES OF ROOMS

Deluxe private room with bath and color TV: $880 per month

Private room with private bath: $780 per month

Private room with hall bath: $660 per month

Deluxe double suite with private bath: $720 per month

Double suite with private bath: $620 per month

Double room with private bath: $560 per month

Double room with shared bath: $540 per month

Double room with hall bath: $500 per month

BATHROOM

Rooms have private and shared baths, with a sink in each room.

PARKING

No parking is available on the premises. You can park on the street with a permit.

HOUSEWARES AND LINENS

Towels and sheets are supplied.

TV/CABLE

The community room has a television. Some deluxe private rooms have color TVs.

TELEPHONE

All rooms have direct-dial phones. Local calls cost 30¢; long-distance calls are a $1 flat fee plus toll (with a $20 limit on long-distance calls). Incoming calls are routed through the switchboard. A 24-hour message service is available free of charge.

MEALS

Breakfast and dinner are served Monday through Saturday. Continental breakfast and brunch are served on Sunday. Meals are included in room rental. (When I stopped by, the menu featured turkey with all the fixings.)

HOUSEKEEPING

Daily maid service is included in the room rental.

LAUNDRY

Coin-operated machines are located in the building.

The Monroe

*1870 Sacramento Street
(between Van Ness Avenue and
Franklin Street)
San Francisco, CA 94109
(415) 474-6200*

Built before the 1906 earthquake, the Monroe survived without a scratch and began its career as a residence club. It started housing U.S. military personnel aiding earthquake victims and then the earthquake homeless themselves. Today, this busy residence hotel serves foreign students and others moving to San Francisco.

The Monroe's elegant interior is decorated with warm mahogany paneling, hardwood-beamed ceilings, and a massive carved wood fireplace. This clean, quiet, softly lit interior could be mistaken for a private business club but is as unstuffy as a college dorm. Guests enjoy plenty of activities, such as billiards, table tennis, chess, and television watching in the lounge. A block away from the Monroe is the Hard Rock Cafe as well as several bus and cable-car lines.

Besides clean and comfortable facilities, the Monroe has a desk clerk on duty 24 hours as well as a 24-hour switchboard that takes messages and provides wake-up calls.

Rooms can be reserved with a $25 deposit. Most rooms are shared rooms, but private ones are available and require an early reservation. The minimum stay at the Monroe is one week. Visa and MasterCard are accepted.

TYPES OF ROOMS

Private room with private bath:
$780 per month

Private room with shared bath:
$740 per month

Private room with hall bath:
$660 per month

Double suite with private bath:
$620 per month

Double room with private bath:
$560 per month

Double room with shared bath:
$540 per month

Double room with hall bath:
$500 per month

BATHROOM
Rooms have private and shared baths.

PARKING
No parking is available on the premises. Neighborhood parking lots cost around $110 to $115 per month. You can park on the street with a permit.

HOUSEWARES AND LINENS
Towels and sheets are supplied.

TV/CABLE
The community room has a giant-screen TV without cable.

TELEPHONE
The rooms have phones to make outgoing calls. All incoming messages are routed through the front desk.

MEALS
Breakfast and dinner are included in the price of the room.

HOUSEKEEPING
Daily maid service is included in the price of the room.

LAUNDRY
No laundry is available on site, but laundromats are in the neighborhood.

Post Hotel
589 Post Street (at Taylor Street)
San Francisco, CA 94102
(415) 441-9378

This no-frills hotel is no match for the swanky Olympic Club and five-star Pan Pacific hotel across the street. The lobby has 1970s-style carpeting and plastic wood furnishings, and iron bars separate the guests from the hotel clerk. The location is good and somewhat safe, and the price is right. Credit cards are not accepted, but cash and traveler's checks are. You must complete a rental application for longer-term stays; a credit check is run. There are no deposits or application fees.

TYPES OF ROOMS

Single with private bath:
$130 per week or $520 per month

Single with shared bath:
$100 per week or $400 per month

BATHROOM
Private and shared baths are available depending on the room rate.

PARKING
No parking is available on the premises. Pricey garages are located nearby.

HOUSEWARES AND LINENS
Towels and sheets are provided.

TV/CABLE
Each room has a color TV without cable.

TELEPHONE
The rooms have no phones. The hotel receives incoming calls for residents, which can be returned on the pay phones located on each floor.

MEALS
The hotel provides no meals and no kitchen access. No cooking is allowed in the rooms, but the rooms have refrigerators.

HOUSEKEEPING
Weekly maid service is included in the price of the room.

LAUNDRY
No laundry facilities are located in the building.

San Francisco Residence Club
851 California Street (at Powell Street)
San Francisco, CA 94108
(415) 421-2220

It advertises itself as a European pension atop of Nob Hill, and it doesn't lie. The charm of this old building is the creaky hardwood floors, worn rug runners, and threadbare velvet parlor furniture. The rooms are on the small side, but if you go stir-crazy, you can visit the TV room. A cable-car ride away you'll find movie theaters, shopping, and restaurants. Meals are included in the price of the room and are served in a dining room that opens to a courtyard garden with outdoor seating.

The residence club is located adjacent to the Fairmont Hotel and two blocks from the heart of the Financial District. Reservations are recommended at least two weeks in advance; a two-week notice to vacate is required. There is no application, just hotel registration. A $100 deposit confirms the reservation, and credit cards are not accepted.

TYPES OF ROOMS

Single: $690 to $1,600 per month

Double: $950 to $1,600 per month

BATHROOM
All rooms have a sink. Most rooms share a bath.

PARKING
There is no parking on the premises. Stanford Court parking is $22 per

day, and other local lots are $17 to $28 per day.

HOUSEWARES AND LINENS
Towels and sheets are provided.

TV/CABLE
No televisions are in the rooms, although guests can bring their own. There is a TV lounge.

TELEPHONE
The rooms are wired for telephones so guests can bring their own and hook them up. The front office has a message service and fax machine.

MEALS
Breakfast and dinner are served Monday through Saturday and are included in the price of the room.

HOUSEKEEPING
Daily maid service is included in the price of the room.

LAUNDRY
Coin-operated machines are located in the building.

Spaulding Hotel
240 O'Farrell Street (at Powell Street)
San Francisco, CA 94102
(415) 788-9419

The lobby is stark, with a couple of folding chairs and fluorescent lighting. The rooms are worn-looking but clean. Each room has a refrigerator and color TV, and in-house movies are shown. MasterCard and American Express are accepted, but checks are not. A credit check and background check are run on guests who want to stay longer term.

The maximum stay is usually 28 days but can "depend on the person"—whatever that means. There's no application fee, but a key deposit is required.

TYPES OF ROOMS
Single with private bath:
$130 per week

Single with shared bath:
$100 per week

BATHROOM
Private and shared baths are available depending on the room rate.

PARKING
No parking is available in the building. There are neighborhood garages, and street parking is very limited.

HOUSEWARES AND LINENS
Towels and sheets are provided and are changed weekly.

TV/CABLE
Each room has a color TV without cable.

TELEPHONE
The rooms don't have phones, but you'll find pay phones on every floor. The front desk takes incoming messages.

MEALS
The hotel has no meals and no kitchen facilities.

HOUSEKEEPING
Weekly maid service is included in the price of the room.

LAUNDRY
Laundry facilities are not available on the premises.

BUDGET-MINDED OPTIONS

Budget-minded options are creative ways to solve your short-term housing crisis without abusing your credit card limits. Places such as youth hostels, the YMCA, and a college dorm may not be homey and quaint, but they can be extremely affordable. Expect to room with other people, sometimes 10 or more to a room. But don't worry; everyone will have his or her own bed. Whether or not you're a people person, bring your patience, tolerance, and sense of humor—and think about all the money you're saving.

The following is a review of some San Francisco hostels, YMCA housing, and a college dorm.

American Youth Hostel (AYH) at Fort Mason

Franklin and Bay Streets, Building 240
San Francisco, CA 94123
(415) 771-7277

American Youth Hostel at Fort Mason is located on the waterfront in the very yuppie Marina neighborhood. Rooms are dorm-style with bunk beds, coed or single-sex, and fit 10 to 12 people in one room. The hostel has smaller four-person rooms, but they require an advance reservation.

The Fort Mason hostel has a communal kitchen with a stove, a TV room that shows nightly movies, a reading room, and a common area. Smoking is not permitted indoors. Laundry machines are on the premises, as is free parking. Although no curfew is in place, this location requires guests to do some chores, such as making beds, vacuuming, and taking out trash (but don't worry, there is no bathroom duty).

Reservations can be made a minimum of 48 hours in advance. During the summer months, the hostel keeps busy, so reservations should be made a couple of weeks in advance. Reservations require a nonrefundable $13 deposit by credit card, which is then applied toward the first night's room rental. The hostel also requires a refundable $5 key deposit. No application paperwork is necessary, and the maximum stay is two weeks due to local residency laws. Though a credit card is used for reservations, only cash and traveler's checks are accepted as payment.

TYPES OF ROOMS

All rooms: $13 per night for AYH members and nonmembers

BATHROOM

Each floor has three male and three female bathrooms.

PARKING

Free parking is available on the premises.

HOUSEWARES AND LINENS

Sheets and towels are supplied.

TV/CABLE

The community room has a television that does not have cable but shows movies nightly.

TELEPHONE

The hostel has pay phones in the hallways and a phone-card machine.

MEALS

No meals are served. A communal kitchen offers a refrigerator, stove, microwave, toaster, sink, pots, pans, dishes, and silverware. Residents must clean up after themselves and put dishes away.

HOUSEKEEPING

Daily housekeeping at the facility handles the messier jobs. Residents are required to do some chores. They are also permitted to change their own sheets and towels daily if they wish.

LAUNDRY

Laundry facilities are on the premises.

American Youth Hostel (AYH) at Union Square

312 Mason Street
San Francisco, CA 94102
(415) 788-5604

American Youth Hostel at Union Square is centered in San Francisco's most famous shopping district. It's conveniently located near many bus, subway, and cable-car lines, not to mention some of the greatest stores around. The hostel has no private rooms; you can choose either three-person rooms or semiprivate two-person rooms. Most rooms share common bathrooms, but a few come with private baths and should be requested ahead of time. Daily housekeeping keeps the place shipshape. Guests are welcome to use the communal kitchen, which has a refrigerator and microwave. The hostel also has a reading room, a smoking room, and a TV room, which shows nightly movies. The good news is that there are no curfews or chores.

Reservations can be made a minimum of 48 hours in advance. During the summer months, the hostel keeps busy, so reservations should be made a month or two in advance. Reservations require a nonrefundable $14 deposit by credit card, which is then applied toward the room rental. The hostel also requires a refundable $5 key deposit. No application paperwork is necessary; the maximum stay is two weeks due to local residency laws. Visa and MasterCard are accepted.

To become a member of American Youth Hostel, you can register when you arrive at the hostel. The annual dues are $25 and provide discounts at hostels around the country.

TYPES OF ROOMS

All rooms: $14 per night for AYH members; $17 per night for nonmembers (no discount for longer stays)

BATHROOM

Shared baths are available. Each room has a sink.

PARKING

No parking is available on the premises. Garages in the area cost around $12 per day.

HOUSEWARES AND LINENS

Sheets are supplied. Bring your own towels.

TV/CABLE

The community room has a television that does not have cable but shows movies nightly.

TELEPHONE

You'll find pay phones in the hallways and a phone-card machine.

MEALS

No meals are served. A communal kitchen offers a refrigerator, microwave, toaster, sink, pots, pans, and dishes, but no stove.

HOUSEKEEPING
Daily housekeeping is provided at the facility, but it does not include bed changes.

LAUNDRY
A laundromat is located two blocks away.

Central YMCA
220 Golden Gate Avenue
San Francisco, CA 94102
(415) 885-0460

The Central YMCA of San Francisco is located in the neighborhood known as Civic Center. This area is the center of city government and culture contrasted by a large homeless population. City Hall is across the street from the famous Opera House. A new main library has been built next door to its old granite, nonretrofitted home. Fast-food chains keep busy throughout the night. This is San Francisco's center of urban life.

The Central Y is an affordable, temporary place to stay in this eclectic neighborhood. Reservations can only be made by sending a letter with the dates of your stay and a money order in the amount of the first night's stay. Visa, MasterCard, traveler's checks, and cash are accepted at checkout time, but personal checks are not. Reservations should be made a month in advance. After staying 28 days, you must complete a tenant/credit application.

TYPES OF ROOMS

Single: $26 per night, $135 per week, or $380 per month

Double: $36 per night, $200 per week, or $550 per month

BATHROOM
The Y offers shared single-sex bath and showers. Each room has a sink.

PARKING
Parking is available for $8.50 per day.

HOUSEWARES AND LINENS
Sheets and towels are supplied.

TV/CABLE
There is a TV lounge without cable. You can request a room with a television for an extra $30 per night.

TELEPHONE
No phones are in the rooms, but you'll find public phones in the building.

MEALS
Continental breakfast is included in the price of the room. A cafeteria on the premises has a reasonably priced fare. There is no kitchen for residents, and no cooking is allowed in the rooms.

HOUSEKEEPING
Daily housekeeping is provided. Sheets are changed every other day, and towels are replaced every day.

LAUNDRY
Laundry machines are on the premises.

University of San Francisco (USF)
Office of Residence Life (summer only)
2130 Fulton Street
San Francisco, CA 94117
(415) 666-6824

USF offers dorm accommodations to students who are taking a summer class or internship at any educational institution in the area. Priority is given to USF students, but some spaces are available for others on a first-come basis. Twenty dollars a day will buy a shared room with a communal bathroom. Everything else you may need, like sheets and towels, you provide yourself. An optional meal program for an additional $10 per day includes breakfast, lunch, and dinner. Inquiries and reservations for this type of housing should be made in May or June. Don't forget you need to be registered for a summer class—any summer class. This might be a good opportunity to take that computer class that will make you more marketable in your job search discussed in Chapter 6.

TYPES OF ROOMS

Shared room with twin beds: $20 per day

BATHROOM

There is a communal bathroom.

PARKING

Street parking is available.

HOUSEWARES AND LINENS

Bring your own sheets and towels.

TV/CABLE

There is cable in the rooms but no television. You can bring your own TV or enjoy the TV lounge.

TELEPHONE

Each room has a phone with voice mail. It requires a $100 deposit.

Other useful sources of rental information are USENET groups or forums offered by your particular Internet provider, such as America Online, or directly on the World Wide Web. Try searching for NEWS:BA.MARKET. HOUSING to link to various housing resources. If you don't see a short-term housing situation that suits you, then post your own and see what kind of response you get. The Internet will also be a valuable resource tool for your job search and for meeting other people in a similar situation.

You can keep abreast of apartment rentals in the city by subscribing to the *Bay Area Rental Guide*. It is published every two weeks, and the cost is about $1.75 an issue. It lists short-term housing options and can give you a head start on the renter's market in San Francisco.

Bay Area Rental Guide Magazine
455 North Point
San Francisco, CA 94133

Many of the apartments and residence hotels discussed in this chapter can provide you with brochures and additional information. Simply write or call them to make your request.

MEALS

You can purchase an optional meal plan for $10 per day.

HOUSEKEEPING

Housekeeping is provided for the communal areas. Residents keep their own dorms clean. Basic cleaning tools such as brooms and vacuums are provided.

LAUNDRY

Coin-operated machines are on the premises.

OVERVIEW OF SHORT-TERM HOUSING OPTIONS

	PRICE RANGE	PARKING ON PREMISES	TV IN ROOM	SHEETS & TOWELS	KITCHEN SUPPLIES	MAID SERVICE	LAUNDRY IN BUILDING AVAILABLE	MEALS	CHECKOUT NOTICE
FURNISHED APARTMENTS									
AMERICAN PROPERTY EXCHANGE	$650–$3,000/mo.	yes	yes	yes	yes	yes	yes	n/a	given at registration
ASHLEE SUITES	$750–$1,300/mo.	no	yes	yes	yes	yes	yes	n/a	30 days
MAYFLOWER HOTEL	$695/mo.	yes	yes	yes	yes	yes	no	n/a	7 days
NOB HILL PLACE	$900–$3,500/mo.	yes	yes	yes	yes	yes	yes	n/a	none
NORTHPOINT SUITES	$950–$2,000/mo.	yes	yes	yes	yes	yes	yes	n/a	2 weeks
OLYMPIC HOTEL	$600/mo.	no	yes	yes	no	no	yes	n/a	30 days
PIERRE CREST	$850–$1,245/mo.	no	yes	yes	yes	yes	yes	n/a	30 days
RESIDENCE HOTELS									
ABIGAIL	$375/week	no	yes	yes	n/a	yes	no	yes	none
ANSONIA	$170–$310/week	no	yes	yes	n/a	yes	yes	yes	none
BRADY ACRES	$650–750/mo.	no	yes	yes	n/a	yes	yes	no	given at registration
CORNELL CLUB	$1,100–$1,450/mo.	no	yes	yes	n/a	yes	no	yes	none
GREEN TORTOISE	$15–$35/day	no	no	yes	n/a	yes	yes	yes	none
THE HARCOURT	$500–$720/mo.	no	no	yes	n/a	yes	no	yes	none
THE KENMORE	$500–780/mo.	no	no	yes	n/a	yes	yes	yes	none
THE MONROE	$500–$780/mo.	no	no	yes	n/a	yes	no	yes	none
POST HOTEL	$400–$520/mo.	no	yes	yes	n/a	yes	no	no	none
S.F. RESIDENCE CLUB	$690–$1,600/mo.	no	no	yes	n/a	yes	yes	yes	2 weeks
SPAULDING HOTEL	$100–$130/week	no	yes	yes	n/a	yes	no	no	none
BUDGET-MINDED OPTIONS									
AYH (FORT MASON)	$13/day	yes	no	yes	yes	yes	yes	no	none
AYH (UNION SQUARE)	$14–$17/day	no	no	yes	yes	yes	no	no	none
CENTRAL YMCA	$380–$550/mo.	yes	no	yes	no	yes	yes	yes	none
USF DORMS	$20–$30/day	no	no	no	no	no	yes	yes	none

WORLD WIDE WEB RESOURCES

The San Francisco Chronicle *and* Examiner *newspapers*
(http://www.sfgate.com)
list their classified sections online, including short-term rentals.

National Interim Housing Network
(http://www2.csn.net/ih)
is a national short-term housing consortium with a directory that lists temporary accommodations.

PART 2

FINDING A PLACE TO CALL HOME

PHOTO BY KITTI HOMME

CHAPTER FOUR

How to Find a Place to Live

FINDING A PLACE TO LIVE is a time-consuming, expensive, and somewhat stressful process, so it's good to get it right the first time. It's time consuming in that a lot of research goes into finding a place you'll call home. It's expensive because the first- and last-month's rent and a security deposit add up. It's stressful because you're not the only one out there looking for an apartment. A great apartment in a great neighborhood that's available for rent could attract many interested people. On the other hand, there are plenty of poorly maintained, undesirable apartments that can make you wonder if decent housing can be found. But this kind of talk isn't meant to discourage you. Research and planning will help you be the boss when it comes to finding housing that meets your needs.

First, you have to figure out what those needs are. Starting an apartment search without knowing what you want is like trying to find a mate just because you want to get married. Don't settle for the first place you see; be patient, know what you want, and you'll find the apartment (and perhaps mate) of your dreams.

Ask yourself the following questions to help clarify the living situation you're looking for:

- What can I afford?

- Do I want to live with roommates or alone?

- How many roommates could I live with?

- Do I want roommates of the same sex or of either sex?

- Do I object to smoking?

- Am I a morning person or a night person?

- Do I want a roommate who's a homebody or someone who's away most of the time?

- Can I live with a roommate who's a party animal?
- Can I live with a roommate whose boyfriend/girlfriend stays over all the time?
- Can I live with a roommate who's a neat freak?
- Am I a neat person or can I live with untidiness?
- If I choose to live alone, do I want a studio or one-bedroom apartment?
- Do I want a front or rear unit?
- Do I prefer a top- or bottom-floor apartment?
- Is parking an issue with me?
- What neighborhood would I prefer to live in?
- Do I have pets to consider?
- Do I want my bedroom facing the street?
- Is street noise an issue?
- Do I want a quiet, residential neighborhood or do I like to be where the action is?
- Am I willing to sign a lease or do I want the freedom of a month-to-month rental?
- Do I want laundry facilities in the building?

Once you've figured out what you want—say, a studio apartment in Russian Hill or North Beach for $600 a month that will allow pets and isn't on any bus or cable-car lines because you can't deal with the noise—then you're ready to start looking. There are different ways to approach an apartment or roommate search:

- Visit the neighborhoods where you think you'd like to live and look for rental signs. In the next chapter, I review the different neighborhoods in San Francisco.

- Read local newspaper classified ads. Local papers include the *San Francisco Chronicle, San Francisco Examiner, Marin Independent,* and *Oakland Tribune.*

- Read the *Bay Area Rental Guide.* I mentioned this as a great resource for finding temporary housing in Chapter 3, "Where to Stay When You Arrive," but the guide also lists many rentals. Another resource for apartment listings outside of San Francisco is *Apartments for Rent,* which is free and available by calling (408) 988-5811; it covers Santa Clara, San Mateo, and Alameda counties.

- Visit real estate agencies in the neighborhood and ask if they have apartment listings. Many real estate agencies will have apartment rental listings in the neighborhood where they do business.

- Call property managers and find out what they have available. They can be found under "Real Estate Management" in the Yellow Pages.

- Let an apartment- or roommate-finding agency do the work for you. Even though a fee is involved, it's usually reasonable and worth the price for all the time and effort you'll save.

The following resources will help you in your apartment search. There's not enough room to list everything available, so I've listed the most well known. If you don't have luck with these, then do some research on your own and you're sure to come up with many more options. Note that prices and services are subject to change.

APARTMENT/ROOMMATE FINDING AGENCIES

Apartments Unlimited
2285 Jackson Street (at Webster Street)
San Francisco, CA 94115
(415) 771-0447

SERVICES

Apartments in Pacific Heights, Marina, Russian Hill, North Beach, and Nob Hill neighborhoods

A new list of vacancies every three days for a period of one month

Listings can be mailed or faxed to you

FEES

$55 fee for total access of listings for one month

NOTE

You can preview listings before you register with them

Berkeley Connection
2840 College Avenue
(near Ashby Avenue)
Berkeley, CA 94705
(510) 845-7821

SERVICES

Listings for rentals in Berkeley, Richmond, Oakland, Alameda, El Cerrito, Claremont, and Rockridge areas

Receives 100 to 200 new listings a day

Get listings by fax, phone, or in person

Roommate searching also available

Fifty percent refund or second month free if you don't find what you're looking for

FEES

$50 per month fee for apartment rental listings

$25 per month fee for shared housing listings

Phone-in service for an extra $5 fee

Fax service for an extra $10 to $20 fee

Community Rentals
470 Castro Street (at 18th Street)
San Francisco, CA 94114
(415) 552-9595

2105 Van Ness Avenue
(at Pacific Avenue)
San Francisco, CA 94109
(415) 474-2787

SERVICES

Around 1,000 listings citywide at any given time

Receives 30 to 60 listings a day

Visit office for detailed listings of properties

FEES

$75 for two months with roommate matching included

Roommate matching separately is $30 for two months

$50 refund if your search is unsuccessful

Homefinders

2158 University Avenue
(near Shattuck Avenue)
Berkeley, CA 94704
(510) 549-6450

SERVICES

Listings in Berkeley, Albany, El Cerrito, and Oakland areas

Get listings by computerized voice mail, fax, e-mail, or in house

Roommate searching also available

Refund of any amount over $25 or the second month free

FEES

$55 per month for apartment rental listings

$25 per month for shared housing listings

Fax and e-mail service for an extra $10 each

Marin Rentals and Roommates

305 Miller Avenue (near Willow Street)
Mill Valley, CA 94941
(415) 383-1161

SERVICES

Complete a form with information about who you are and what you are looking for; this information is entered into a computer, generating a list of rentals

Fax or mail you listings at no extra charge

Listings throughout Marin county, from Sausalito to Novato

FEES

$55 for two months for rental listings *or* roommate searches

$65 for two months for both rental listings *and* roommate searches

Metro Rent

2021 Fillmore Street
(between California and Pine Streets)
San Francisco, CA 94115
(415) 563-7368

SERVICES

Claims to have San Francisco's largest database of listings: all areas, prices, and unit types

Rental books organized by area and price

Detailed full-page descriptions of rentals

Custom computer searches

Join-by-phone option

Twenty to fifty new listings each day

Credit report service

Fax service (searches database for match and faxes info to you)

Free phone access on the premises to call for appointments

Neighborhood maps

FEES

$95 to join by phone and have info faxed to you or told over the phone

$65 for in-office service (visit office and look through rental books organized by area and price)

$25 credit report service

NOTE

Membership lasts for 40 days, and a $40 refund is guaranteed if you're not successful.

Original San Francisco Roommate Referral Service

610A Cole Street
(between Haight and Waller Streets)
San Francisco, CA 94117
(415) 626-0606 information recording
(415) 626-7056 Roommates Now
call-in service
(415) 558-9191 office

SERVICES

Over 500 listings for gay, straight, and coed households

Express registration by phone

Temporary and permanent rental situations available

Rents range from $250 to $800 a month

Vacancies updated every week

Phone access 24 hours a day to daily updated information

Computer matching 24 hours a day

Complete information about prospective roommates, including

a recorded message from the roommate

Add your profile to the rental database so people can call you

FEES

$29 for walk-in service

$29 per month call-in service with additional months costing $10 each

$34 for deluxe access, which includes one month of call-in access plus four months of walk-in access

NOTES

Sign up by phone with a credit card 24 hours a day

In business for 20 years

Rental Solutions

1200 Gough Street
(at Geary Boulevard)
San Francisco, CA 94109
(415) 929-5100

2213 Dwight Way, #1
(near Fulton Street)
Berkeley, CA 94704
(510) 644-2522

437 Cambridge Street
Palo Alto, CA 94306
(415) 473-3000

SERVICES

Full-service rental search company

Agent works with you to meet your needs (for example, if you want a one-bedroom in Potrero Hill, that's where the agent will look)

FEES

One-half month's rent of the property you choose

$25 for interview and prescreening

Roommate Network

3129 Fillmore Street (between Filbert and Greenwich Streets)
San Francisco, CA 94123
(415) 441-2309 information message
(415) 441-6334 main office

SERVICES

Lists share rentals, empty rental units, as well as roommate searches

San Francisco's largest, catering to working professionals and graduate students

Only service with custom computer searches, matches, and multimedia previewing

Sign up and get immediate results by fax, phone, or in person

Quality listings with references

Satisfaction guaranteed

Unlimited updates to your search

No time limit on the membership

FEES

$55 for a share rental service only

$80 for apartment search and share rental service combined

NOTE

Seventy percent of clientele is repeat business.

Roommate Resource

2285 Jackson Street (at Webster Street)
San Francisco, CA 94115
(415) 771-0223

SERVICES

Largest selection of premium share rentals and vacant apartments in San Francisco

Detailed information profiles that describe apartment, roommates, and what they're looking for

Hundreds of listings in binders and on the computer

Phone access to computer database

FEES

$35 in-office binder service for three months and a $10 upgrade for computer matching

$45 computer database service with information faxed or mailed to you

REAL ESTATE/PROPERTY MANAGEMENT COMPANIES

Founders Realty Rental Department

585 8th Avenue (at Balboa Street)
San Francisco, CA 94118
(415) 668-5822

They have listings on voice mail including address, brief description, rental price, and contact.

McGuire Real Estate

2001 Lombard Street
San Francisco, CA 94123
(415) 929-1500

Listings are mostly in Pacific Heights, Marina, and Cow Hollow neighborhoods. The listings are mostly upper-end in price; for example the average price of a one-bedroom apartment is $1,500.

Paragon Management

185 Berry Street, Suite 4601
San Francisco, CA 94107
(415) 777-5200

This is a property management company that has rental listings in the South of Market and Potrero Hill neighborhoods. Call them and they'll tell you what's available and let you visit. If you're interested, complete an application and pay the processing fee for a credit check.

PLS (Property and Loan Services)

599 8th Avenue (at Balboa Street)
San Francisco, CA 94118
(415) 751-0599

You'll become familiar with these initials if you scan the rental ads in the Sunday paper regularly. This is a no-fee property management company. Call them and ask about their current listings, which are all over the city. A representative will set up an appointment and show you the places that interest you.

SAXE

1188 Franklin Street, Suite 204
San Francisco, CA 94109
(415) 474-2435 or
(415) 661-8110

An agent will take down your information over the phone or in person and call when there's something that matches what you're looking for. This is a no-fee agency that lists in the *Bay Area Rental Guide.*

Skyline Realty Rental Department

2101 Market Street (at Church Street)
San Francisco, CA 94114
(415) 861-2284

This agency lists studios, one- and two-bedroom apartments, flats, and hotel rooms. It's a no-fee agency. Call for their current listings.

Taisch Property

301 Jersey Street
San Francisco, CA 94114
(415) 826-4223

This no-fee agency has apartment rentals throughout the city. There is a $30 credit-check fee.

TCO

1364 Haight Street
San Francisco, CA 94117
(415) 621-1100

This is a Haight Street establishment, and most of their rental properties are in the neighborhood. Visit their offices to review binders of listings. If there's a property you like, you can check out a key and visit on your own. An application needs to be completed along with a credit check by interested renters.

The Union Group (TUG)

1700A Union Street (at Gough Street)
San Francisco, CA 94123
(415) 202-7444

This no-fee agency will tell you what they have available and give you the address so you can drive by. If you like it on the outside, then they can show you the inside. If you want to rent it, then complete an application and they'll run a credit check for a fee. They have listings all over the city.

Trinity Properties
333 Bay Street
(between Mason and Powell Streets)
San Francisco, CA 94133
(415) 433-3333

They own and manage all the buildings they rent. There's no fee for their service. Simply call them, tell them what you're looking for and your price range, and they'll tell you what they have available. They have buildings all over the city except in the Marina and Cow Hollow neighborhoods. The buildings are modern with wall-to-wall carpeting. No pets are allowed. Parking is available in all buildings for an extra charge. Units are always available for rent. An agent or apartment manager will show you the unit and if you like it, then you complete an application and hand over a $100 check for the credit check. This $100 will be applied toward your rent. It takes about three days from the time you find an apartment to when you can move in. There's a first- and last-month's deposit required and a $25 key fee.

GETTING YOUR APARTMENT

Now that you've found some listings that sound appealing and you've made your calls, be ready for the meetings with landlords or managers. As in any city, good apartments, especially affordable ones, are hard to find. Some neighborhoods, such as Pacific Heights, are considered more prime than others. Chances are you will be competing with other people for the same places. Here are some tips to gain the advantage:

Try to be the first appointment of the day. This way, if you like the place, you can let the landlord or manager know right away. Many times managers are just interested in getting a new tenant in a vacant apartment as soon as possible because they're losing money.

Come prepared. Be prepared to make a decision on the spot. Good apartments don't stay vacant for long. Bring your checkbook with enough money for down payments and security deposits. Also, bring a completed rental application, which can be found in most office supply stores, and a copy of your credit report. The three major credit reporting agencies are Equifax (800-685-1111), TRW (800-392-1122), and Trans Union (216-779-2378). Some information you'll need for your rental application is:

- Names, addresses and telephone numbers of your current and past employers

- Names, addresses and telephone numbers of your current and past landlords

- Names, addresses and telephone numbers of references

- Social Security number
- Driver's license number
- Bank account numbers
- Credit card numbers for credit reference

Look presentable. First impressions do count. Someone who shows up in business clothes or nice casual clothes will look more responsible, professional, and mature than someone who just came off the beach. Landlords want to make sure they're renting to responsible people who can pay their rent on time and take care of the property.

GETTING WHAT YOU WANT

Asking the right questions to a landlord or apartment manager before you move in can prevent unpleasant situations. The following are some key questions to ask:

- If there's a plumbing problem or some other emergency, how would I handle it with you?
- How long does it take for things to get fixed?
- What bills am I responsible for? What are you responsible for (e.g., trash, water)?
- Who else will have keys to my apartment?
- Who are the tenants upstairs and downstairs? (You don't want to be stuck with an aspiring tap dancer upstairs.)
- When is the rent due?
- When will I be receiving interest payments for my deposits? (California law states that landlords must pay interest on deposits they hold.)
- If you or someone you supervise, like a repairperson, needs to enter my apartment, how much notice will you give me? (California law states a minimum of 24 hours.)
- Are pets allowed?

Try to get a written rental agreement for your records. Even though an oral rental agreement is binding, there is no proof of the terms if you should have a disagreement with your landlord. For more information on tenant rights, send a self-addressed, stamped, 7-by-10-inch envelope to California Tenants, P.O. Box 310, Sacramento, CA 95802. You will receive a free copy of *California Tenants, Your Rights and Responsibilities.*

Nobody said apartment hunting was easy. Depending on the circumstances, you could take six days or six months to find a decent place to live. If you have to settle for a quick fix, make sure no lease is involved. Good luck!

WORLD WIDE WEB RESOURCES

The Gate
(http://www.sfgate.com/)
is the Web site for San Francisco's two major newspapers, the *San Francisco Chronicle* and *Examiner*. Select "classifieds" and you'll find a breakdown of apartment rentals in San Francisco, East Bay, Peninsula, and Marin, both furnished and unfurnished. There are also classified listings for rooms for rent, residential hotels, and rentals to share.

Rent Net
(http://www.inetbiz.com:1000/cgi-bin/rentnet/CA/Greater_SF_ &_Bay_Area)
is a service that will help you find an apartment anywhere in the San Francisco Bay Area according to your specifications. The first screen asks you to choose the desired apartment size. You are then linked to a screen where you choose your price range. The next screen shows apartments available in that size and price range; click on those you're interested in for more details and contact information. You can also narrow your search to a specific city in the Bay Area, say, San Rafael.

San Francisco Property Report
(http://www.izad.com/izad/urbanjmf/sfnews.htm)
is a newsletter for the San Francisco real estate industry but holds valuable information on the rental market.

CHAPTER FIVE

Where to Find a Place to Live

AN FRANCISCO is comprised of more than 30 different neighborhoods, each with a flavor of its own. North Beach is considered the Little Italy of the city with its abundance of Italian eateries and European-style cafés. The Mission is a mostly Hispanic neighborhood where many artists are taking advantage of low rents and enjoying the cafés, used-book stores, and art house theaters. The Marina is for yuppies who enjoy bayfront recreation and a pristine shopping district full of chain stores such as Starbucks and Pottery Barn. Whatever your lifestyle, there is sure to be a neighborhood that will suit your personality or satisfy your alter ego.

This chapter will describe some of the many different neighborhoods in San Francisco. The neighborhoods I will not detail are those that are suburban, family-style communities, because they don't offer many opportunities for renters. I will, however, venture outside of San Francisco city limits to mention some Bay Area communities that are an alternative to city living.

The resources I list for each San Francisco neighborhood have not been rated and do not represent the best of their type. The reason some businesses are listed over others is because they are the most well known or convenient to that neighborhood. For example, in a neighborhood that has many dry cleaners, I may name only the dry cleaner on the main business strip that is therefore easy to find. The purpose of the resource list is to assist new community residents to locate basic services in their neighborhood, such as a post office, grocery store, or laundromat. As you familiarize yourself with your community, you many find businesses and services that better suit your needs.

THE BIG PICTURE

The northern section of San Francisco has many opportunities for renters. This is a desirable section of the city, with many great outdoor spaces for sports and recreation. Along the waterfront is a running and biking path. Park Presidio is located in the northwest corner of the city and is another recreation area for hikers, bikers, runners, and golfers. Also, the north side of Golden Gate Park runs along the Richmond District neighborhood. This side of the park has various museums, tennis courts, the conservatory of flowers, and a golf course. Neighborhoods in the northern part of San Francisco include North Beach, Russian Hill, Nob Hill, Pacific Heights/Lower Pacific Heights, Marina, Presidio Heights/Laurel Heights, and Richmond District.

The central part of the city includes the neighborhoods right below the northern neighborhoods. Though there is no waterfront access, some areas still have great views of the bay, and others are located near Golden Gate Park. This section of the city is more diverse and gentrified than its northern neighbors. For example, the funky Haight-Ashbury neighborhood borders the gay Upper Market neighborhood, which borders a homey Noe Valley community. As you head out toward the ocean, neighborhoods tend to get more suburban and family-oriented. For example, if you choose to live in the Sunset District, Inner Sunset is a young, vibrant neighborhood located near the University of California, San Francisco, with a main street full of coffee shops and local bars for people to meet and hang out. If you go to Outer Sunset, which is near the ocean, you'll find mostly single-family homes with few social areas but lots of parking. Neighborhoods in the central part of the city include Western Addition, South of Market, Upper Market, Civic Center, Haight-Ashbury, Potrero Hill, Mission, Bernal Heights, Twin Peaks, Noe Valley, Glen Park, and Sunset District.

The southern section of the city is a combination of "bad" neighborhoods to the east and residential "family" neighborhoods to the west. Bayview has many housing projects and high crime. Excelsior, Visitation Valley, Crocker Amazon, and Outer Mission are lower-middle to middle-class areas with diverse ethnic populations, mostly families. Ocean View, Lakeshore, Parkside, and Mount Davidson/Diamond Heights are located closer to the ocean and are more solid, middle-class, family neighborhoods. In the Lakeshore district, San Francisco State University has the largest college student attendance in the city. This part of town also has public golf courses such as Harding Park and private clubs such as the tony Olympic Club. Lake Merced is a recreational park with a man-made lake located near the San Francisco Zoo.

Now that you have a flavor of what to find in each section of the city, it's time to get a more detailed look. Each neighborhood profile includes the following information:

- Average monthly rents were gathered from the *San Francisco Chronicle/Examiner* Sunday classified section

- Demographics are cited from *UPCLOSE San Francisco Bay Area 1991* (Up Close Publishing, 1991)

- Crime, as interpreted from statistics in *UPCLOSE San Francisco Bay Area 1991* (Up Close Publishing, 1991), is categorized as:

- Below average: fairly safe

- Average: still safe, but take precautions

- Above average: watch your back and belongings

• Street parking availability, as based on my own experience and informal interviews with residents, is categorized as:

- Good: you'll always find something, usually near your destination

- Moderate: you'll find parking, but you may have to circle the block a few times

- Difficult: think about public transportation

BERNAL HEIGHTS

Located on a hill rising above the Mission District and Noe Valley, this neighborhood has lower-than-average city rents and a diverse population of younger, creative types. You'll find a small-town quaintness here reflected in the architecture of Queen Anne cottages and Victorian bungalows and also in the bustling main street with an eclectic mix of small shops and cafés. This neighborhood offers city living with many suburban charms.

Bordered by Cesar Chavez (Army) Street, San Jose Avenue, U.S. 101, and Interstate 280

Bus lines: 9X, 12, 14, 14L, 14X, 23, 24, 27, 49, 67

Main street: Cortland Avenue between Mission and Bocana Streets

**BERNAL HEIGHTS
NEIGHBORHOOD RESOURCES**

Community Organizations
Bernal Heights Neighborhood Center
515 Cortland Avenue
(415) 206-2140 or 648-0330

Post Office
30 29th Street
(415) 695-1703

Library
Bernal Heights Library
500 Cortland Avenue
(415) 695-5160

Recreation Center
St. Mary's Park Recreation Center
On Crescent Street at Murray Street
(415) 695-5006

Parks
Bernal Heights Park
Bernal Heights Boulevard at
Folsom Street

Holly Park
Holly Park Circle on Elsie Street

St. Mary's Park
Crescent Avenue at Benton Avenue

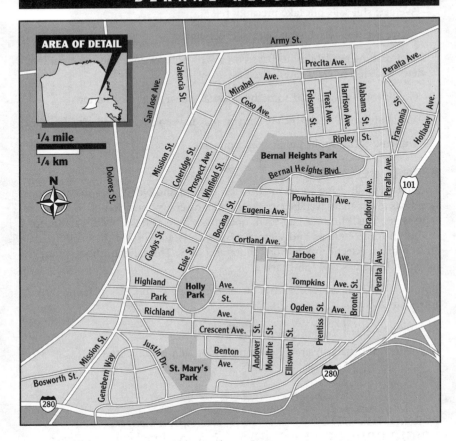

BERNAL HEIGHTS

AREA OF DETAIL

1/4 mile

1/4 km

N

Churches

St. Anthony's Catholic Church
3215 Cesar Chavez (Army) Street
(415) 647-2704

St. John the Evangelist Episcopal Church
1661 15th Street
(415) 861-1436

St. Kevin's Catholic Church
704 Cortland Avenue
(415) 648-5751

Banks

Bank of America
433 Cortland Avenue
(415) 615-4700

Supermarkets/Grocery Store

All-American Meat Market
615 Cortland Avenue
(415) 647-4776

Bernal Heights Produce
800 Cortland Avenue
(415) 282-7308

The Good Life Grocery
448 Cortland Avenue
(415) 648-3221

JC Supermarket
820 Cortland Avenue
(415) 648-4656

Pharmacy
Arrow Pharmacy
439 Cortland Avenue
(415) 648-5618

Cleaners/Laundromats
Bell's Cleaners
629 Cortland Avenue
(415) 285-3239

Bill's Whirl-O-Mat
600 Cortland Avenue
(415) 282-5912

Cortland One Hour Cleaners
331 Cortland Avenue
(415) 282-3700

Health Clubs
Navarro's Gym
3470 Mission Street
(415) 550-1694

Video Rentals
Four Star Videos
402 Cortland Avenue
(415) 641-5380

Video Oasis
448 Cortland Avenue
(415) 648-3569

Shoe Repair
Alexander's Shoe Repair
3296 Mission Street
(415) 648-4947

Oscar Montenegro Shoe Repair
1796 San Jose Avenue
(415) 585-1155

Hardware Store
Cole Hardware
3312 Mission Street
(415) 647-8700

Goodman's Lumber Company
445 Bayshore Boulevard between Cesar
Chavez (Army) Street and Alemany
Boulevard
(415) 285-2800

Pizza
Pizza Express
919 Cortland Avenue
(415) 282-2333

Miscellaneous
Bernal Books
401 Cortland Avenue
(415) 550-0293

Brown Bear Realty
303 Cortland Avenue
(415) 285-5700

Prince Charming Barber Shop
434 Cortland Avenue
(415) 285-0233

San Francisco Auto Repair Center
611 Florida Street near 18th Street
(415) 285-8588

BERNAL HEIGHTS NEIGHBORHOOD STATISTICS

Average Monthly Rent

Studio: $550 to $800

One-bedroom: $595 to $895

Two-bedroom: $950 to $1,200

Ethnic/Racial Distribution

White: 38%

African American: 10%

Asian: 22%

Hispanic: 30%

Median Age: 33

Percentage of Population

Male: 50%

Female: 50%

Percentage of Renters: 51%

Crime

Violent crime: Above average, with robbery the highest

Property crime: Slightly above average, with auto theft the highest

Street Parking

Permit required: No

Availability: Moderate

Local Newspaper: *New Bernal Journal*, (415) 206-2144

DOWNTOWN/UNION SQUARE/CIVIC CENTER

This neighborhood is a blend of the upscale Union Square shopping district, socially distressed Tenderloin community, and San Francisco city government. The lines between these communities are usually clear but sometimes blurred. The division is clear when you cross the street from the luxurious San Francisco Hilton hotel in Union Square and find yourself in the midst of the homeless on the other side. But if you wander up Hayes Street from the elegant Opera House, what at first appears to be a bad neighborhood quickly turns into a hip commercial strip with specialty shops, art galleries, cafés, and restaurants.

The Union Square residential neighborhood is full of sturdy old apartment buildings built in a time when no detail was too extravagant. Their elegant exterior architecture disguises poor interior maintenance. Many residents are elderly and have been there from better times or have relocated because of housing subsidies. The Academy of Art is located here, so you'll find a young artist population that brings a hip accent to the community. In the nearby Tenderloin, a growing immigrant Asian population has made its home in this community. Their presence and small businesses, such as markets and restaurants, have improved the neighborhood slightly. Even so, it is still considered one of the worst neighborhoods in the city, and visible signs are the prostitutes and drunks loitering in the streets.

The Civic Center neighborhood is home to San Francisco city government and the homeless. Surrounding city hall are cultural and civic landmarks such as Davies Symphony Hall, War Memorial Opera House, Herbst Theater, and the San Francisco Main Library. Nearby Hayes Street between Franklin and Webster is a perfect example of a once-shabby neighborhood that has been redeveloped into a thriving commercial strip.

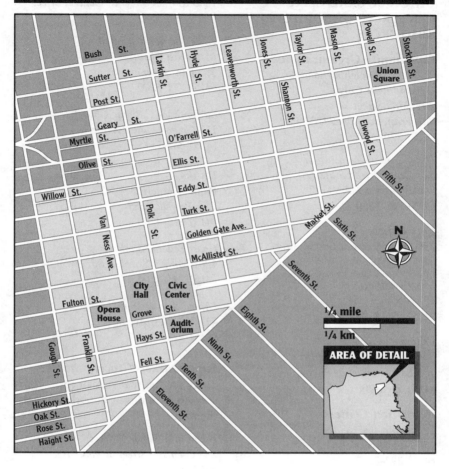

DOWNTOWN/UNION SQUARE/CIVIC CENTER

Bordered by Bush Street, Stockton Street, Market Street, Gough Street, Ellis Street, and Van Ness Avenue

Bus lines: 2, 3, 4, 5, 8, 21, 27, 30, 31, 38, 38L, 42, 45, 47, 49, 76

Main streets: Van Ness Avenue and Market Street (this is a shopping district with many commercial streets)

DOWNTOWN/ UNION SQUARE/CIVIC CENTER NEIGHBORHOOD RESOURCES

Community Organizations
Tenderloin Neighborhood
Development Corp.
201 Eddy Street
San Francisco, CA 94102
(415) 776-2151

Union Square Association
323 Geary Street, Suite 710
San Francisco, CA 94102
(415) 781-7880

Post Offices
1500 Pine Street at Larkin Street
(415) 284-0755

Macy's Station
121 Stockton Street
(415) 956-3570

Library
San Francisco Main Library
100 Larkin Street at Fulton Street
(415) 557-4400

Recreation Centers
Tenderloin Rec Center
570 Ellis Street
(415) 292-2162

Park
Union Square
At Stockton, Post, Powell,
and Geary Streets

Churches
Advent of Christ
the King Episcopal Church
261 Fell Street between Franklin
and Gough Streets
(415) 431-0454

First Baptist Church of California
1800 Market Street at Octavia Street
(415) 863-3382

Glide Memorial United
Methodist Church
330 Ellis Street
(415) 771-6300

St. Boniface Catholic Church
133 Golden Gate Avenue
(415) 863-7515

Banks
Bank of America
One Powell Street
(415) 615-4700

Coast Federal Bank
1201 Market Street at 8th Street
(415) 241-8700

United Savings Bank
711 Van Ness Avenue
(415) 928-0700

Supermarkets/Grocery Stores
There are too many small corner grocery stores in this neighborhood to list
them all.

Bread and Butter Market
888 O'Farrell Street at Polk Street
(415) 563-8985

City Hall Market
424 Hayes Street
(415) 863-1372

Hayes Valley Natural Foods
559 Hayes Street
(415) 241-9560

Hayes Valley Supermarket
580 Hayes Street
(415) 431-3527

Sutter Fine Foods
988 Sutter Street
(415) 776-7079

Pharmacies
A-P Pharmacy
1000 Larkin Street at Post Street
(415) 673-9130

Merrill's Drug Center
Market Street near 7th Street
(415) 431-7240

Walgreen
790 Van Ness Avenue
(415) 292-4899; and
500 Geary Street
673-8411

Cleaners/Laundromats
There are too many laundromats and
cleaners scattered about this neighborhood to list them all.

Abell Martinizing
441 Eddy Street
(415) 776-6662

Apple Cleaners
849 Leavenworth Street
(415) 776-9391

Coin Wash and Launderette
609 Hayes Street

Dry Image
455 Market Street
(415) 882-7351

Golden Launderette
445 Leavenworth Street
(415) 885-1144

Hyde-O'Farrell Dry Cleaners and
Finished Laundry
467 Hyde Street
(415) 474-3522

Health Clubs
Central YMCA
220 Golden Gate Avenue
(415) 885-5207

In Shape
371 Hayes Street
(415) 922-3700

Muscle Fitness
364 Hayes Street
(415) 863-4701

Video Rental
Wherehouse
1303 Van Ness Avenue
(415) 346-1978

Shoe Repair
Anthony's Shoe Service, Inc.
30 Geary Street
(415) 781-1338

Hyde Shoe Repair
112 Hyde Street
(415) 474-5622

Renato Shoe Repair
1405 Market Street at 10th Street
(415) 626-0481

ShoeWiz
865 Market Street
San Francisco Shopping Center
(415) 546-6986

Hardware Store
Double Eagle Hardware
530 O'Farrell Street near Jones Street
(415) 673-6724

Fox Hardware
70 Fourth Street
(415) 777-4400

Haji's Hardware
1170 Sutter Street
(415) 885-6321

Pizza

Blondie's
63 Powell Street
(415) 982-6168

Brooklyn Pizza
491 O'Farrell Street
(415) 474-3997

Escape from New York
7 Stockton Street
(415) 421-0700

Round Table Pizza
973 Market Street between
5th and 6th Streets
(415) 777-1888

Miscellaneous

Harold's International Newsstand
524 Geary Street
(415) 441-2665

Kwik Kopy Printing
1201 Sutter Street
(415) 775-2444
439 O'Farrell Street
(415) 885-3324

Mail Boxes Etc.
588 Sutter Street
(415) 834-1555
601 Van Ness Avenue at Opera Plaza
(415) 775-6644

PIP Printing
1101 Post Street
(415) 441-7227

DOWNTOWN/ UNION SQUARE/CIVIC CENTER NEIGHBORHOOD STATISTICS

Average Monthly Rent

Studio: $400 to $675

One-bedroom: $625 to $900

Two-bedroom: $1,050 to $1,300

Ethnic/Racial Distribution

White: 52%

African American: 14%

Asian: 26%

Hispanic: 8%

Median Age: 39

Percentage of Population

Male: 64%

Female: 36%

Percentage of Renters: 98%

Crime

Violent crime: Way above average, with robbery being the highest

Property crime: Way above average. with auto theft being the highest

Street Parking

Permit required: No, but mostly parking meters

Availability: Difficult

Local Newspaper: None

GLEN PARK

Glen Park is the place to go if you want quiet living yet proximity to freeways and public transportation that will get you to work. This is a homey community tucked between Bernal Heights and Diamond Heights, with narrow, winding streets and lots of trees and foliage. You'll find the best of both worlds here—city living with suburban touches.

Bordered by San Jose Avenue, 30th Street, Bosworth Street, and Elk Street

Bus lines: 26, 35, 44, 52

Main street: Chenery Street, from Diamond Street to Castro Street

GLEN PARK NEIGHBORHOOD RESOURCES

Community Organizations

Glen Park Association
P.O. Box 31292
San Francisco, CA 94131

Glen Park Neighbors
333 Bryant Street, Suite 220
San Francisco, CA 94107

Post Office

Diamond Heights Station
5265 Diamond Heights Boulevard
(415) 550-6412

Library

Glen Park Branch of the Library
653 Chenery Street
(415) 337-4740

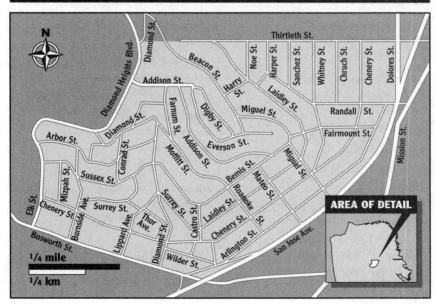

Recreation Center
Glen Park Rec Center
70 Elk Street at O'Shaughnessy
Boulevard
(415) 337-4705

Parks
Dorothy Erskine Park
On Bosworth Street at Burnside Avenue

George Christopher Playground
Off of Diamond Heights Boulevard at
Gold Mine Street

Glen Canyon Park
On O'Shaughnessy Boulevard
and Elk Street

Walter Haas Playground
On Diamond at Beacon Streets

Churches
Shepherd of the Hills Lutheran Church
Diamond Heights Boulevard at
Addison Street
(415) 586-3424

St. Francis Episcopal Church
399 San Fernando Way
(415) 334-1590

St. Phillips Catholic Church
725 Diamond Street
(415) 282-0141

Banks
Bank of America
2810 Diamond Street
(415) 615-4700

California Federal
2895 Diamond Street
(415) 239-4500

Supermarkets/Grocery Stores
Diamond Supermarket
2815 Diamond Street
(415) 587-8851

Safeway
Diamond Heights Shopping Center
5290 Diamond Heights Boulevard
(415) 824-7744

Cleaners/Laundromats
Ernie's Laundromat
636 Chenery Street
(415) 585-6911

Glen Park Cleaners
701 Chenery Street
(415) 239-8247

Health Clubs
SOL Gym
2838 Diamond Street
(415) 334-7697

Video Rentals
Diamond Video
5214 Diamond Heights Boulevard
(415) 550-1087

Shoe Repair
Alexander's Shoe Repair
3296 Mission Street
(415) 648-4947

Glen Park Shoe Care
2912 Diamond Street
(415) 334-0826

Hardware Store
Glen Park Hardware
685 Chenery Street
(415) 585-5761

Pizza
Sunset Pizza
2842 Diamond Street
(415) 239-1355

Miscellaneous
Excellent Haircuts
630 Chenery Street
(415) 585-5790

Glen Park Books
2788 Diamond Street
(415) 586-3733

Glen Park Flowers and Gifts
654 Chenery Street
(415) 584-4536

Glen Park Hardware
685 Chenery Street
(415) 585-5761

GLEN PARK NEIGHBORHOOD STATISTICS

Average Monthly Rent

Studio: not available

One-bedroom: $785 to $1,100

Two-bedroom: $975 to $1,200

Ethnic/Racial Distribution

White: 38%

African American: 10%

Asian: 22%

Hispanic: 30%

Median Age: 39

Percentage of Population

Male: 64%

Female: 36%

Percentage of Renters: 98%

Crime

Violent crime: Below average, highest being robbery

Property crime: Below average, highest being auto theft

Parking

Permit required: Yes

Availability: Moderate

Local Newspaper: The Noe Review, (415) 648-5898

HAIGHT-ASHBURY/COLE VALLEY

This community has a lively, nonconformist atmosphere. It was the 1960s mecca for America's hippies and the center of the counter-culture movement. It still retains some of that sixties flavor along Haight Street, where a new wave of Gen X hippies hang outside of funky secondhand clothing stores and paraphernalia shops. For more traditional living, Cole Valley is just south of Haight Street; the streets are narrow and tree-lined, and parking is impossible. Cole Valley has a small, quaint business district, so you never have to venture to the griminess of the Haight. The Haight-Ashbury/Cole Valley neighborhoods are situated near Golden Gate Park, Buena Vista Park, and the Panhandle, which are great areas for outdoor recreation and relaxing. University of California, San Francisco, and its hospital is also nearby. If you make this your home, you'll share the community with young, rebellious student types, old hippies, drug dealers, and the avant garde. Living here is sure to be an experience.

Bordered by Divisadero Street, Buena Vista Avenue, Stanyan Street, and Fulton Street

Bus lines: 6, 7, 22, 24, 33, 37, 43, 66, 71

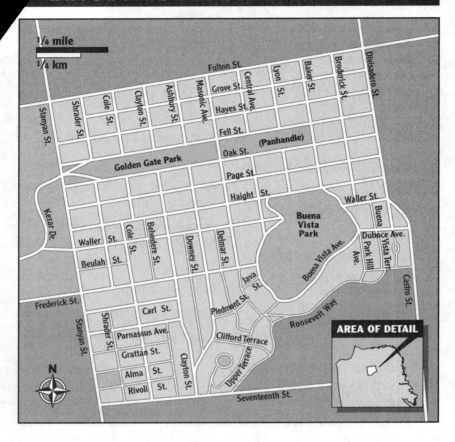

Main streets: Haight Street, from Masonic to Stanyan Streets; in Cole Valley, Cole Street from Waller to Carl Streets

HAIGHT-ASHBURY/COLE VALLEY NEIGHBORHOOD RESOURCES

Community Organization
Haight-Ashbury Neighborhood Council
P.O. Box 170518
San Francisco, CA 94117

Post Office
Clayton Street Station
554 Clayton Street
(415) 621-7445

Library
1833 Page Street near Cole Street
(415) 666-7155

Recreation Center
Hamilton Rec Center
1900 Geary Street at Steiner Street
(415) 292-2008

Parks
Buena Vista Park
Haight and Lyon Streets

Corona Heights Park
Castro and 15th Streets

Richard Gamble Memorial Park
Cole and Carl Streets

Churches
All Saints Episcopal Church
1350 Waller Street
(415) 621-1862

Hamilton United Methodist Church
1525 Waller Street
(415) 566-2416

Mt. Zion Baptist Church
1321 Oak Street
(415) 863-4109

St. Agnes Catholic Church
1025 Masonic Street
(415) 863-2485

Banks
First Interstate Bank
1653 Haight Street
(415) 765-4500

Supermarkets/Grocery Stores
Alpha Market
960 Cole Street
(415) 564-8910

Cala Foods
690 Stanyan Street
(415) 752-3940

Diamond Supermarket
199 Parnassus Avenue
(415) 664-3034

Haight Ashbury Produce
1615 Haight Street
(415) 861-5672

Haight Natural Foods
1621 Haight Street
(415) 487-1540

Real Foods
1023 Stanyan Street
(415) 564-2800

Say Cheese and Food
856 Cole Street
(415) 665-5020

Sun Country Foods
1101 Stanyan Street
(415) 566-2511

Pharmacy
Pacific Drug
1530 Haight Street
(415) 431-8559

Val-Grin Drug Store
925 Cole Street
(415) 661-1216

Cleaners/Laundromats
Cole Cleaners
947 Cole Street
(415) 566-8841

Lucky Cleaners
1300 Haight Street
(415) 621-7867

New Russ Cleaners
701 Schrader Street
(415) 750-9590

Parkview Launderette
618 Stanyan Street

Prosperity Cleaners
912 Cole Street
(415) 566-9040

Quality Wash and Dry
1431 Haight Street
(415) 431-1330

Son Loy Laundry and Cleaners
784 Stanyan Street
(415) 752-7686

Health Club
Cole Valley Fitness
957 Cole
(415) 665-3330

Video Rentals
Into Video
1439 Haight Street
(415) 864-2346

Video Nook
858 Cole Street
(415) 731-6265

Shoe Repair
Elite Shoe Repair
1614 Haight Street
(415) 863-3260

Hardware Store
Cole Hardware
956 Cole Street
(415) 753-2653

Roberts Hardware
1629 Haight Street
(415) 431-3392

Pizza
Cybelles Pizza
1535 Haight Street
(415) 552-4200

Escape from New York Pizza
1737 Haight Street
(415) 668-5577

Papadoro Pizza
1649 Haight Street
(415) 621-7272

Movie Theater
Red Vic Movie House
1727 Haight Street
(415) 668-3994

Miscellaneous
Cole Garage
930 Cole Street
(415) 753-2280

Copy Central
1685 Haight Street
(415) 863-4304

Haight Mail
1388 Haight Street
(415) 621-0975

Hair on Haight
1783 Haight Street
(415) 221-4247

The Postal Chase
915 Cole Street
(415) 566-9777

Tassajara Bakery
1000 Cole Street
(415) 664-8947

TCO (Rentals/Real Estate)
1364 Haight Street
(415) 621-1600

Trimmers Hair
1576 Haight Street
(415) 431-7340

HAIGHT-ASHBURY/COLE VALLEY NEIGHBORHOOD STATISTICS

Average Monthly Rent

Studio: $485 to $695

One-bedroom: $725 to $995

Two-bedroom: $975 to $1,295

Ethnic/Racial Distribution

White: 76%

African American: 10%

Asian: 10%

Hispanic: 4%

Median Age: 32

Percentage of Population

Male: 57%

Female: 43%

Percentage of Renters: 82%

Crime

Violent crime: Slightly above average, with robbery being the highest

Property crime: Above average, with auto theft being the highest

Street Parking

Permit required: Yes

Availability: Difficult

Local Newspaper: None

LAKESHORE

Though this neighborhood appears to be mostly residential, it is the home of San Francisco State University and its population of college students. San Francisco State offers on-campus housing, which is a good thing, because the area doesn't have many apartment buildings. If you choose to live in this part of the city, you'll enjoy Lake Merced and Harding Park, two recreational areas that have, among other things, golf, biking, and running. It's also home to one of the nicest shopping centers in the city, Stonestown Galleria. This mall has a Nordstrom anchor store and quality shops such as Ann Taylor and Banana Republic. If you don't end up living here, you're sure to be visiting for sports or shopping.

Bordered by Junipero Serra Boulevard, Sloat Boulevard, and Ocean Avenue

Bus lines: 17, 18, 28, 28L, 29, 88, M

Main street: There is no clearly defined street; Stonestown Galleria and Lakeside Village offer shopping and strolling

LAKESHORE NEIGHBORHOOD RESOURCES

Community Organization

Lake Merced Hill Association
1150 Lake Merced Boulevard
San Francisco, CA 94132

Post Office

565 Buckingham Way
(415) 759-1660

Library

155 Winston Drive at 19th Avenue
(415) 337-4780

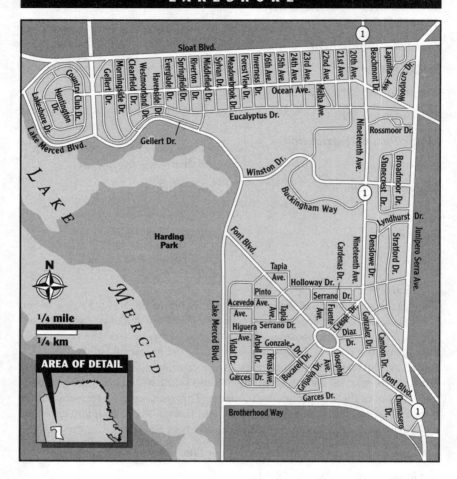

Recreation Center
Ocean View Recreation Center
Capitol Avenue and Montana Street
(415) 337-4710

Parks
Lake Merced
Lake Merced Boulevard

Pine Lake Park
Crestlake Drive at Paraiso Place

Churches
First United Presbyterian Church
1740 Sloat Boulevard
(415) 759-3700

Incarnation Episcopal Church
1750 29th Avenue
(415) 564-2324

Lakeside Presbyterian Church
19th Avenue and Eucalyptus Drive
(415) 564-8833

Lutheran Church of Our Savior
Junipero Serra Boulevard and
Garfield Street
(415) 586-7890

St. Cecilia's Catholic Church
2555 17th Avenue
(415) 664-8481

St. Stephen's Catholic Church
475 Eucalyptus Drive
(415) 681-2444

St. Thomas More Catholic Church
1300 Junipero Serra Boulevard
(415) 584-4613

Temple Baptist Church
3355 19th Avenue
(415) 566-4080

Temple United Methodist Church
19th Avenue and Junipero Serra
Boulevard
(415) 586-1444

West Portal Lutheran Church
200 Sloat Boulevard
(415) 661-0242

Banks
Bank of America
1007 Taraval Street;
1515 Sloat Street at the Lakeshore
Plaza Lucky;
245 Winston Drive
(415) 615-4700

Bank of the West
495 Buckingham Way
(415) 665-5252

California Federal
2600 Ocean Avenue
(415) 239-2000

First Nationwide Bank
3160 20th Avenue
(415) 566-8212

Glendale Federal
2499 Ocean Avenue
(415) 586-9292

Wells Fargo Bank
599 Buckingham Way
(415) 781-2235

World Savings and Loan
140 Serramonte Center.
(415) 994-2550

Supermarkets/Grocery Stores
Lucky's Supermarket
1515 Sloat Boulevard
(415) 681-4300

Parkside Farmer's Market
555 Taraval Street
(415) 681-5563

Petrini's Stonestown Market
255 Winston Drive
(415) 753-0189

Safeway Marketplace
730 Taraval Street
(415) 665-4136

Pharmacies
Barron's Pharmacy
2621 Ocean Avenue
(415) 333-4883

Merrill's Drugs
Winston Avenue at Stonestown
(415) 681-4035

Thrifty Junior
445 Taraval Street
(415) 564-9437

Walgreen
2250 Ocean Avenue
(415) 587-911

Cleaners/Laundromats
Lakeshore Cleaners
1513 Sloat Boulevard
(415) 753-5854

Stonestown Cleaners
285 Winston Drive
(415) 564-5881

Video Rental
Blockbuster Video
1503 Sloat Boulevard
(415) 753-1404

Shoe Repair
Lakeshore Shoe Service
1553 Sloat Boulevard
(415) 664-1344

Hardware Store
Lakeshore Lock and Hardware
1583 Sloat Boulevard
(415) 665-5300

Miscellaneous
Kinko's
555 Buckingham Way
(415) 566-0572

Postal Annex
2570 Ocean Avenue
(415) 587-7661

Super Crown Bookstore
1591 Sloat Boulevard
(415) 664-1774

United Artists Stonestown Twin Theater
501 Buckingham Way
(415) 221-8182

LAKESHORE NEIGHBORHOOD STATISTICS

Average Monthly Rent
Studio: $775 to $995

One-bedroom: $995 to $1,100

Two-bedroom: $975 to $1,275

Ethnic/Racial Distribution
White: 64%

African American: 8%

Asian: 20%

Hispanic: 8%

Median Age: 38

Percentage of Population
Male: 41%

Female: 59%

Percentage of Renters: 75%

Crime
Violent crime: Below average, with homicide being the highest

Property crime: Below average, with auto theft being the highest

Street Parking
Permit required: Yes

Availability: Good

Local Newspaper: None

MARINA

The Marina was created on landfill for the Pan Pacific Expo back in 1915. Because of this, it sustained some of the worst damage in the 1989 Loma Prieta earthquake. But that doesn't stop it from being a popular community for young, white-collar singles and couples who pay some of the highest rents in the city. This attraction could be because of the proximity to the Marina Green, a grassy open space bordering the San Francisco Bay from Fort Mason to the Golden Gate Bridge. There's always a flurry of athletic activity along here, including jogging and rollerblading. It gets especially active on the weekends with sunbathers, kite-flyers, and volleyball enthusiasts. Another attraction could be the active day and night life along Chestnut Street, which has lots of bars, boutiques, and cafés. The residential portion of the neighborhood consists of well-tended streets lined with elegant Mediterranean-style buildings, some with views of the bay. This is the place to be if you want to experience hip, yuppie, urban living.

Bordered by Van Ness Avenue, Green Street, Lyon Street, and Marina Boulevard

Bus lines: 22, 28, 30, 30X, 43, 76

Main street: Chestnut Street, between Fillmore and Divisadero Streets

MARINA

1/4 mile
1/4 km

San Francisco Bay

AREA OF DETAIL

Yacht Harbor
Marina Green Park
Fort Mason

Marina Blvd.
Jefferson St.
Beach St.
North Point St.
Bay St.
Francisco St.
Chestnut St.
Richardson Ave.

Casa Wy.
Rico Wy.
Prado St.
Cervantes Blvd.
Pierce Wy.
Avila St.
Capra Wy.
Alhambra St.
Mallorca Wy.
Toledo Wy.

Marina Blvd.
Beach St.
North Point St.
Bay St.
Moscone Rec. Center

Laguna St.
Octavia St.
Gough St.
Franklin St.
Van Ness Ave.

Lombard St.
Greenwich St.
Filbert St.
Union St.
Green St.

Lyon St.
Baker St.
Broderick St.
Divisadero St.
Scott St.
Pierce St.
Steiner St.
Fillmore St.
Webster St.
Buchanan St.

101

101

N

MARINA NEIGHBORHOOD RESOURCES

Community Organizations

Marina Neighborhood Association
3727 Fillmore Street, #201
San Francisco, CA 94123

Cow Hollow Neighbors in Action
2742 Baker Street
San Francisco, CA 94123

Post Office
2055 Lombard Street
(415) 284-0755

Library
1890 Chestnut at Webster Streets
(415) 292-2006 or 292-2150

Recreation Center
Moscone Center
1800 Chestnut at Buchanan Streets
(415) 292-2006

Parks
Marina Green
Along Marina Boulevard

Churches
Calvary Presbyterian Church
2515 Fillmore Street at Jackson Street
(415) 346-3832

St. Mary the Virgin Episcopal Church
2325 Union Street
(415) 921-3665

St. Vincent de Paul Catholic Church
2320 Green Street
(415) 922-1010

Banks
Bank of America
2460 Lombard Street
2200 Chestnut Street
(415) 615-4700

Citibank
2197 Chestnut Street
(415) 923-1123

First Interstate Bank
2300 Chestnut Street
(415) 544-5009

Great Western Bank
2166 Chestnut Street
(415) 931-3391

Home Savings of America
2750 Lombard Street
(415) 474-5052

San Francisco Federal
2198 Chestnut Street
(415) 346-2900

Wells Fargo Bank
2055 Chestnut Street
(415) 781-2235

World Savings and Loan
2298 Chestnut Street
(415) 346-9658

Supermarkets/Grocery Stores
High Health Shoppe Natural Foods
2172 Chestnut Street
(415) 921-1400

Lucca Deli
2120 Chestnut Street
(415) 921-7873

Marina Supermarket
2323 Chestnut Street
(415) 346-7470

Safeway
15 Marina Boulevard
(415) 563-4946

Pharmacy
Burton's Pharmacy
2016 Chestnut Street
(415) 567-1166

Walgreen
2125 Chestnut Street
(415) 567-9322
Divisadero and Lombard Streets
(415) 931-6415

Cleaners/Laundromats
B & M Launderesse
2371 Chestnut Street
(415) 921-0405

Fine Arts Cleaners
2379 Chestnut Street
(415) 885-4416

Launderland (Laundromat)
3320 Fillmore Street
(415) 921-7813

The Laundry Basket
2228 Chestnut Street
(415) 567-9888

Walnut Cleaners
2266 Chestnut Street
(415) 921-0495

Health Clubs
Advantage Fitness
3741 Buchanan Street
(415) 563-3535

Marina Club
3333 Fillmore Street
(415) 563-3333

Video Rentals
Captain Video
2398 Lombard Street
(415) 921-2839

Shoe Repair
James Bros. Shoe Repair
2176 Chestnut Street
(415) 921-9032

Hardware Store
Fredericksen Hardware
3029 Fillmore Street
(415) 292-2950

Pizza
Cybelles Pizza
2105 Chestnut Street
(415) 563-0620

Movie Theater
Cinema 21
2141 Chestnut Street
(415) 921-6720

Miscellaneous
Kimmel's Stationery
2144 Chestnut Street
(415) 921-8828

Mail Boxes Etc.
2269 Chestnut Street
(415) 922-4500

Marina Pet Hospital
2024 Lombard Street
(415) 921-0410

Nice Cuts
2224 Chestnut Street
(415) 441-1235

Ole's Hair Salon
2072 Chestnut Street
(415) 346-7967

Radio Shack
1799 Lombard Street
(415) 922-2973

Silver Shears Barber Shop
2272 Chestnut Street
(415) 563-9773

Supercuts
2244 Chestnut Street
(415) 771-9934

Waldenbooks
2169 Chestnut Street
(415) 563-1658

MARINA NEIGHBORHOOD STATISTICS

Average Monthly Rent

Studio: $700 to $995

One-bedroom: $850 to $1,500

Two-bedroom: $1,400 to $1,850

Ethnic/Racial Distribution

White: 84%

African American: 2%

Asian: 10%

Hispanic: 4%

Median Age: 38

Percentage of Population

Male: 42%

Female: 58%

Percentage of Renters: 85%

Crime

Violent crime: Below average, with robbery being the highest

Property crime: Above average, with auto theft being the highest

Street Parking

Permit required: Yes

Availability: Difficult

Local Newspaper: Marina Times, (415) 928-1398

MISSION DISTRICT

The Mission District was once prime land for the Ohlone Native Americans and then for Spanish missionaries. Today it's known as a Latino neighborhood with gang activity and high crime, especially at night. But change is coming about in the northern part of the district, thanks to a contingent of artists, musicians, and lesbians that are calling this low-rent neighborhood home. North Mission is becoming quite the artsy scene, especially along Valencia and 16th Streets, where you'll find grunge cafés, secondhand bookstores, and plenty of thrift shops. The Women's Building serves, among others things, as a meeting place for progressive and radical political groups that tend to congregate in this part of town. This neighborhood is for you if you want a bohemian kind of living experience.

Bordered by Market Street, Dolores Street, Cesar Chavez (Army) Street, and U.S. 101

Bus lines: 12, 14, 14L, 22, 26, 27, 33, 49, 53

Main streets: Valencia Street, from 16th Street to about 19th Street, and 16th Street, from Dolores to Valencia Streets

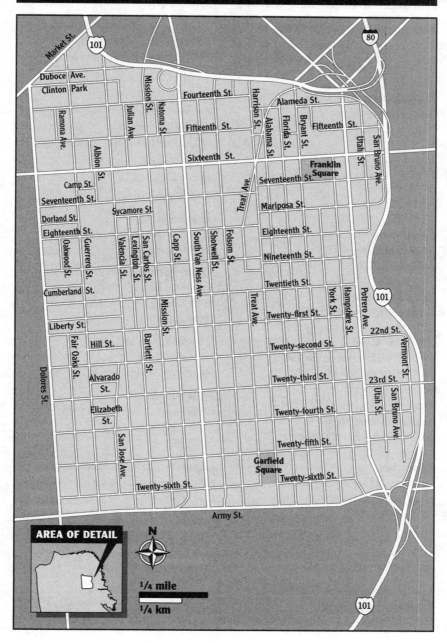

Market St.

101

80

Duboce Ave.

Clinton Park

Ramona Ave.

Mission St.

Julian Ave.

Natoma St.

Fourteenth St.

Alameda St.

Harrison St.

Alabama St.

Florida St.

Bryant St.

Fifteenth St.

Utah St.

San Bruno Ave.

Albion St.

Fifteenth St.

Sixteenth St.

Camp St.

Seventeenth St.

Franklin Square

Treat Ave.

Seventeenth St.

Dorland St.

Sycamore St.

Mariposa St.

Eighteenth St.

Oakwood St.

Guerrero St.

Valencia St.

Lexington St.

San Carlos St.

Capp St.

South Van Ness Ave.

Shotwell St.

Folsom St.

Eighteenth St.

Nineteenth St.

Cumberland St.

Twentieth St.

Treat Ave.

York St.

Hampshire St.

Potrero Ave.

101

Liberty St.

Fair Oaks St.

Hill St.

Mission St.

Bartlett St.

Twenty-first St.

22nd St.

Vermont St.

Dolores St.

Alvarado St.

Twenty-second St.

Twenty-third St.

23rd St.

Utah St.

San Bruno Ave.

Elizabeth St.

Twenty-fourth St.

San Jose Ave.

Twenty-fifth St.

Garfield Square

Twenty-sixth St.

Twenty-sixth St.

Army St.

101

AREA OF DETAIL

N

1/4 mile

1/4 km

MISSION DISTRICT NEIGHBORHOOD RESOURCES

Community Organizations

Inner Mission Neighbors
1250 Treat Avenue
San Francisco, CA 94110

North Mission Association
286 Guerrero Street
San Francisco, CA 94103

Post Office

1198 South Van Ness Avenue
at 23rd Street
(415) 284-0755

Library

3359 24th Street
(415) 695-5090

Recreation Center

Mission Rec Center
2450 Hamson Street (gym)
745 Treat Avenue (theater arts
and cultural programs for kids)
(415) 695-5012 or 695-5014

Park

Mission Dolores Park
Dolores Street at 18th Street

Churches

Golden Gate Lutheran Church
601 Dolores Street at 19th Street
(415) 647-5050

Mission Dolores Catholic Church
16th and Dolores Streets
(415) 621-8203

Mission Presbyterian Church
23rd and Capp Streets
(415) 647-8295

St. John the Evangelist Episcopal Church
1661 15th Street
(415) 861-1436

St. Matthew's Lutheran Church
3281 16th Street at Dolores Street
(415) 863-6371

Banks

Bank of America
2701 Mission Street
(415) 615-4700

Bayview Federal Bank
2601 Mission Street
(415) 826-8410

Wells Fargo Bank
3027 16th Street
(415) 781-2235

Supermarkets/Grocery Stores

Rainbow Grocery
1899 Mission Street
(415) 863-0620

Safeway Supermarket
2020 Market Street
(415) 861-7660

Pharmacy

Walgreen
1979 Mission Street
(415) 558-8905

Cleaners/Laundromats

Fabri Care Dry Cleaners
2345 Mission Street
(415) 647-2345

Mission Quick Cleaners
3270 24th Street
(415) 285-5313

Launderland Laundromat
3800 24th Street
(415) 282-9839

Laundryworld Laundromat
2799 24th Street
(415) 648-5081

Health Clubs
See Upper Market or Noe Valley listings.

Video Rentals
See Upper Market or Noe Valley listings.

Shoe Repair
Mission Shoe Repair Shop
2589 Mission Street
(415) 285-3767

Montano Shoe Repair
199 Guerrero Street
(415) 626-7638

Hardware Store
Cole Hardware
3312 Mission Street
(415) 647-8700

Pizza
Arinell Pizza
509 Valencia Street
(415) 255-1303

Pauline's Pizza
260 Valencia Street
(415) 552-2050

Pizza Pop!
3274 21st Street
(415) 695-1615

Movie Theater
The Roxie Cinema
3117 16th Street
(415) 863-1087

Miscellaneous
The Women's Building
3543 18th Street
(415) 431-1180

MISSION DISTRICT NEIGHBORHOOD STATISTICS

Average Monthly Rent

Studio: $475 to $650

One-bedroom: $670 to $900

Two-bedroom: $850 to $1,200

Ethnic/Racial Distribution

White: 28%

African American: 8%

Asian: 14%

Hispanic: 50%

Median Age: 31

Percentage of Population

Male: 51%

Female: 49%

Percentage of Renters: 87%

Crime

Violent crime: Way above average, with robbery being the highest

Property crime: Way above average, with auto theft being the highest

Street Parking

Permit required: Yes, in most but not all areas

Availability: Moderate

Local Newspaper: New Mission News, (415) 695-8702

NOB HILL

For over a century, this has been the home of San Francisco high society. But scattered amongst the luxurious high-rises are affordable apartment buildings housing working professionals. The many professionals that live here enjoy the proximity to work in the Financial District as well as restaurants and shopping in Chinatown and on Polk Street. The steep hills that comprise this neighborhood offer excellent Stairmaster-like workouts, so there's hardly a need for a gym membership. Some attractions in this neighborhood are the Gothic-style Grace Cathedral and the famous Fairmont Hotel.

Bordered by Bush Street, Powell Street, Broadway, and Van Ness Avenue

Bus lines: 1, 27

Main streets: California Street, between Powell and Polk Streets, and Polk Street, between California Street and Broadway

NOB HILL

Broadway Tunnel
Bernard St.
Himmelmann Place
Broadway
Polk St.
Morrell St.
Auburn
Pacific Ave.
Larkin St.
Hyde St.
Leavenworth St.
Jones St.
Taylor St.
Mason St.
Powell St.
Jackson St.
Washington St.
Pleasant St.
Sproule Lane
Cushman St.
Fairmont Hotel
Clay St.
Van Ness Ave.
Grace Cathedral
Sacramento St.
California St.
Pine St.
Austin St.
Bush St.

AREA OF DETAIL

1/4 mile
1/4 km

NOB HILL NEIGHBORHOOD RESOURCES

Community Organizations
Nob Hill Association
588 Sutter Street, #433
San Francisco, CA 99102

Nob Hill Neighbors
1525 Grant Avenue
San Francisco, CA 94133

Post Offices
1400 Pine Street at Larkin Street
(415) 284-0755

Chinatown Branch
867 Stockton Street
(415) 956-3566

Library
Chinatown Branch
445 Grant Avenue near Pine Street
(415) 274-0275

Recreation Center
Chinese Recreation Center
1199 Mason Street
(415) 292-2017

Park
Huntington Square Park
On Taylor Street across from
Grace Cathedral

Churches
First St. John United Methodist Church
1600 Clay Street at Larkin Street
(415) 474-6219

Grace Cathedral Episcopal Church
California and Taylor Streets
(415) 776-6611

Notre Dame Des Victoires
Catholic Church
566 Bush Street
(415) 397-0113

Old First Presbyterian Church
1751 Sacramento Street at
Van Ness Avenue
(415) 776-5552

Old St. Mary's Catholic Church
660 California Street
(415) 288-3800

Banks
American Savings Bank
1500 Polk Street
800-788-7000

Bank of America
1640 Van Ness Avenue at
California Street
(415) 615-4700

First Nationwide Bank
1541 Polk Street
(415) 776-9322

Wells Fargo Bank
1560 Van Ness Avenue at
California Street
(415) 781-2235

Supermarkets/Grocery Stores
Better Life Whole Foods
1058 Hyde Street
(415) 474-3053

Cala Foods
Hyde and California Streets
(415) 776-3650

Chico's Market
1168 Leavenworth Street
(415) 885-9500

Le Beau Nob Hill Market
1263 Leavenworth Street
(415) 885-3030

Nob Hill Produce
1000 Hyde Street
(415) 441-2220

Pharmacy

Fairmont Hotel Pharmacy
801 Powell Street at California Street
(415) 362-3000

Walgreen
1524 California Street at Polk Street
(415) 673-4809

Cleaners/Laundromats

American Cleaners
1400 Hyde Street
(415) 885-3360

Cable Car Cleaners
1398 California Street
(415) 928-0219

Clean Express Coin Laundry
(Laundromat)
1566 Hyde Street

Larkin Street Laundromat
1868 Larkin Street

Marvel Cleaners
1501 California Street
(415) 775-0897

Stanford Cleaners and Tailors
1018 Hyde Street
(415) 474-5524

Today's Laundromat
1438 California Street

Top Elegance Cleaners
1156 Taylor Street
(415) 931-8963

Health Clubs

Chinatown YMCA
855 Sacramento Street
(415) 982-4412

Club One
950 California Street
(415) 397-6363

Video Rental

Video Movie Center II
1414 California Street
(415) 775-5505

Shoe Repair

Crazy Cobbler Shoe Repair
1042 Hyde Street
(415) 776-5033

Hardware Store

Brownies Hardware
1552 Polk Street
(415) 673-8900

Pizza

California Pizza
1534 California Street
(415) 775-2525

Front Room Pizza
California Street
(415) 771-1591

Movie Theaters

Lumiere Theater
1572 California Street
(415) 885-3200

Royal Theater
1529 Polk Street
(415) 474-0353

Miscellaneous

Copy Central
1475 Polk Street
(415) 775-0200

NOB HILL NEIGHBORHOOD STATISTICS

Average Monthly Rent

Studio: $450 to $825

One-bedroom: $650 to $1,200

Two-bedroom: $1,000 to $2,300

Ethnic/Racial Distribution

White: 44%

African American: 2%

Asian: 50%

Hispanic: 4%

Median Age: 38

Percentage of Population

Male: 52%

Female: 48%

Percentage of Renters: 88%

Crime

Violent crime: Below average, with robbery being the highest

Property crime: Below average, with auto theft being the highest

Street Parking

Permit required: Yes

Availability: Difficult

Local Newspaper: *Nob Hill Gazette,* (415) 227-0190

NOE VALLEY

It could be a slice of small-town America along 24th Street: mothers strolling their babies, yuppie singles walking their dogs, couples holding hands and window-shopping. Welcome to Noe Valley, one of San Francisco's best-kept secrets. Up the hill from the Castro, this neighborhood offers a respite from the hustle and bustle of the city below. This is a place where small business is king and corporate chain stores and restaurants are practically nonexistent (Walgreen and Thrifty drug stores have opened). Noe Valley is a tight-knit, friendly community with a small-town feel. Residents are hip and progressive, interested in environmental good and a good latte.

Bordered by Diamond Heights, Dolores Street, 30th Street, Portola Drive, and 21st Street

Bus lines: 24, 48, J

Main street: 24th Street, between Castro and Church Streets

NOE VALLEY
NEIGHBORHOOD RESOURCES

Community Organizations
Friends of Noe Valley
3922 22nd Street
San Francisco, CA 94114

Noe Valley Neighborhood Association
995 Duncan Street
San Francisco, CA 994131

Post Office
4083 24th Street
(415) 821-0776

Library
451 Jersey Street near Castro Street
(415) 695-5095

Recreation Center
Upper Noe Recreation Center
285 Day Street at Sanchez Street
(415) 695-5011

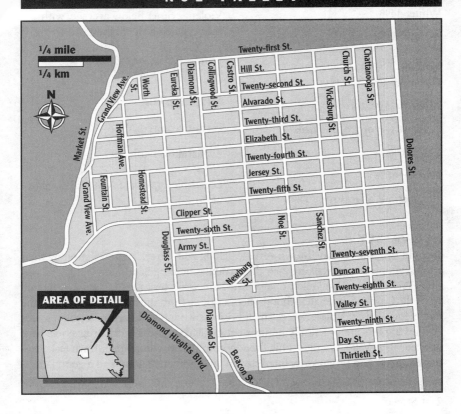

NOE VALLEY

Churches

Bethany United Methodist Church
1268 Sanchez Street
(415) 647-8393

Holy Innocents Episcopal Church
455 Fair Oaks Street
(415) 824-5142

St. James Catholic Church
1086 Guerrero Street
(415) 824-4232

St. Paul's Catholic Church
221 Valley Street
(415) 648-7538

St. Philip's Catholic Church
725 Diamond Street
(415) 282-0141

Banks

Bank of America
4098 24th Street
(415) 622-4301

Coast Federal Savings and Loan
2998 24th Street
(415) 285-3040

Wells Fargo Bank Express Stop
24th Street, between Noe and
Castro Streets

Supermarkets/Grocery Stores
Bell Markets
3950 24th Street
(415) 648-0876

Jim and Sons Produce
3813 24th Street
(415) 647-0755

Mikey Tom Market
1747 Church Street
(415) 826-5757

Noe Valley Community Store
(a food cooperative)
1599 Sanchez Street
(415) 824-8022

Real Food Company
3939 24th Street
(415) 282-9500

Pharmacies
Thrifty Drugs
4045 24th Street
(415) 648-8660

Walgreen
1333 Castro Street
(415) 826-8998

Cleaners/Laundromats
Best Cleaners and Laundry
3783 24th Street
(415) 648-2378

Launderland Coin-Op Laundry
3800 24th Street
(415) 282-9839

Suzie's Laundry Service
3812 24th Street
(415) 647-1597

Health Clubs
Back Room Yoga and Bodyworks
1199 Sanchez Street
(415) 821-2979

Video Rentals
West Coast Video
1201 Church Street
(415) 648-0300

Shoe Repair
The Wooden Heel
4071 24th Street
(415) 824-9399

Hardware Store
Tuggey's Hardware
3885 24th Street
(415) 282-5081

Pizza
Haystack Pizza
3881 24th Street
(415) 647-1929

Noe Valley Pizza
3898 24th Street
(415) 647-1664

Miscellaneous
Carroll's Books
1193 Church Street
(415) 647-3020

Colorcrane Office Supplies
3957 24th Street
(415) 285-1387

Dan's Smog and Auto Service
3865 24th Street
(415) 282-1552

Goodnews Newsstand
3920 24th Street
(415) 821-3694

J & S Barbering Co.
1298 Church Street
(415) 642-1556

Mail Boxes Etc.
4104 24th Street
(415) 824-1070

Noe Valley Bakery and Bread Co.
4073 24th Street
(415) 550-1405

Radio Shack
4049 24th Street
(415) 285-3300

RMC Real Estate Management Co.
1234 Castro Street
(415) 821-3167

Supercuts
4031 24th Street
(415) 282-5929

Twin Peaks Properties
4072 24th Street
(415) 824-0872

Zephyr Real Estate
404 24th Street
(415) 695-7707

NOE VALLEY NEIGHBORHOOD STATISTICS

Average Monthly Rent

Studio: $595 to $775

One-bedroom: $735 to $1,200

Two-bedroom: $885 to $1,495

Ethnic/Racial Distribution

White: 72%

African American: 6%

Asian: 10%

Hispanic: 12%

Median Age: 34

Percentage of Population

Male: 54%

Female: 46%

Percentage of Renters: 66%

Crime

Violent crime: Below average, with robbery being the highest

Property crime: Slightly above average, with auto theft being the highest

Street Parking

Permit required: No

Availability: Difficult

Local Newspaper: Noe Valley Voice, (415) 821-3324

NORTH BEACH/TELEGRAPH HILL

This once Italian immigrant community is still known San Francisco's "Little Italy" even though the predominant ethnic group today is Asian. There is still an abundance of Italian restaurants, cafés, pastry shops, and delis. This neighborhood is conveniently located near the Financial District, two main bridges, and the

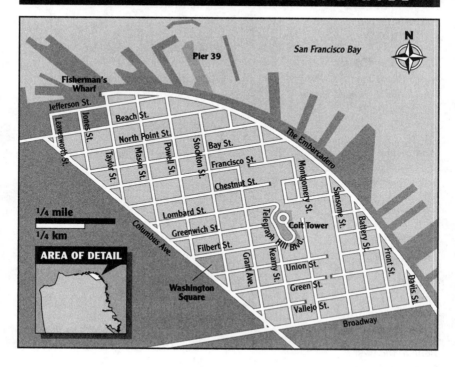

freeways. North Beach was home to the Beat generation, and landmarks such as City Lights Bookstore and Vesuvio Bar remain. The Beats were around in the 1950s, writing poetry and protesting against conformity. Instead of Beats, today your neighbors might be Gen Xers, hippies, and the occasional artist mixed in with some professionals. This is a nonconformist neighborhood with a lot of pizzazz.

Bordered by Columbus Avenue, Broadway, and the Embarcadero

Bus lines: 15, 30, 39, 41, 42, 45

Main streets: Columbus Avenue and Grant Avenue

NORTH BEACH/TELEGRAPH HILL NEIGHBORHOOD RESOURCES

Community Organizations
North Beach Neighbors
P.O. Box 330115
San Francisco, CA 94133

Telegraph Hill Dwellers
P.O. Box 330159
San Francisco, CA 94133

Post Office
North Beach Post Office
1640 Stockton Street
(415) 956-3581

Library
North Beach Library
2000 Mason Street
(415) 274-0270

Recreation Center
North Beach Pool and Playground
Powell and Lombard Streets
(415) 274-0200

Parks
Washington Square Park
Stockton, Union, Columbus,
and Filbert Streets

Churches
St. Peter and Paul Catholic Church
666 Filbert Street
(415) 421-0809

Banks
Bank of America
1445 Stockton Street
(415) 615-4700

Bank of the West
580 Green Street
(415) 982-1344

Bayview Federal Bank
480 Columbus Avenue
(415) 433-6110

Wells Fargo Bank
468 Columbus Avenue
(415) 781-2235

Supermarkets/Grocery Stores
Nature Stop
1336 Grant Avenue
(415) 398-3810

Rossi's Supermarket
627 Vallejo Street
(415) 986-1068

Safeway Supermarket
350 Bay Street
(415) 781-4374

Pharmacy
Walgreen Pharmacy
320 Bay Street
(415) 296-0108
1344 Stockton Street
(415) 981-6244

Laundromats/Cleaners
Comet Cleaners
930 Columbus Avenue
(415) 474-2161

Doowash Laundromat and Cafe
817 Columbus Avenue
(415) 885-1222

Little Bubbles Coin Wash Laundromat
1535 Grant Avenue
(415) 398-2247

Price Cleaners
800 Bay Street
(415) 885-1717

Health Clubs
24 Hour Nautilus Fitness Center
350 Bay Street
(415) 395-9595

Bay Club
150 Greenwich Street
(415) 433-2200

North Point Health Club
2310 Powell Street
(415) 989-1449

Video Rentals
Blockbuster Video
350 Bay Street
(415) 982-4800

North Beach Video
1398 Grant Avenue
(415) 398-7773

Shoe Repair
Galletti Brothers Shoe Repair
427 Columbus Avenue
(415) 982-2897

Hardware Stores
Figone Hardware
1351 Grant Avenue
(415) 392-4765

Tower Hardware
1300 Grant Avenue
(415) 788-1188

Pizza
North Beach Pizza
1499 Grant Avenue
(415) 433-2444

Movie Theater
Northpoint Movie Theater
2290 Powell Street
(415) 989-6060

Miscellaneous
Danilo Bakery
516 Green Street
(415) 989-1806

Sario's Barber Shop
128 Columbus Avenue
(415) 421-4062

NORTH BEACH/TELEGRAPH HILL NEIGHBORHOOD STATISTICS

Average Monthly Rent

Studio: $685 to $735

One-bedroom: $775 to $1,400

Two-bedroom: $1,250 to $2,850

Ethnic/Racial Distribution

White: 50%

African American: 5%

Asian: 45%

Median Age: 38

Percentage of Population

Male: 52%

Female: 48%

Percentage of Renters: 83%

Crime

Violent crime: Above average, with robbery being the highest

Property crime: Above average, with auto theft being the highest

Street Parking

Permit required: Yes

Availability: Difficult

Local Newspaper: North Beach NOW, (415) 391-1043

PACIFIC HEIGHTS/LOWER PACIFIC HEIGHTS

Like its neighbor the Marina District, Pacific Heights caters to a young, educated, dog-loving professional crowd that enjoys outdoor sports and hanging out in the cafés on Union and Fillmore Streets. Pacific Heights is known as an upscale neighborhood and lives up to its reputation off of Union Street near the Presidio, where mansions are inhabited by the old, moneyed elite. The views from this part of town are great and so is the shopping along Union Street, with its many boutiques and specialty stores. Lower Pacific Heights is just over a hill south of Union Street. It centers around Fillmore Street, with its shops and services. This part is also very yuppie but not as upscale. The further south you go on Fillmore Street, the grittier the neighborhood gets. Pacific Heights and Lower Pacific Heights are for those who want clean-cut living with no surprises.

Bordered by Union Street, Van Ness Avenue, California Street, Presidio Avenue, and Lyon Street

Bus lines: 1, 22, 41, 45

Main streets: Union Street, between Van Ness Avenue and Fillmore Street, and Fillmore Street, between Jackson and California Streets

PACIFIC HEIGHTS/LOWER PACIFIC HEIGHTS NEIGHBORHOOD RESOURCES

Post Office
2055 Lombard Street
(415) 284-0755

Community Organizations
Pacific Heights Residents Association
2585 Pacific Avenue
San Francisco, CA 94115

Libraries
Presidio Branch
3150 Sacramento Street
(415) 292-2155

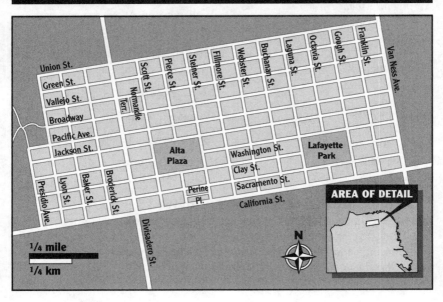

PACIFIC HEIGHTS/LOWER PACIFIC HEIGHTS

Golden Gate Valley Branch
1801 Green Street
(415) 292-2195

Western Addition
1550 Scott Street
(415) 292-2160

Recreation Center
There's only a recreation playground
with tennis courts and basketball courts:
Presidio Heights Playground
Clay Street near Walnut Street
(415) 292-2005

Parks
Alta Plaza Park
Jackson and Steiner Streets

Lafayette Park
Washington Street between Gough and
Laguna Streets

Churches
Calvary Presbyterian Church
2515 Fillmore at Jackson Streets
(415) 346-3832

Congregation Sherith Israel
2266 California Street
(415) 346-1720

The Episcopal Church of St. Mary
the Virgin
2325 Union Street
(415) 921-3665

St. Dominic's Catholic Church
Bush and Steiner Streets
(415) 567-7824

St. Vincent de Paul Catholic Church
2320 Green Street
(415) 922-1010

Trinity United Methodist Church
1675 California Street
(415) 626-0913

Banks
Bank of America
1995 Union Street
2310 Fillmore Street
(415) 615-4700

Wells Fargo Bank
1900 Union Street
2100 Fillmore Street
(415) 781-2235

Supermarkets/Grocery Stores
Auntie Pasta
3101 Fillmore Street
(415) 921-7576

California Street Creamery
2413 California Street
(415) 929-8610

City Pantry
2190 Union Street
(415) 923-9771

Full Moon Foods
2263 Union Street
(415) 567-5755

Grand Central Market
2435 California Street
(415) 567-4902

Little Venice Fine Foods
2066 Fillmore Street
(415) 292-9800

Martha Bros. Food Inc.
2800 California Street
(415) 931-2281

Mayflower Market
2498 Fillmore Street
(415) 346-1700

Pacific Heights Market
1971 Fillmore Street
(415) 921-9300

The Straw Jar and the Bean
(Natural/Organic Food Store)
2047 Fillmore Street
(415) 922-3811

Thriftway Market
2174 Union Street
(415) 922-4545

Pharmacies
Dave's Pharmacy
2230 Union Street
(415) 567-0122

Pacific Heights Pharmacy
2436 Fillmore Street
(415) 346-0707

Walgreen
1899 Fillmore Street
(415) 771-1568

Cleaners/Laundromats
Best Cleaners
1699 Union Street
(415) 292-4073

Bond Cleaners
2442 Fillmore Street
(415) 567-2158

Clean Image Cleaners
3141 Fillmore Street
(415) 922-2080

Esrik Quality Cleaners
2429 California Street
(415) 346-0626

Fabricare Dry Cleaners
1919 Fillmore Street
(415) 346-1919

Italy Cleaners
2502 Clay Street
(415) 673-7525

Master Cleaners
3005 Union Street
(415) 921-8830

Pacific Heights Cleaners
2437 Fillmore Street
(415) 567-5999

Perfect Cleaners
1909 Fillmore Street
(415) 775-1638

Self Service Wash Center (Laundromat)
2434 California Street

Silver Cleaners
2235 Greenwich
(415) 929-8647

Union French Cleaners
1718 Union Street
(415) 923-1212

Wash Palace
2056 Fillmore Street
(415) 922-4093

Health Clubs
In Shape
3214 Fillmore Street
(415) 922-3700

Pacific Heights Health Club
2358 Pine Street
(415) 563-6694

Video Rentals
Castro Video
2410 California Street
(415) 441-3111

Wherehouse
2083 Union Street
(415) 346-0944

See Western Addition listing for Block-buster Video.

Shoe Repair
SF Boot and Shoe Repair
2448 Fillmore Street
(415) 567-6176

Hardware Stores

Fillmore Hardware
1930 Fillmore Street
(415) 346-5240

Fredericksen Hardware
3029 Fillmore Street
(415) 292-2950

Pacific Heights Hardware
2828 California Street
(415) 346-9262

Pizza

Amici's East Coast Pizzeria
2033 Union Street
(415) 885-4500

Roamin' Pizza
2142 Union Street
(415) 921-7272

Movie Theaters

United Artists Metro Theater
2055 Union Street
(415) 931-1685

Clay Theater
2261 Fillmore Street
(415) 346-1123

Miscellaneous

The Brown Bag Office Supplies
2000 Fillmore Street
(415) 922-0390

Copy Net
2404 California Street
(415) 567-5888

Copymat
1898 Union Street
(415) 567-8933

Good Haircuts
2208 Filbert Street
(415) 928-0785

Hill & Co. Real Estate
2107 Union Street
(415) 921-6000

Jet Mail
2130 Fillmore Street
(415) 922-9402

Jon Douglas Real Estate
2259 Fillmore or Clay
(415) 771-8500

Juicy News (Newsstand)
2453 Fillmore Street
(415) 441-3051

Kinko's
3225 Fillmore Street
(415) 441-2995

Lombardo's Barber Shop
1508 Union Street
(415) 441-0356

Mail Boxes Etc.
2443 Fillmore Street
(415) 922-6245

Mason-McDuffie Real Estate
2200 Union Street
(415) 921-0113

Nice Cuts
2187 Union Street
(415) 929-7744

Packaging Store
2427 California Street
(415) 931-3751

The Postal Chase
3053 Fillmore Street
(415) 567-7447

Speedway Copy
2425 California Street
(415) 346-8111

Supercuts
2306 Fillmore Street
(415) 474-9652

PACIFIC HEIGHTS/LOWER PACIFIC HEIGHTS NEIGHBORHOOD STATISTICS

Average Monthly Rent

Studio: $575 to $950

One-bedroom: $745 to $1,800

Two-bedroom: $1,275 to $2,550

Ethnic/Racial Distribution

White: 84%

African American: 4%

Asian: 8%

Hispanic: 4%

Median Age: 38

Percentage of Population

Male: 50%

Female: 50%

Percentage of Renters: 84%

Crime

Violent crime: Way below average, with robbery being the highest

Property crime: Above average, with auto theft being the highest

Street Parking

Permit required: Yes

Availability: Difficult

Local Newspaper: None

POTRERO HILL

This neighborhood is becoming very trendy, attracting artists, computer people, hip couples with kids, and others who enjoy quiet residential living, great views, and a sunny microclimate. The main retail area is 18th Street, where the true community spirit can be felt. Among the many gathering spots and neighborhood watering holes is Farleys Cafe, where trendy residents enjoy their coffee and paper. You're sure to run into your neighbors browsing at Christopher Books or enjoying a treat at the Daily Scoop Ice Cream Shop. The only problem with this cozy neighborhood is the proximity of housing projects, making crime a problem.

Bordered by Cesar Chavez (Army) Street, 3rd Street, U.S. 101, and 16th Street

Bus lines: 19, 22, 53

Main street: 18th Street, between York and Alabama Streets

POTRERO HILL NEIGHBORHOOD RESOURCES

Community Organizations
Lower Potrero Hill Neighborhood Association
934 Minnesota Street
San Francisco, CA 94107

Post Offices

4304 18th Street
(415) 621-5317

4083 24th Street
(415) 821-0776

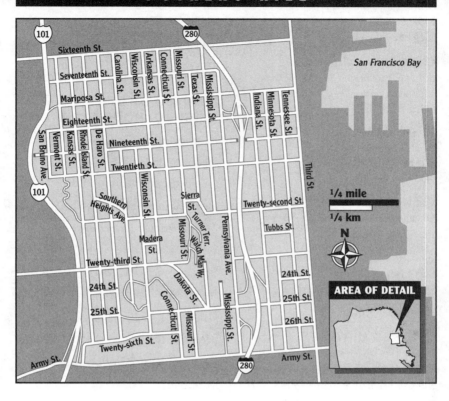

POTRERO HILL

San Francisco Bay

1/4 mile
1/4 km
N

AREA OF DETAIL

Library
1616 20th Street near Connecticut Street
(415) 695-6640

Recreation Center
801 Arkansas Street at 22nd Street
(415) 695-5009

Park
Esprit Park
On Minnesota Street between
18th and 22nd Streets

Churches
St. Gregory Nyssen Episcopalian Church
500 De Haro Street
(415) 255-8100

St. Peter's Catholic Church
1200 Florida Street
(415) 282-1652

St. Teresa's Catholic Church
1490 19th Street
(415) 285-5272

Banks
Banks are not located in this neighborhood. See Mission District listings for
the nearest ones.

Supermarket/Grocery Store
Good Life Grocery
1524 20th Street
(415) 282-9204

Pharmacy
Atchinson's Pharmacy
1607 20th Street
(415) 824-3590

Cleaners/Laundromat
Billy's Cleaners and Laundry
1503 20th Street
(415) 826-0422

Health Club
World Gym
260 De Haro Street
(415) 703-9650

Video Rental
Dr. Video
1521 18th Street
(415) 826-2900

Shoe Repair
See Mission District listing.

Hardware Store
See Mission District listing.

Pizza
Goat Hill Pizza
300 Connecticut Street at 18th Street
(415) 641-1440

Miscellaneous
Christopher's Books
1400 18th Street
(415) 255-8802

The Daily Scoop Ice Cream Shop
1401 18th Street
(415) 824-3975

Farleys Coffeehouse
1315 18th Street
(415) 648-1545

Ford Real Estate
1542 20th Street
(415) 824-7200

Potrero Mail 'n More
1459 18th Street
(415) 826-8757

Sally's Bakery
300 De Haro Street
(415) 626-0838

POTRERO HILL NEIGHBORHOOD STATISTICS

Average Monthly Rent
Studio: $525 to $795

One-bedroom: $650 to $1,095

Two-bedroom: $1,095 to $1,800

Ethnic/Racial Distribution
White: 58%

African American: 22%

Asian: 8%

Hispanic: 12%

Median Age: 35

Percentage of Population
Male: 54%

Female: 46%

Percentage of Renters: 61%

Crime
Violent crime: Way above average, with robbery being the highest

Property crime: Above average, with auto theft being the highest

Street Parking
Permit required: No

Availability: Good

Local Newspaper: Potrero View, (415) 824-7516

PRESIDIO HEIGHTS/LAUREL HEIGHTS

This is a most pristine community neighboring the city's newest national park, the Presidio. Thanks to the meticulous care and respect former Presidio army base residents have given to this neighborhood, Presidio Heights/Laurel Heights is one of the truly civilized areas left in the city. Wealthier residents live in beautifully maintained mansions looking over acres of eucalyptus trees that fill Presidio National Park. For the rest of us, equally nice apartments are for rent, which, if available, can cost a bundle. Retail activity is concentrated along Sacramento Street (between Lyon and Spruce Streets) and also along California Street near California Pacific Medical Center.

Bordered by West Pacific Avenue, Arguello Boulevard, Geary Boulevard, Masonic Avenue, and Presidio Avenue

Bus lines: 1, 2, 4, 28, 28L, 33, 38, 38L, 43, 44

Main streets: Sacramento Street, between Lyon and Spruce Streets, and Laurel Village Shopping Center at the 3000 block of California Street

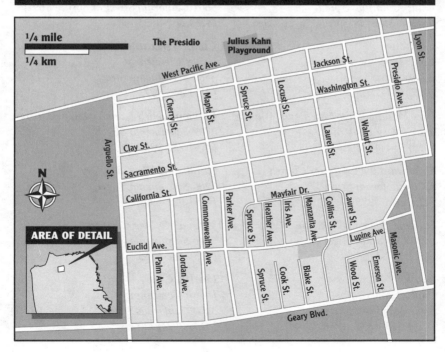

PRESIDIO HEIGHTS/LAUREL HEIGHTS NEIGHBORHOOD RESOURCES

Community Organization
Presidio Heights Association
of Neighbors
P.O. Box 29503
San Francisco, CA 94129

Post Office
950 Lincoln Boulevard
(415) 563-4975

Library
3150 Sacramento Street near
Baker Street
(415) 292-2155

Parks/Playgrounds
Laurel Hill Playground
Euclid Avenue at Blake Street

Julius Kahn Playground
Jackson Street at Spruce Street

Churches
Congregation Emanu-El
2 Lake Street
(415) 751-2535

Park Presidio United Methodist Church
4301 Geary Boulevard
(415) 751-4438

St. Edward the Confessor Church
3320 California Street
(415) 346-0958

St. James Episcopal Church
4620 California Street
(415) 751-1198

Banks
Bank of America
3565 California Street
(415) 615-4700

Citibank
3296 Sacramento Street
(415) 922-0400

First Interstate Bank
3431 California Street
(415) 544-5065

Wells Fargo Bank
3150 California Street
(415) 781-2235

Supermarkets/Grocery Stores
Cal-Mart Supermarket
3585 California Street
(415) 751-3516

Laurel Super Mart
3445 California Street
(415) 752-0179

Pharmacy
Walgreen
3601 California Street at Spruce Street
(415) 668-3555

Cleaners/Laundromats
Locust Cleaners
3587 Sacramento Street
(415) 346-9271

Peninou French Laundry and Cleaners
3707 Sacramento Street
(415) 751-9200

Sacramento Wash and Dry
3200 Sacramento Street
(415) 922-8899

Veteran's Deluxe Cleaners
3300 Sacramento Street
(415) 567-6585

Health Clubs
Jewish Community Center
3200 California Street
(415) 292-1220

Video Rentals
California Video Express
4355 California Street
(415) 752-8504

Shoe Repair
Cobblers Bench Shoe Repair
3308 Sacramento Street
(415) 567-3555

Hardware Store
Hardware Unlimited
3326 Sacramento Street
(415) 931-9133

Pizza
The Front Room
823 Clement Street
(415) 386-6000

Mr. Pizza Man
3409 Geary Boulevard
(415) 387-3131

Village Pizzeria
1 Clement Street
(415) 221-2100

Movie Theater
United Artists Vogue Theater
3290 Sacramento Street
(415) 221-8183

Miscellaneous
Asano's Barber Shop
3312 Sacramento Street
(415) 567-3335

Jewish Community Center
3200 California Street
(415) 346-6040

Professional Mailing and Shipping
3450 Sacramento Street
(415) 921-6644

Standards 5&10
3545 California Street
(415) 751-5767

PRESIDIO HEIGHTS/LAUREL HEIGHTS NEIGHBORHOOD STATISTICS

Average Monthly Rent
Studio: $750 to $1,295

One-bedroom: $775 to $1,300

Two-bedroom: $1,195 to $3,200

Ethnic/Racial Distribution
White: 74%

African American: 6%

Asian: 16%

Hispanic: 4%

Median Age: 36

Percentage of Population
Male: 47%

Female: 53%

Percentage of Renters: 74%

Crime
Violent crime: Below average, with homicide being the highest

Property crime: Slightly above average, with auto theft being the highest

Street Parking
Permit required: Yes

Availability: Moderate

Local Newspaper: None

RICHMOND DISTRICT

This used to be a graveyard district, but the bodies have been moved to Colma to make way for the living. Today, the Richmond District is a solid middle-class neighborhood with a diverse ethnic population, great restaurants, convenient shopping, and low crime. The Inner Richmond along Clement Street reflects the influence of a growing Asian population and is sometimes referred to as the "New Chinatown." In fact, Asians replaced a significant Russian population that settled here after the revolution. If you choose to live in the Richmond, you'll have access to Presidio National Park as well as Golden Gate Park. The University of San Francisco campus is near the Inner Richmond; Lincoln Park Golf Course, one of the nicest public courses in the city, is in the Outer Richmond. The weather is usually foggy in this part of town.

Bordered by Fulton Street, Masonic Avenue, Geary Boulevard, Arguello Boulevard, West Pacific Avenue, Lobos Creek, California Street, Clement Street, and 49th Avenue

Bus lines: 1, 2, 28, 28L, 29, 31, 33, 38

Main streets: Clement Street, between Arguello and 8th Avenue, and Geary Boulevard, between 9th and 25th Avenues

RICHMOND DISTRICT NEIGHBORHOOD RESOURCES

Community Organizations

Richmond Community Association
240 4th Avenue
San Francisco, CA 94118

Lincoln Park Neighborhood Association
270 32nd Avenue
San Francisco, CA 94121

Post Offices

Geary Station
5654 Geary Boulevard at 21st Avenue
(415) 752-0231

Golden Gate Station
3245 Geary Boulevard at Lake Street
(415) 284-0755

Library

351 9th Avenue near Clement Street
(415) 666-7165

Recreation Center

The nearest recreation center is in the Sunset District:
28th Avenue and Lawton Street
(415) 753-7098

Park

Mountain Lake Park
Lake Street between 8th and 12th Avenues

Churches

Congregation Beth Sholom Conservative
1301 Clement Street
(415) 221-8736

First United Lutheran Church
6555 Geary Boulevard
(415) 751-8101

Pine United Methodist Church
426 33rd Avenue
(415) 387-1800

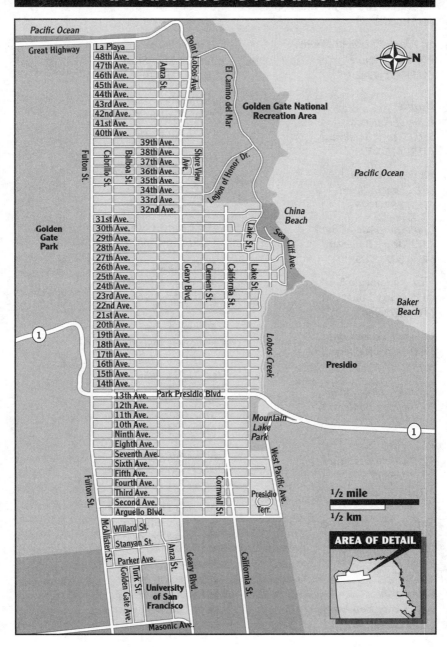

N

Pacific Ocean

Great Highway

La Playa
48th Ave.
47th Ave.
46th Ave.
45th Ave.
44th Ave.
43rd Ave.
42nd Ave.
41st Ave.
40th Ave.

Anza St.

Point Lobos Ave.

El Camino del Mar

**Golden Gate National
Recreation Area**

Fulton St.

Cabrillo St.

Balboa St.

39th Ave.
38th Ave.
37th Ave.
36th Ave.
35th Ave.
34th Ave.
33rd Ave.
32nd Ave.

Shore View Ave.

Legion of Honor Dr.

Pacific Ocean

China
Beach

31st Ave.
30th Ave.
29th Ave.
28th Ave.
27th Ave.
26th Ave.
25th Ave.
24th Ave.
23rd Ave.
22nd Ave.
21st Ave.
20th Ave.
19th Ave.
18th Ave.
17th Ave.
16th Ave.
15th Ave.
14th Ave.

**Golden
Gate
Park**

Geary Blvd.

Clement St.

California St.

Lake St.

Lake St.

Sea Cliff Ave.

Baker
Beach

Presidio

Lobos Creek

(1)

13th Ave.
12th Ave.
11th Ave.
10th Ave.
Ninth Ave.
Eighth Ave.
Seventh Ave.
Sixth Ave.
Fifth Ave.
Fourth Ave.
Third Ave.
Second Ave.
Arguello Blvd.

Park Presidio Blvd.

*Mountain
Lake
Park*

West Pacific Ave.

(1)

Fulton St.

Cornwall St.

Presidio
Terr.

¹/₂ mile

¹/₂ km

Willard St.
Stanyan St.
Parker Ave.

McAllister St.

Anza St.

Geary Blvd.

California St.

Turk St.

Golden Gate Ave.

**University
of San
Francisco**

Masonic Ave.

AREA OF DETAIL

St. Ignatius Catholic Church
650 Parker Avenue at Fulton Street
(415) 666-0123

St. Peter's Episcopal Church
420 29th Avenue
(415) 751-4942

Banks
Bank of America
5500 Geary Boulevard
(415) 615-4700

Bank of the West
801 Clement Street
(415) 387-1425

California Federal Bank
4373 Geary Boulevard
(415) 387-7705

First Nationwide Bank
4455 Geary Boulevard
(415) 752-4602

Glendale Federal Bank
6100 Geary Boulevard
(415) 387-5112

Great Western Bank
5600 Geary Boulevard
(415) 221-5220

Wells Fargo Bank
5455 Geary Boulevard
599 Clement Street
(415) 781-2235

Supermarkets/Grocery Stores
Appel & Dietrich Fine Food Market
6001 California Street
(415) 221-7600

Cala Foods
4041 Geary Boulevard
(415) 221-9191

Fruit Basket
661 Clement Street
(415) 221-0656

Happy Supermarket
400 Clement Street
(415) 221-3195

Pacific Food Market
2147 Clement Street
(415) 387-6210

Safeway
3132 Clement Street
(415) 752-1244

Seven-Eleven Store
900 Clement Street
(415) 668-3537

State Market
4751 Geary Boulevard
(415) 752-3466

Pharmacies
Evergreen Pharmacy
5601 Geary Boulevard
(415) 221-0065

Hall's Pharmacy
6157 Geary Boulevard
(415) 751-1320

Joe's Pharmacy
5199 Geary Boulevard
(415) 751-2326

Merrill's Drug Center
5280 Geary Boulevard
(415) 668-2040

Walgreen
719 Clement Street
(415) 668-3939
5411 Geary Boulevard
(415) 752-6727

Cleaners/Laundromat

A1 Launderette and Cleaning
5523 California Street
(415) 751-1237

Aurora Clean Center Laundromat
1744 Clement Street
(415) 752-0909

Certified Cleaners
2601 Clement Street
(415) 752-0659

Clean Express Laundromats
4726 Geary Boulevard at 11th Avenue
(415) 668-9538
5211 Geary Boulevard at 16th Avenue
(415) 668-8181

Geary Cleaners
5911 Geary Boulevard
(415) 751-9218

Lux Cleaners & Shoe Repair
5331 Geary Street
(415) 387-1030

Qualitech Cleaners
5530 Geary Boulevard
(415) 668-1175

Rite-Way Cleaners
4105 California Street
(415) 221-0545

Snow White Cleaners
2650 Clement Street
(415) 751-6539

Health Clubs

Jewish Community Center
3200 California Street
(415) 292-1220

Richmond YMCA
360 18th Avenue
(415) 668-2060

Video Rentals

Blockbuster Video
5240 Geary Boulevard
(415) 668-2675

California Video Express
4355 California Street
(415) 752-8504

Wherehouse
3301 Geary Boulevard
(415) 751-3711

Shoe Repair

Clement Shoe Repair
1909 Clement Street
(415) 752-4500

Geary Shoe Repair
5430 Geary Boulevard
(415) 387-1268

Geary Shoe Repair and Service
6242 Geary Boulevard
(415) 221-6101

Hardware Stores

Ace Hardware
1019 Clement Street
(415) 221-1888

Bay View Hardware
6114 Geary Boulevard
(415) 221-4948

Pizza

Bella Pizza
4124 Geary Boulevard
(415) 668-4150

The Front Room
823 Clement Street
(415) 386-6000

Mr. Pizza Man
3409 Geary Boulevard
(415) 387-3131

Theaters

Bridge Theater
3010 Geary Boulevard
(415) 751-3212

United Artists Alexandria Theater
5400 Geary Boulevard
(415) 752-5100

Miscellaneous
Geary Print Shop
3452 Geary Boulevard
(415) 751-1212

Mail Boxes Etc.
3145 Geary Boulevard
(415) 751-6644

PIP Printing
3569 Geary Boulevard
(415) 221-0997

RICHMOND DISTRICT NEIGHBORHOOD STATISTICS

Average Monthly Rent

Studio: $575 to $725

One-bedroom: $695 to $950

Two-bedroom: $775 to $1,300

Ethnic/Racial Distribution

White: 44%

African American: 4%

Asian: 48%

Hispanic: 4%

Median Age: 34

Percentage of Population

Male: 46%

Female: 54%

Percentage of Renters: 70%

Crime

Violent crime: Way below average, with robbery and rape tying as the highest

Property crime: Below average, with auto theft being the highest

Street Parking

Permit required: Yes

Availability: Moderate to difficult

Local Newspaper: None

RUSSIAN HILL

This hilly community was named after the Russian seal hunters and traders buried there. Russian Hill is located between North Beach and Pacific Heights. Instead of the morbid burial ground it used to be, it is a hip, yuppie neighborhood with great shops and views. Polk Street, from Union Street to California Street, is the main commercial street in this community with neighborhood bars, ethnic restaurants, gourmet grocery stores, and movie theaters. Go south of California Street, and you'll find yourself in the Polk Gulch, once the gay heart of San Francisco. Today it is the second most prominent gay community next to the Castro. Compared to the coziness on the north side, the south side of Polk shows the grittier side of urban life, including drugs and prostitution.

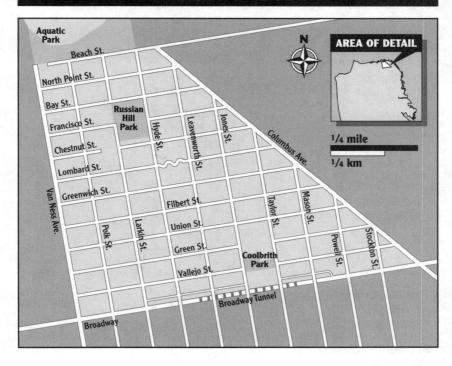

Bordered by Columbus Avenue, Broadway, and Van Ness Avenue

Bus lines: 19, 41, 42, 45, 49

Main street: Polk Street, between Union and California Streets

RUSSIAN HILL NEIGHBORHOOD RESOURCES

Community Organizations
Russian Hill Neighbors
2040 Polk Street
San Francisco, CA 94109

Post Office
Nearby ones are in North Beach and Marina District.

Library
Nearby ones are in North Beach and Marina District.

Recreation Center
Nearby ones are in North Beach and Marina District.

Parks
Russian Hill Park
On Bay Street between Hyde and Larkin Streets

Churches

See North Beach, Nob Hill, or Pacific Heights listings.

Bank

Coast Federal Savings and Loan
1850 Polk Street
(415) 928-6400

Supermarkets/Grocery Stores

Auntie Pasta
2139 Polk Street
(415) 776-9420

Big Apple Grocery Express
1650 Polk Street
(415) 775-9090

Food Warehouse
1732 Polk Street
(415) 292-5659

Grand Meat Market
1806 Polk Street
(415) 885-5030

Polk and Green Produce
2222 Polk Street
(415) 776-3099

Polk Vallejo Market
2150 Polk Street
(415) 673-4176

Real Food Co.
2164 Polk Street
(415) 673-7420

Pharmacies

Home Drug Co.
1200 Union Street
(415) 474-0281

Walgreen
2254 Polk Street
(415) 474-9750

Cleaners/Laundromats

Holiday Cleaners
1850 Polk Street
(415) 928-5707

Marvin's Cleaners
2052 Polk Street
(415) 885-6944

Michael's Cleaners
2235 Polk Street
(415) 771-0660

Missing Sock Laundromat
1958 Hyde Street
(415) 673-5640

San Francisco Cleaners
2123 Polk Street
(415) 776-7890

Silk Tech Cleaners
2221 Polk Street
(415) 474-1120

Health Club

Karate One
1830 Polk Street
(415) 474-3322

Video Rentals

Movie Magic
1590 Pacific Avenue
(415) 771-1290
2325 Polk Street
(415) 775-3735

Shoe Repair

Frank's Shoe Repair
1561 Polk Street
(415) 775-1694

Hardware Store

Brownie's Hardware
1552 Polk Street
(415) 673-8900

Pizza

That's Amore
2109 Polk Street
(415) 771-4222

Victor's Pizza
1411 Polk Street
(415) 885-1660

Za Gourmet Pizza
1919 Hyde Street
(415) 771-3100

Movie Theater

Alhambra Movie Theater
2330 Polk Street
(415) 775-2137

Miscellaneous

Fred's Barber Shop
1714 Polk Street
(415) 885-9957

Insta-Tune Car Repair
1601 Pacific Avenue
(415) 775-4044

Lombardi Sports
1600 Jackson Street
(415) 771-0600

Mail Boxes Etc.
2040 Polk Street
(415) 441-4954

Pet Wash
1840 Polk Street
(415) 928-8788

Radio Shack
1841 Polk Street
(415) 673-9414

Russian Hill Book Store
2234 Polk Street
(415) 929-0997

RUSSIAN HILL NEIGHBORHOOD STATISTICS

Average Monthly Rent

Studio: $700 to $850

One-bedroom: $750 to $2,150

Two-bedroom: $1,200 to $2,800

Ethnic/Racial Distribution

White: 48%

African American: 1%

Asian: 50%

Hispanic: 1%

Median Age: 40

Percentage of Population

Male: 46%

Female: 54%

Percentage of Renters: 80%

Crime

Violent crime: Below average, with robbery being the highest

Property crime: Slightly above average, with auto theft being the highest

Street Parking

Permit required: Yes

Availability: Difficult

Local Newspaper: None

SOUTH OF MARKET

South of Market (SoMa) is quickly redeveloping from an abandoned warehouse district into a hip place to live and work. Warehouses and industrial spaces are being transformed into live/work lofts, trendy restaurants, art galleries, and nightclubs. Many of life's conveniences have come to this part of town, including food stores like Costco and Trader Joe's and factory outlet stores. There's also a plethora of auto repair shops and auto bodywork garages. If you choose to live in SoMa, you'll feel like you have a lot of elbow room. This part of town is still not densely populated like most of San Francisco. Parking won't be a problem, but your car getting stolen will. Crime is still high because of the population of vagrants that lives on the streets. But it's the price you pay if you want to live on the cutting edge in a neighborhood that's about to explode with exciting development. The new modern art museum and Yerba Buena Gardens are signs of what to expect. The CalTrain station on 4th and Townsend Streets is a convenient way to get to the peninsula. SoMa is quickly becoming one of the city's most vibrant new neighborhoods.

Bordered by 16th Street, U.S. 101, Market Street, 4th Street, Folsom Street, and the Embarcadero

Bus lines: 9, 12, 14, 14L, 15, 19, 22, 26, 27, 30, 42, 45, 76

Main street: A main street has not been established, but there are pockets of activity, and it will take some exploring on your part. South Park at 2nd and Bryant Streets is like a Parisian square lined with cafés and restaurants and in the center is a playground and grassy area to hang out; around the 11th and Folsom Streets area is a thriving nightlife scene with Slim's performance club, Hamburger Mary's burger joint, and the DNA Lounge; the streets closer to Market Street have convenience stores and clothing shops

SOUTH OF MARKET NEIGHBORHOOD RESOURCES

Community Organizations
South of Market Neighborhood Association
737 Folsom Street, #314
San Francisco, CA 94107

Post Offices
460 Brannan Street
(415) 543-7729

Rincon Center
180 Steuart Street
(415) 543-3340

Library
The closest one is the Main Library at Civic Center.

Recreation Center
270 6th Street
(415) 554-9532

Park
South Park
Between 2nd and 3rd Streets
and Brannan and Bryant Streets

Churches
St. Joseph's Catholic Church
1415 Howard Street
(415) 552-0406

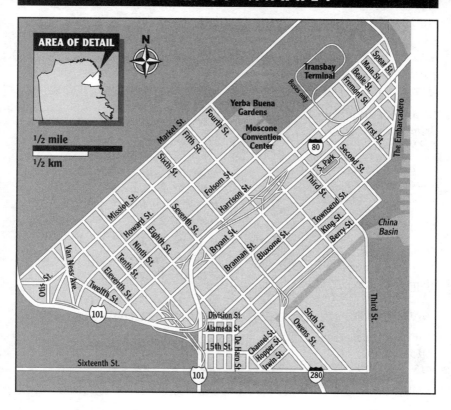

St. Patrick's Catholic Church
756 Mission Street
(415) 421-0547

Banks

Bank of America
501 Brannan Street
(415) 615-4700

First Interstate Bank
490 Brannan Street
(415) 544-5024

Wells Fargo Bank
601 3rd Street
201 3rd Street
(415) 781-2235

Supermarkets/Grocery Stores

Bayside Market
140 Brannan Street
(415) 227-0151

Costco
450 10th Street
(415) 626-4288

Museum Parc Supermarket
725 Folsom Street
(415) 543-9753

Trader Joe's
555 9th Street
(415) 863-1292

Welcome Supermarket
1141 Folsom Street
(415) 431-7007

Pharmacy
Costco
450 10th Street
(415) 626-4341

Cleaners/Laundromats
Brain Wash
1122 Folsom Street
(415) 431-9274

Museum Parc Dry Cleaning
and Laundry
300 3rd Street
(415) 777-2520

Health Clubs
24 Hour Nautilus
Marathon Plaza
303 2nd Street
(415) 543-7808

Club One Museum Parc
350 3rd Street
(415) 512-1010

Gold's Gym
501 2nd Street
(415) 777-4653

Video Rental
South Beach Video
151 Brannan Street
(415) 882-9953

Shoe Repair
Magic Shoe Repair
345 3rd Street
(415) 512-7123

Hardware Stores
Fox Hardware
70 4th Street
(415) 777-4400

Hundley Hardware Co.
617 Bryant Street
(415) 777-5050

Pizza
Mama Gorilla Pizza
555 9th Street
(415) 552-4286

Pizza Love
1245 Folsom Street
(415) 252-1111

Miscellaneous
A & T Mail Center
1072 Folsom Street
(415) 252-1496

Office Depot
855 Harrison Street
(415) 243-9959

SOUTH OF MARKET NEIGHBORHOOD STATISTICS

Average Monthly Rent

Studio: $425 to $575

One-bedroom: $600 to $1,150

Two-bedroom: $795 to $1,850

Ethnic/Racial Distribution

White: 30%

African American: 20%

Asian: 38%

Hispanic: 12%

Median Age: 45

Percentage of Population

Male: 67%

Female: 33%

Percentage of Renters: 96%

Crime

Violent crime: Way above average, with robbery being the highest

Property crime: Way above average, with auto theft being the highest

Street Parking

Permit required: Yes, in a few areas

Availability: Good

Local Newspaper: None

SUNSET (INNER)

The Inner Sunset is a lively part of town, home to University of California, San Francisco, and neighbor to Golden Gate Park. Unlike its residential, family-oriented Outer Sunset sister, this neighborhood has lots of singles and many convenient local businesses. This neighborhood lifestyle resembles that of the Marina and Pacific Heights, except there's more of a diversity of people: university students and young married couples, artsy types and ethnic residents. If you choose to live here, you'll enjoy all the recreational activities Golden Gate Park has to offer and lots of neighborhood camaraderie.

Bordered by Lincoln Way, Ocean Avenue, Rivera Street, Quintara Street, 10th Avenue, Ortega Street, Clarendon Avenue, and Stanyan Street

Bus lines: 6, 44, 66, 71, N Judah

Main street: Irving Street, between 5th and 9th Streets

INNER SUNSET NEIGHBORHOOD RESOURCES

Community Organizations
Inner Sunset Neighborhood Association
1309 12th Avenue
San Francisco, CA 94122

Sunset Neighbors Unite
1831 Lincoln Way
San Francisco, CA 94122

Post Office
Fisk Station
1317 9th Avenue
(415) 759-1901

Library
1305 18th Avenue
(415) 753-7130

Recreation Center
Sunset Recreation Center
2201 Lawton Street at 28th Avenue
(415) 753-7098

Parks
Golden Gate Park
Interior Park Belt
Stanyan and Belgrave Streets

Grandview Park
Quintara and Cragmont Streets

Churches
19th Avenue Baptist Church
1370 19th Avenue between Judah and Irving Streets
(415) 564-7721

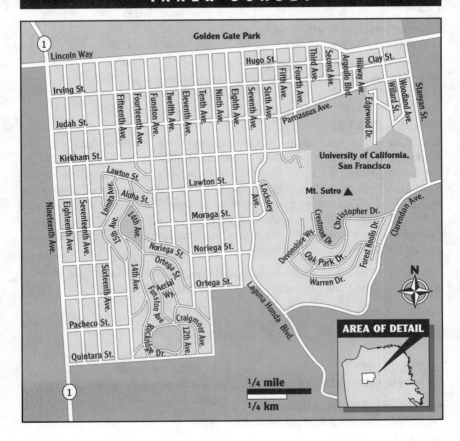

Calvary United Methodist Church
19th Avenue and Judah Street
(415) 566-3704

Christ Church Lutheran
20th Avenue and Quintara Street
(415) 664-0915

Seventh Avenue Presbyterian Church
1329 7th Avenue
(415) 664-2543

St. Anne of the Sunset Catholic Church
850 Judah Street
(415) 665-1600

Sunset Baptist Church
3010 Noriega Street
(415) 731-1780

Banks

Bank of America
800 Irving Street
(415) 615-4700

Bank of the West
750 Irving Street
(415) 566-7111

San Francisco Federal
701 Irving Street
(415) 661-2550

Wells Fargo Bank
725 Irving Street
(415) 781-2235

Supermarkets/Grocery Stores
Irving Market
828 Irving Street

Parks Farmers Market
840 Irving Street
(415) 665-1154

Pharmacies
Dessel's Pharmacy
756 Irving Street
(415) 681-3300

Reliable Drugs
801 Irving Street
(415) 664-8800

West Coast Drug Store
601 Irving Street
(415) 664-0470

Cleaners/Laundromats
Daya Cleaners
617 Irving Street
(415) 566-8005

Irving Laundry World
1932 Irving Street
(415) 665-0911

Health Club
Muscle Fitness Center
1247 9th Avenue
(415) 564-4343

Video Rental
Le Video
1239 9th Avenue
(415) 566-3606

Shoe Repair
Sunset Shoe Repair
621 Irving Street
(415) 661-8259

Hardware Store
Progress True Value Hardware
724 Irving Street
(415) 731-2038

Pizza
Pasquales Pizzeria
700 Irving Street
(415) 661-2140

Miscellaneous
Irving Variety 5 & 10
647 Irving Street
(415) 731-1286

Karl's Service Center
1259 9th Avenue
(415) 731-0227

Park Animal Hospital
1207 9th Avenue
(415) 753-8485

Radio Shack
827 Irving Street
(415) 661-4360

Supercuts
715 Irving Street
(415) 664-4777

Tart to Tart 24-Hour Bakery
641 Irving Street
(415) 753-0643

INNER SUNSET NEIGHBORHOOD STATISTICS

Average Monthly Rent

Studio: $550 to $800

One-bedroom: $700 to $895

Two-bedroom: $975 to $1,325

Ethnic/Racial Distribution

White: 48%

African American: 2%

Asian: 44%

Hispanic: 6%

Median Age: 37

Percentage of Population

Male: 47%

Female: 53%

Percentage of Renters: 42%

Crime

Violent crime: Way below average, with robbery being the highest

Property crime: Below average, with auto theft being the highest

Street Parking

Permit required: Yes

Availability: Good to moderate

Local Newspaper: *The Sunset Beacon,* (415) 241-0539

UPPER MARKET/EUREKA VALLEY

Also known as the Castro, this is San Francisco's largest gay community. This is a well-maintained neighborhood with a great sense of pride and style. Small businesses tend to have a creative flair and cater to their market. Castro Street is the heart of this neighborhood and is always full of street life. The neighborhood outside of this high-traffic area can be very charming and quiet. Being gay is not a prerequisite for living here, but it does add to the experience.

Bordered by Duboce Avenue, Dolores Street, 21st Street, and Buena Vista Avenue

Bus lines: K, L, and M streetcars

Main streets: Castro Street, between Market and 21st Streets, and Market Street, from Castro to Sanchez Streets

UPPER MARKET/EUREKA VALLEY NEIGHBORHOOD RESOURCES

Community Organizations
Duboce Triangle Neighborhood Association
2235 15th Street
San Francisco, CA 94114

Post Office
4083 24th Street
(415) 821-0776

4304 18th Street
(415) 621-5317

Library
The nearest one is the Noe Valley Branch.

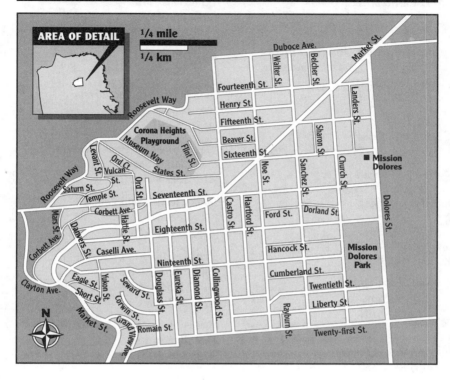

Recreation Center
Eureka Valley Rec Center
100 Collingwood Street at 18th Street
(415) 554-9528

Park
Mission Dolores Park
18th and Church Streets

Churches
Golden Gate Lutheran Church
601 Dolores Street
(415) 647-5050

Most Holy Redeemer Catholic Church
100 Diamond Street
(415) 863-6259

St. Aidan's Episcopal Church
101 Gold Mine Drive
(415) 285-9540

St. Francis Lutheran Church
152 Church Street at Market Street
(415) 621-2635

Banks
Bank of America
501 Castro Street
(415) 615-4700

California Federal Bank
2099 Market Street
(415) 861-5554
444 Castro Street
(415) 861-3161

Eureka Bank
443 Castro Street
(415) 431-6700

Supermarkets/Grocery Stores
Buffalo Whole Food and Grain Co.
598 Castro Street
(415) 626-7038

Cala Foods
4201 18th Street
(415) 431-3822

Harvest Ranch Market
2285 Market Street
(415) 626-0805

Nora's Produce
4360 19th Street
(415) 621-0689

Ryan's Food Emporium
4230 18th Street
(415) 621-6131

Safeway
2020 Market Street
(415) 861-7660

Seven-Eleven Food Store
3998 18th Street
(415) 552-8611

Valley Pride Market
474 Castro Street
(415) 431-1292

Pharmacies
Castro Village Pharmacy
4122 18th Street
(415) 434-8600

Walgreen
498 Castro Street
(415) 861-6276
1333 Castro Street
(415) 826-8998

Cleaners/Laundromats
As the Suds Turn
4172 18th Street

Castro Cleaners
4051 18th Street
(415) 552-2988

Little Hollywood Launderette
1906 Market Street
(415) 252-9357

Martinizing One Hour Cleaners
2233 Market Street
(415) 552-6035

Toni's Cleaners and Laundry
270 Noe Street
(415) 861-6993

Health Clubs
City Athletic Club
2500 Market Street
(415) 552-6680

Market Street Gym
2301 Market Street
(415) 626-4488

Muscle System
2275 Market Street
(415) 863-4700

Video Rentals
Blockbuster Video
160 Church Street
(415) 255-0600

Castro Video
525 Castro Street
(415) 552-2448

Take 1 Video
445 Castro Street
(415) 864-1456

Tower Video
2278 Market Street
(415) 255-5920

US Video
2330 Market Street
(415) 552-9080

Shoe Repair
The Pioneer Renewer Shoe Repair
4501 18th Street
(415) 255-4576

Hardware Store
Cliff's Variety Store
479 Castro Street
(415) 431-5365

Pizza
Sparky's Pizza
246 Church Street
(415) 626-8666

Movie Theater
Castro Theater
429 Castro Street
(415) 621-6120

Miscellaneous
Copy Central
2336 Market Street
(415) 431-6725

Copymat
2370 Market Street
(415) 864-2679

Kinko's
1967 Market Street
(415) 252-0864

Mail Access
2261 Market Street
(415) 626-2574

Radio Shack
2288 Market Street
(415) 255-8595

Skyline Realty
2101 Market Street
(415) 861-1111

UPPER MARKET/EUREKA VALLEY NEIGHBORHOOD STATISTICS

Average Monthly Rent

Studio: $595 to $675

One-bedroom: $680 to $975

Two-bedroom: $1,200 to $1,600

Ethnic/Racial Distribution

White: 80%

African American: 5%

Asian: 7%

Hispanic: 8%

Median Age: 34

Percentage of Population

Male: 69%

Female: 31%

Percentage of Renters: 79%

Crime

Violent crime: Above average, with homicide being the highest

Property crime: Below average, with auto theft being the highest

Street Parking

Permit required: Yes

Availability: Difficult

Local Newspaper: San Francisco Bay Times (gay/lesbian/bi/trans newspaper for the Bay Area), (415) 227-0800

WESTERN ADDITION

This is one of San Francisco's most diverse neighborhoods. It is home to the Japanese Cultural and Trade Center along with a Japanese-American community. Also in the neighborhood is the Center for African and African American Art, supported by a large African American population.

Japantown revolves around the Cultural and Trade Center on Geary Street. Once you cross south of Geary Street, the neighborhood doesn't have the polish of its northern side, but you can tell it's trying. This south-of-Geary neighborhood has seen considerable redevelopment, including subsidized housing and urban renewal projects. Some wonderful Victorian architecture has been restored in Alamo Park, and new luxury high-rise apartments have been built with amenities such as views, health club, security, and parking. The one downside to this part of town, especially south of Geary Street, is the higher-than-average crime due in part to the many housing projects in the area.

Bordered by Geary Street, Van Ness Avenue, Hayes Street, and Divisadero Street

Bus lines: 22, 24, 42, 47, 49, 5, 31, 21, 38, 38L

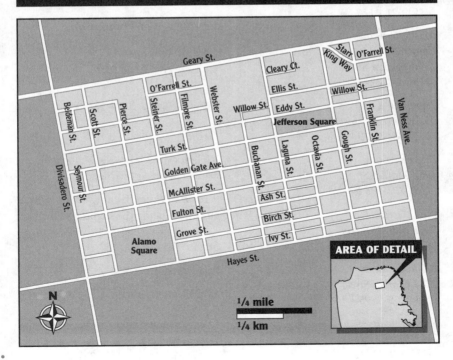

Main street: The closest main street is Fillmore Street in Lower Pacific Heights; on Webster Street at Geary Boulevard is a business area with a Safeway and other practical services

WESTERN ADDITION NEIGHBORHOOD RESOURCES

Community Organizations

Western Addition Neighborhood
Association
1948 Sutter Street
San Francisco, CA 94115

Post Office

1550 Steiner Street at Geary Street
(415) 284-0755

Library

1550 Scott Street at Geary Street
(415) 292-2160

Recreation Center

Hamilton
Geary and Steiner Streets
(415) 292-2008

Parks

Alamo Square
Fulton and Steiner Streets

Jefferson Square
Eddy and Gough Streets

Churches

Ebenezer Baptist Church
275 Divisadero Street
(415) 621-3996

First Friendship Institutional Baptist
Church
501 Steiner Street
(415) 431-4775

First Union Baptist Church
1001 Webster Street
(415) 929-9738

Hamilton Square Baptist Church
1212 Geary Street at Franklin Street
(415) 673-8586

Sacred Heart Catholic Church
546 Fillmore Street
(415) 861-5460

St. Cyprian's Episcopal Church
2097 Turk Street
(415) 567-1855

St. Mary's Catholic Cathedral
1111 Gough Street
(415) 567-2020

St. Mary's Lutheran Church
1111 O'Farrell Street
(415) 928-7770

St. Paulus Lutheran Church
950 Gough Street at Eddy Street
(415) 673-8088

Banks

See Lower Pacific Heights listings.

Supermarkets/Grocery Stores

Safeway
1335 Webster Street
(415) 921-4557

Woori Food Market
1528 Fillmore Street
(415) 673-9888

Pharmacies

Walgreen
Divisadero and O'Farrell Streets
(415) 931-9971

See other Walgreen listing under the Pacific Heights section.

Cleaners/Laundromat

European Cleaners
1468 Fillmore Street
(415) 921-1900

Health Clubs

Cathedral Hill Plaza Athletic Club
1333 Gough Street
(415) 346-3868

San Francisco Athletic Club
1755 Fillmore Street
(415) 776-2260

Video Rental

Blockbuster Video
1495 Webster Street
(415) 771-5620

Shoe Repair

K-Shoe Repair
1426 Fillmore Street
(415) 929-8422

Hardware Store

Divisadero Lock and Hardware
1649 Divisadero Street
(415) 673-5300

Pizza

Pizza Inferno
1800 Fillmore Street
(415) 775-1800

Miscellaneous

Jerry's Barber Shop
1250 Fillmore Street
(415) 921-7733

WESTERN ADDITION NEIGHBORHOOD STATISTICS

Average Monthly Rent

Studio: $475 to $825

One-bedroom: $625 to $1,275

Two-bedroom: $890 to $1,500

Ethnic/Racial Distribution

White: 38%

African American: 38%

Asian: 16%

Hispanic: 8%

Median Age: 34

Percentage of Population

Male: 53%

Female: 47%

Percentage of Renters: 89%

Crime

Violent crime: Way above average, with robbery being the highest

Property crime: Above average, with auto theft being the highest

Street Parking

Permit required: Yes, in some areas

Availability: Moderate to difficult

Local Newspaper: The New Fillmore, (415) 931-0515

BAY AREA COMMUNITIES

If you choose to avoid fast-paced city living, there are many flourishing communities in the outskirts of San Francisco. Though these suburbs, like most, are family-oriented, some have a congregation of young and single professionals. These folks typically choose suburban living because their jobs are located nearby or they want to have more open space for sports and recreation, or they want to pay less rent and get more for the rental buck. The following is an overview of three San Francisco Bay regions and their counties. I've listed all the communities in each county but only go into detail with those that attract a young, single, professional, nonfamily crowd.

NORTH BAY

MARIN COUNTY

Instead of becoming overdeveloped, this waterside county has carefully preserved its natural resources such as Mount Tamalpais, Point Reyes National Park Seashore, Marin Headlands, and the Tennessee Valley. Communities in this region include Belvedere, Corte Madera, Fairfax, Larkspur, Mill Valley, Novato, Ross, San Anselmo, San Rafael, Sausalito, and Tiburon.

Larkspur

Situated along the bay, Larkspur is an easy ferryboat commute to the San Francisco Financial District. Once you step off that ferry after a hectic day in the city, you'll find yourself in a pretty, woodsy community that has a town shopping center with movie theaters and restaurants.

Mill Valley

This town attracts writers and artists and therefore has a great appreciation for the arts. It hosts an annual film festival, and its Lytton Square town center has quaint galleries and boutiques. Mill Valley is situated in the shadow of Mount Tamalpais, which has great hiking trails. The town also has a nine-hole golf course, doggie parks, and bike paths.

San Rafael

This town boasts a civic center designed by Frank Lloyd Wright. You'll also find a college and a downtown area with shops and eateries. Like everywhere else in Marin, San Rafael has many outdoor activities, including golf, baseball, biking, and hiking. If you want to live here, stay away from the Canal area, where crime is high and there is a drug problem. Other parts of the town are very suburban and well kept.

Sausalito

This is Marin County's most popular tourist spot. The commercial strip along the waterfront has many galleries, clothing boutiques, and eateries. An easy commute to San Francisco by ferry or bus makes it a popular rental area for city workers. Rents aren't cheap, with studios averaging around $900 and one-bedrooms around $1,400. If you can afford it, you'll be rewarded with low-stress living.

Tiburon

This is a wealthy harbor village with great views of San Francisco and Angel Island. Its downtown (Main Street) is a popular weekend spot for city dwellers who ride their bikes over the Golden Gate Bridge to enjoy brunch at Sam's Cafe on the waterfront. There are many shops, galleries, and restaurants along Tiburon Boulevard. Crime is low and rents are high. A studio apartment will average $850, while a one-bedroom ranges between $1,200 to $2,600 per month.

EAST BAY

ALAMEDA COUNTY
This county is located 15 minutes to a half hour east of San Francisco across the Bay Bridge. It is a suburban metropolis surrounded by rolling hills and recreational parks. Alameda County communities include Alameda, Albany, Berkeley, Dublin, Emeryville, Fremont, Hayward, Livermore, Newark, Oakland, Claremont/Rockridge, Eastmont, Elmhurst/Brookfield Village, Forest Park, Fruitvale, Lakeshore/Trestle Glen, Melrose/Seminary, Millsmont, Montclair/Piedmont Pines, Oak Knoll/Sheffield Village, Oakmore/Diamond, Temescal, Piedmont, Pleasanton, San Leandro, Union City, Ashland/Cherryland, Castro Valley, and San Lorenzo.

Berkeley
In Berkeley, you can choose to live on the south side by U.C. Berkeley, which is like a suburban Haight-Ashbury, or on the north side, which is more residential. Life on the south side is not for the quiet soul. There is much street life along Telegraph Avenue, and the college town reputation is definitely maintained. Crime is higher here due in part to a population of young street people. The north side, on the other hand, is a quieter, gentler community. For the most part, Berkeley is an extremely liberal city that attracts creative, innovative types like artists, educators, and computer professionals. Berkeley is an easy BART commute to San Francisco.

Oakland
This is an ethnically diverse city that's home to the Oakland A's baseball team, the Golden State Warriors basketball team, museums, theater, ballet, symphony, zoo, and a convention center. It's a big city just like San Francisco. Choose your neighborhood carefully, though. Crime is high in the western section; the east and in the hills are safer. If you live here, you'll enjoy affordable rents, mild weather year-round, and lots of activities both in town and over the Bay Bridge in San Francisco.

CONTRA COSTA COUNTY
Once considered a bedroom community, this has developed into an important business and commercial region. Communities include Antioch, Brentwood, Clayton, Concord, Danville, El Cerrito, Hercules, Lafayette, Martinez, Moraga, Orinda, Pinole, Pittsburg, Pleasant Hill, Richmond, San Pablo, San Ramon, and Walnut Creek.

Concord
This is a bedroom community with a thriving business district that creates thousands of white-collar jobs. Some industries here are Bank of America and Chevron. You can shop at Sun Valley Mall; Cal State Hayward has a satellite campus nearby.

There are also 19 parks, golf courses, a community center, and Co[...] concert hall. If you need to get to San Francisco, you're in luck—[...] BART station that will take you directly downtown.

Walnut Creek

Even though Walnut Creek has a large retirement community, it attracts many single professionals to its active city. Some highlights are Mount Diablo and its surrounding parklands, which offer many great outdoor activities. There are also 15 parks, two golf courses, two libraries, and a brand new Regional Center for the Arts. You can also enjoy many restaurants, bookstores, shops, and movie theaters in its downtown. The commute to San Francisco is a pleasant and easy BART train ride.

PENINSULA

SAN MATEO COUNTY

This area covers Daly City to Menlo Park, encompassing the San Francisco International Airport. Bioscience, industrial, and business parks are located along Highway 101, the county's main business corridor. San Mateo County communities include Atherton, Belmont, Brisbane, Burlingame, Colma, Daly City, East Palo Alto, Foster City, Half Moon Bay, Hillsborough, Menlo Park, Millbrae, Pacifica, Redwood City, San Bruno, San Carlos, San Mateo, and South San Francisco.

Burlingame

Burlingame is a peaceful bedroom community with ranch-style homes and sycamore-lined streets. San Francisco International Airport is minutes away, which is a plus if you do a lot of traveling for your job, but the noise can be intrusive at times. If you live here, you'll enjoy many activities thanks to 15 parks, tennis and basketball courts, a recreation center, and a fishing pier.

Foster City

This pleasant and attractive town was built from scratch by a rags-to-riches orphan named Jack Foster. His success was helped by the fact that he bought a piece of land that sits on an island with three sides surrounded by water. This makes for wonderful outdoor activities along the many trails that wander along the shore. No need to worry about fog, because the town is sheltered by hills and is close to the bay. Foster City has everything a resident could want or need, including a library, recreation center, 18 parks, and opportunity for employment at more than 600 businesses, including the headquarters for Visa. The neighborhood residences are a mix of apartments, townhouses, and modest homes, and crime is low.

Menlo Park

This is a clean, well-cared-for suburb with tree-lined streets, nine parks, and a popular farmer's market. This is also home to some Bay Area industry biggies like Sun Microsystems, *Sunset* magazine, and the U.S. Geological Survey. Under construction is a one million square foot engineering and research park that will employ close to 3,600 people. Commutes to San Francisco can either be done by CalTrain or SamTrans buses.

Redwood City

Redwood City is an established, attractive, tree-filled city that has a port and little crime. It doesn't have the polish of its neighboring Menlo Park and Foster City, but it does have many of the same features. There are seven parks, two municipal swimming pools, three libraries, a nine-hole golf course, four marinas, and a farmer's market in the summers. Redwood City is known as the headquarters for software giant Oracle.

San Mateo

This city has it all: four parks, golf course, marina, farmer's market, arts center, horse racing, wildlife center, bay beach, two big shopping malls, and plenty of open space. If that's not enough for you, then an easy commute along Highways 101 and 280 or on public transportation will get you to San Francisco. This is a well-maintained, middle-class city that offers a comfortable lifestyle.

PART 3

JOB HUNTING

PHOTO BY KITTI HOMME

CHAPTER SIX

Temporary and Permanent Job Placement

WHEN YOU ARE NEW to a city and need to find work, signing up with an employment agency is a quick and easy way to do it. Most agencies have temporary and permanent job placement departments. While the permanent job placement side searches for full-time work, the temporary side can set you up with short-term job assignments. Temp work is a great way to earn quick cash and get your foot in the door at many companies. It's not uncommon for temporary jobs to turn into full-time permanent jobs. Be warned, though, that most employment agencies, both temporary and permanent, deal with administrative jobs. To the college-educated, this may sound unappealing, but if you have a good attitude and some foresight, these jobs will turn into something better. I'm a good example of this.

When I moved to San Francisco after graduate school, I needed to find work right away. Like most people, I had no savings to support me until the perfect job came along. I signed up with eight temp agencies with the attitude that I was happy to be working and perhaps I'd find permanent work and eventually get promoted. Well, this attitude paid off. I temped for a big bank in a very boring department. I was a hard worker, doing every menial task that was given to me with a positive attitude. I established a good reputation in my department and soon started getting more interesting and challenging projects. I developed a good working relationship with my manager and started telling her about my talents as a writer. I offered to help her with proposals and communication materials for the department. Soon she hired me for the vacant administrative assistant position I was filling as a temp. She kept using my writing skills, and, because I worked for a big bank, I was able to take that experience to a different department and into a more interesting, nonadministrative position.

Now I'd like to give those of you who have never used an employment agency an overview of what to expect.

The more agencies you sign up with, the better chance you have of finding work. This chapter only lists a few of the many agencies in the Bay Area. Your best bet is to supplement my agency list with the classified ads in the Sunday paper and the Yellow Pages. When you review the classified ads, you'll notice that many of the listed jobs are offered through employment agencies. You can pick your agencies by how interesting you find the jobs they list. The Yellow Pages will list all agencies in town, sometimes with a description of their services.

Once you choose your agencies, call and make appointments. You'll be asked if you're interested in temporary or permanent work or both. It's suggested you register with both sides so all your bases are covered. Besides, you don't want to have to go through the registration process twice (temporary and permanent departments are usually run separately in the same agency). I mentioned in Chapter 2 that you should call ahead to make your appointment before you move to San Francisco. This is because you may have to wait up to three weeks before meeting with an agent.

When preparing for your meeting with the agency, make sure you have several copies of your resume to distribute. If possible, write different versions of your resume to market yourself for different positions. For example, have a resume that shows exactly how talented you are, a resume that highlights your administrative skills, and a resume that emphasizes your transferable skills.

How you look and dress is also important for these meetings. Even though you're not going to be working for the actual agency per se, you will be representing them when you go out on interviews or temp assignments. San Francisco is a fairly conservative city despite what you may hear. If you get a chance, have lunch in the Financial District to get an idea of what type of wardrobe professionals wear.

Arrive at the agency on time even though you'll probably have to wait. Bring the Sunday newspaper classified section with the jobs the agency is advertising that interest you. During this wait you will be asked to complete an application and show a passport for proof of U.S. residency and a driver's license for identification.

Be prepared to take a battery of tests before you even get to see an agent. Testing is a normal part of the registration and screening process, and you'll probably find some of the tests laughably easy. You'll be tested on your typing speed, knowledge of certain software programs such as Microsoft Word, Excel, WordPerfect, and PageMaker. They may give you a 10-key, spelling, grammar, math, and filing test. You'll probably wonder why you went to college when you're completing your filing test, but everyone has to do it.

When you finally get to meet with an agent, he or she will review your test scores and ask you what type of job you're looking for. You can say anything you want, but they'll probably tell you they fill support positions. If there's an industry you want to get into, say advertising, the agent can focus on that.

You will then be handed some time sheets and told how the agency works. If you're temping, you'll be told to call the agency once a day. I recommend calling in three times a day—first thing in the morning, once at 10 A.M., and then around 4 P.M. to be put on the list for the next day. For permanent work, call in once a week or when you see an interesting job listing the agency has put in the paper.

To help you select the right employment agencies to register with, the following are some questions to ask before you schedule an appointment and/or at the time you're meeting with your counselor:

What type of job placement do you do—temporary, permanent, executive, or a combination? Most agencies will have temporary and permanent placements, usually with different counselors working in each area. As I mentioned earlier, it's best to register in both areas so your bases are covered.

What are some typical temporary and permanent positions you fill at your agency? If you're looking for a technical writing job and the agency mainly gets administrative jobs, then that's not a good fit. Also, be clear with the agency about what you're looking for, because if they can't help you, they may refer you to another agency that can.

What's the hourly rate for a temporary job at your agency? Depending on the job, ranges will be anywhere from $8 per hour for clerical to $35 per hour for computer programmers. Here is a very general average of temp wages:

Receptionist/Clerical	$8 to $10
Administrative/Secretarial	$10 to $15
Accounting/Bookkeeping/Finance	$14 to $17
Desktop Publishing/Graphics	$15 to $18
Legal/Paralegal	$18 to $20
Medical Workers	$8 to $14
Dental Workers	$13 to $30

What's the typical salary for a permanent job found through your agency? This will give you an idea of the job market in the area. Salaries may appear to be high if you're not from California, but you'll soon discover the high cost of living in San Francisco makes up for this. If you want a realistic look of competitive salaries in different industries, contact professional organizations or visit your local library for the information.

What skills and qualifications would make me most marketable in the workforce your agency deals with? This will help you assess your own skills and decide where you need more training. In general, computer skills and knowledge of many software programs is always a plus in the temporary job force. Also, more specialized agencies that handle medical, dental, legal, and insurance professions may require certain licensing or minimum experience.

How long will it take to find a temporary or permanent job once I register? This usually depends on your skill level and market conditions. Also, those people who have been registered with the agency for a while will probably get priority on jobs because of their experience and reputation.

Who are some of your clients? Agencies may not always reveal who their clients are. If this is the case and you have some specific companies in mind you'd like to work for, say, The Gap or Levi's, they can tell you if they're a client or perhaps refer you to the agency handling their account. Another option is to call the company's human resources department and ask what temp agencies they use.

How soon can I get an appointment with the agency? Depending on how popular the agency is, this can range from one day to three weeks. Call early to be on the safe side.

How much time should be set aside for the appointment? Registration will take about one to two hours, so plan your schedule accordingly.

What should I bring with me? The state of California requires that all job applicants present a passport or other form of identification that proves eligibility to work in the U.S. Besides that, agencies may ask for the following: copies of your resume, letters of recommendation, references, driver's license or other form of identification, and school transcripts.

Which tests do you administer to applicants? There will be basic evaluation tests such as math, filing, spelling, grammar, accounting, and whatever else is appropriate for the agency. There will also be tests on the computer for typing speed and knowledge of different software programs like Microsoft Word and Excel. Ask the agency for the ones they administer so you can brush up ahead of time.

Do you offer any training or benefits? Most agencies will offer some type of benefits and training, whether a discounted health plan, a software tutorial, or vacation pay after working a certain number of hours.

How often would I need to call in for work? Some agencies will say to call in once every couple of days, while others are specific about the time and frequency you should check in. When you're starting out, it's better to call more frequently so the office receptionist and your counselor become familiar with you.

What advice do you give to your temps? This is a great question to get insight about the temporary workforce from people who know it best. Counselors will talk to you about things like dress code and attitude. On specific assignments, they can tell you about your supervisor's personality or the experience the last temp had. This is all good to get you in the right frame of mind for work.

PERSONNEL AGENCIES

The following is a list of some local Bay Area temporary personnel agencies. This is a list that incorporates some of the top agencies in the Bay Area, as named in the *1995 Book of Lists* produced by the *San Francisco Business Times*. Also included are a number of agencies that answered a survey for this chapter. Remember, the phone book and newspapers are also good resources for finding agencies in the area.

ABA Staffing
2121 South El Camino Real
San Mateo, CA 94403
(415) 349-9200

Industries: Accounting, retail, general office, secretarial, banking, finance, telemarketing, sales, technical, marketing, legal, direct mail, hospitality

Service area: Entire Bay Area except Marin

Benefits and training: Both

ABAR Personnel
595 Market Street
San Francisco, CA 94105
(415) 243-9700

Industries: Finance, accounting, administration, technical, systems, clerical, hospitality

Service area: Entire Bay Area

Benefits and training: Both

Accountants On Call
44 Montgomery Street
San Francisco, CA 94104
(415) 398-3366

Industries: Finance, accounting, clerical

Service area: Entire Bay Area

Benefits and training: Benefits only

Accountemps
388 Market Street, Suite 1400
San Francisco, CA 94111
(415) 434-1900

Industries: Finance, accounting

Service area: Entire Bay Area

Benefits and training: Both

Adia Personnel Services
100 Redwood Shores Parkway
Redwood City, CA 94065
(415) 610-1000

Industries: Finance, accounting, sales, management, engineering, marketing, administration, technical, systems, clerical, hospitality, executives

Service area: Entire Bay Area

Benefits and training: Both

Alper & Associates Personnel Service
353 Sacramento Street, #1760
San Francisco, CA 94111
(415) 397-6611

Industries: Administration, corporate and legal

Service area: Entire Bay Area

Benefits and training: Both

AppleOne
1515 South El Camino Real
San Mateo, CA 94402
800-266-9991

Industries: Finance, accounting, administration, clerical

Service area: Entire Bay Area

Benefits and training: Both

Bradford Personnel, Inc.
130 Battery Street, Suite 600
San Francisco, CA 94111
(415) 362-0435

Industries: Finance, accounting, sales, management, marketing, administration, clerical, hospitality

Service area: Entire Bay Area

Benefits and training: Both

Certified Personnel
233 Sansome Street
San Francisco, CA 94111
(415) 677-9900

Industries: Finance, accounting, marketing, administration, technical, clerical, hospitality, legal

Service area: Entire Bay Area except Marin

Benefits and training: Both

Innovations PSI
345 California Street, Suite 1750
San Francisco, CA 94104
(415) 392-4022

Industries: Finance, accounting, sales, marketing, administration, clerical, executives

Service area: Entire Bay Area

Benefits and training: Both

Interim Services, Inc.
160 Pine Street, Suite 300
San Francisco, CA 94111
(415) 391-5979

Industries: Finance, accounting, sales, marketing, administration, technical, clerical, hospitality

Service area: Entire Bay Area

Benefits and training: Both

Kelly Services
One Walnut Creek Center
Walnut Creek, CA 94596
(510) 933-6293

Industries: Finance, accounting, sales, engineering, marketing, administration, technical, systems, clerical, hospitality

Service area: Entire Bay Area

Benefits and training: Both

McCall Staffing Services
351 California Street, Suite 1200
San Francisco, CA 94104
(415) 981-3400

Industries: Finance, accounting, administration, clerical

Service area: Entire Bay Area

Benefits and training: Both

Nelson Personnel Services
425 California Street, Suite 600
San Francisco, CA 94104
(415) 989-9911

Industries: Finance, accounting, engineering, administration, technical, clerical, executives

Service area: Entire Bay Area

Benefits and training: Both

Office Team
388 Market Street, Suite 1400
San Francisco, CA 94111
(415) 434-2429

Industries: Finance, accounting, administration, clerical

Service area: Entire Bay Area
except Marin

Benefits and training: Both

Olsten Staffing Services
120 Montgomery Street, Suite 700
San Francisco, CA 94104
(415) 362-3244

Industries: Finance, accounting, sales,
engineering, marketing, administration, technical, systems, clerical

Service area: Entire Bay Area

Benefits and training: Both

The People Connection
100 California Street
San Francisco, CA 94111
(415) 397-5517

Industries: Administration, clerical

Service area: Entire Bay Area

Benefits and training: Benefits only

ProServ
110 Sutter Street, Suite 600
San Francisco, CA 94104
(415) 781-6100

Industries: Finance, accounting, sales,
management, marketing, administration, technical, systems, clerical,
hospitality

Service area: Entire Bay Area

Benefits and training: Both

Remedy Intelligent Staffing
595 Market Street, Suite 1150
San Francisco, CA 94105
(415) 243-8566

Industries: Finance, accounting, sales,
management, engineering, administration, technical, systems, clerical,
hospitality, executives

Service area: Entire Bay Area

Benefits and training: Both

The Right People
155 Montgomery Street, #1600
San Francisco, CA 94104
(415) 705-5333

Industries: Clerical, word processing,
administrative, graphics, desktop
publishing, reception

Service area: Entire Bay Area

Benefits and training: Both

Roberta Enterprises, Inc.
44 Montgomery Street, Suite 1430
San Francisco, CA 94104
(415) 433-7624

Industries: Administration, clerical

Service area: San Francisco and San
Mateo

Benefits and training: Benefits only

Temporary Skills Unlimited
2380 Salvio, Suite 300
Concord, CA 94520
(510) 827-5627

Industries: Finance, accounting,
marketing, administration, technical,
clerical

Service area: Entire Bay Area

Benefits and training: Both

Toner Corporation
27 Maiden Lane, Suite 300
San Francisco, CA 94108
800-339-5339 (within California);
(415) 788-8488

Industries: Technical, programming,
engineering, computers

Service area: Entire Bay Area

Benefits and training: Benefits only

World Wide Web:
http://www.toner.com

Truex Associates
456 Montgomery Street, 22nd Floor
San Francisco, CA 94111
(415) 433-6222

Industries: Finance, accounting, sales,
management, engineering, marketing,
administration, technical, systems,
clerical, hospitality, executives

Service area: Alameda, San Francisco,
San Mateo

Benefits and training: Both

Volt Services Group
340 Pine Street, Suite 504
San Francisco, CA 94108
(415) 391-6830

Industries: Finance, accounting,
engineering, marketing, administration, technical, systems, clerical,
hospitality

Service area: Entire Bay Area
except Marin

Benefits and training: Both

Western Temporary Services
301 Lennon Lane
Walnut Creek, CA 94598
(510) 930-5300

Industries: Finance, accounting, sales,
management, engineering, marketing,
administration, technical, systems,
clerical, hospitality, executives

Service area: Entire Bay Area

Benefits and training: Both

SPECIALIZED TEMPORARY EMPLOYMENT AGENCIES

DENTAL

Dental Fill-Ins Placement Agency
2027 Van Ness Avenue
San Francisco, CA 94109
(415) 771-2426

Dental Plus Medical (DPM)
490 Post Street, Suite 1701
San Francisco, CA 94102
(415) 677-0961

INSURANCE

Insurance Personnel Service
120 Montgomery Street, Suite 2500
San Francisco, CA 94104
(415) 391-5900

The Tetsell Group
350 California Street, Suite 1750
San Francisco, CA 94104
(415) 392-4000

LEGAL

The Affiliates
388 Market Street, Suite 1420
San Francisco, CA 94111
(415) 982-2001

Chapman Williams International

300 Montgomery Street, Suite 860
San Francisco, CA 94104
(415) 392-2729

Exclusively Legal

311 California Street, Sixth Floor
San Francisco, CA 94104
(415) 616-9733

Legal Staff

433 California Street, Suite 904
San Francisco, CA 94104
(415) 433-3230

Mark Associates

300 Montgomery Street, Suite 860
San Francisco, CA 94104
(415) 392-1835

Specialists Group

655 Montgomery Street, Suite 515
San Francisco, CA 94111
(415) 421-9400

MEDICAL

Medical Center Agency

870 Market Street, Suite 650
San Francisco, CA 94102
(415) 397-9440

Medi-Quest Personnel Services

220 Sansome Street, Eighth Floor
San Francisco, CA 94104
(415) 421-7183

The local phone company has a Local Talk tips line to give you information about temporary agencies. The main number is (415) 837-5050, and the choices are:

1510 How a temporary agency works
1515 Information you may need
1520 Fees
1525 The interview

CHAPTER SEVEN

More Job-Finding Ideas

I N THE LAST CHAPTER, I talked about the different temporary and permanent job placement agencies in San Francisco. If you're new to the city and/or need to find work right away, enlisting an agency's help is probably the quickest and easiest way to do it. You can combine that method of job searching with your own efforts. There are many other ways to find work in San Francisco. The most obvious is to look through the newspaper classified ads. If your goal is a managerial job, then executive recruiters are a good bet. You can also research different Bay Area companies and contact them yourself. In this chapter, I will list different options for finding a job in San Francisco. I will also reference several excellent resources to help you with your own research.

EXECUTIVE RECRUITERS

Executive recruiters deal with people who have held management positions, make over $40,000 a year, or are proven in their field. The following is a list of the 10 largest contingency executive search firms in the Bay Area as ranked in the *1995 Book of Lists* by the *San Francisco Business Times*. Many more can be found either in the Yellow Pages under "Executive Search" or researching the job-finding books listed at the end of the chapter.

Culver Personnel Services
1555 Old Bayshore Highway, Suite 100
Burlingame, CA 94010
(415) 692-9090

Areas of specialization: Sales and sales management

Enterprise Solutions International
235 Pine Street, Suite 1800
San Francisco, CA 94104
(415) 421-1400

Areas of specialization: Sales teams for early state high-tech companies

Interim Accounting Professionals
200 Pringle Avenue, Suite 325
Walnut Creek, CA 94596
(510) 934-7092

Areas of specialization: Accounting and finance

Management Recruiters and Sales Consultants
480 Roland Way
Oakland, CA 94621
(510) 569-6231

Areas of specialization: Biotechnology, medical, telecommunications, industrial, mechanical, chemical

Management Recruiters International
591 Redwood Highway, Suite 2225
Mill Valley, CA 94941
(415) 383-7044

Areas of specialization: Health care, high-tech engineering and marketing, environmental, software, multimedia

PFC Inc.
455 Market Street, Suite 1850
San Francisco, CA 94105
(415) 957-1400

Areas of specialization: Systems and technology, management, consulting services

Robert Grant Associates, Inc.
100 Pine Street, Suite 2225
San Francisco, CA 94111
(415) 981-7424

Areas of specialization: Health care, consumer products, medical sales, MIS, high-tech

Schlatter & Associates
388 Market Street, Suite 400
San Francisco, CA 94111
(415) 433-8100

Areas of specialization: CFO and controllers for small to medium-size companies

Search West
100 Pine Street
San Francisco, CA 94111
(415) 788-1770

Areas of specialization: Real estate, health care, insurance, engineering, sales, multimedia

SmartSource Inc.
1700 North Broadway, Suite 320
Walnut Creek, CA 94596
(510) 935-4200

Area of specialization: Telecommuni-cations, PC/LAN, information systems

COMPANY JOB LINES
Company job lines are a good way to find out if a company has job opportu-nities without making cold calls. List-ings are usually updated weekly.

Academy of Sciences
Golden Gate Park
San Francisco, CA 94118
(415) 750-7333

Industry: Science

Asian Art Museum
Golden Gate Park
San Francisco, CA 94118
(415) 379-8802

Industry: Art

Bank of California
433 California Street
San Francisco, CA 94104
(415) 765-3535

Industry: Banking

Brøderbund Software
500 Redwood
Novato, CA 94948
(415) 382-4404

Industry: Software developer and publisher

California Biotechnology
Silus Nova Incorporated
2450 Bayshore Parkway
Mountain View, CA 94043
(415) 962-5990

Industry: Specialty hospitals, general medical and surgical hospitals

California School Library Association

1499 Old Bayshore Highway, Suite 142
Burlingame, CA 94010
(415) 697-8832

Industry: Library

California State Automobile Association

100 Van Ness Avenue
San Francisco, CA 94102
(415) 565-2194

Industry: Auto, insurance

Charles Schwab

101 Montgomery Street
San Francisco, CA 94104
(415) 627-7227

Industry: Brokerage and financial services

World Wide Web:
http://www.schwab.com

Chevron Corp.

P.O. Box 7318
San Francisco, CA 94120
(415) 894-2552
Walnut Creek and Concord:
(510) 680-3152
Richmond: (510) 242-5523 or 242-4948

Industry: Petroleum refining

World Wide Web:
http://www.chevron.com/

Cisco Systems

501 East Middlefield Road
Mountain View, CA 94043
(415) 326-1941 (ask to be transferred to the employment hotline)

Industry: Computer peripheral equipment

World Wide Web:
http://www.cisco.com

Clorox Co.

1221 Broadway
Oakland, CA 94612
(510) 271-7625

Industry: Specialty cleaners, polishes, and sanitation goods

Davies Medical Center

Castro and Duboce Streets
San Francisco, CA 94114
(415) 565-6104

Industry: General medical and surgical hospital

Esprit

900 Minnesota Avenue
San Francisco, CA 94107
(415) 550-3998

Industry: Women's clothing

Exploratorium

3601 Lyon Street
San Francisco, CA 94123
(415) 561-0328

Industry: Science museum

World Wide Web:
http://www.exploratorium.edu/

Failure Analysis Associates

149 Commonwealth Drive
Menlo Park, CA 94025
(415) 688-6700

Industry: Engineering services

Federal Job Information Center

(415) 744-5627

Industry: Federal jobs

World Wide Web:
http://www.clubfed.com/

Federal Reserve Bank of San Francisco
101 Market Street
San Francisco, CA 94105
(415) 974-3330

Industry: Federal reserve bank

Franklin Resources
777 Mariners Island Boulevard
San Mateo, CA 94404
(415) 312-JOBS

Industry: Mutual funds and investment management

Gap Incorporated
1 Harrison Street
San Francisco, CA 94105
(415) 737-4495

Industry: Clothes manufacturer

Genentech Inc.
460 Point San Bruno Boulevard
South San Francisco, CA 94080
(415) 225-2580

Industry: Biotechnology/
biopharmaceuticals

World Wide Web:
http://www.gene.com

Golden Gate Transit
1011 Andersen Drive
San Rafael, CA 94901
(415) 257-4545

Industry: Transportation

World Wide Web:
http://server.berkeley.edu/transit/

Good Guys
7000 Marina Boulevard
Brisbane, CA 94005
(415) 615-6051 (corporate)
800-JOB-GUYS (stores)

Industry: Retail consumer electronics

Gymboree Corp.
700 Airport Boulevard
Burlingame, CA 94010
(415) 579-0600 (ask to be connected to
the hotline)

Industry: Children's Apparel and Retail

World Wide Web:
http://www.service.com/gymboree/
home.html

Hilton Hotel
1 Hilton Square
San Francisco, CA 94102
(415) 923-5068

Industry: Hotels and hospitality

World Wide Web:
http://www.hilton.com/

Kaiser Permanente
One Kaiser Plaza
Oakland, CA 94612
(415) 202-2500

Industry: Health care

World Wide Web:
http://www.kpga.org/

KGO Channel 7
900 Front Street
San Francisco, CA 94111
(415) 954-7958

Industry: Television broadcasting

World Wide Web:
http://www.kgo-tv.com/~jcasabel/channel7.html

KPIX Channel 5

855 Battery Street
San Francisco, CA 94111
(415) 765-8609

Industry: Television broadcasting station

World Wide Web:
http://www.kpix.com/

KQED Channel 9

2601 Mariposa Street
San Francisco, CA 94110
(415) 553-2303

Industry: Public television station

World Wide Web:
http://www.kqed.org/

KRON Channel 4

1001 Van Ness Avenue
San Francisco, CA 94109
(415) 561-8662 (ext. 1)

Industry: Television broadcasting station

World Wide Web:
http://www.kron.com

Levi Strauss and Co.

1155 Battery Street
San Francisco, CA 94111
(415) 544-7828

Industry: Clothing manufacturer

World Wide Web:
http://www.levi.com/menu

Lucasfilm

P.O. Box 2009
San Rafael, CA 94912
(415) 662-1999

Industry: Film

World Wide Web:
http://lum.com/thx/thxmain.html

McKesson Corp.

McKesson Plaza
One Post Street
San Francisco, CA 94104
(415) 983-8409

Industry: Drug and toiletries distribution

NASA Ames Research Center

Allied Technical Services Corp.
Nasa Mail Stop 2448
Mountain View, CA 94035
(415) 604-8000

Industry: Management services

World Wide Web:
http://huminfo.arc.nasa.gov/

Pacific Bell and Pacific Telesis

130 Kearny Street
San Francisco, CA 94108
(415) 542-0817
800-924-JOBS

Industry: Telephone communications and telecommunications

World Wide Web:
http://www.pactel.com/

Pacific Gas and Electric (PG&E)

77 Beale Street
San Francisco, CA 94177
(415) 973-5195

Industry: Utility company

PC World Communications

501 2nd Street
San Francisco, CA 94107
(415) 978-3100

Industry: Computer magazines

World Wide Web:
http://www.pcworld.com

San Francisco Federal Savings and Loan
88 Kearny Street
San Francisco, CA 94108
(415) 291-9932

Industry: Savings and loan

San Francisco Museum of Modern Art
151 Third Street
San Francisco, CA 94103
(415) 357-4000 (ext. 1, selection 9)

Industry: Modern art museum

World Wide Web:
http://www.sfmoma.org

San Francisco Newspaper Agency
925 Mission Street
San Francisco, CA 94103
(415) 777-7642 (ext. 2 and ext. 4)

Industry: Newspaper publisher

World Wide Web:
http://www.sfgate.com

San Francisco State University
1600 Hollaway Avenue
San Francisco, CA 94132
(415) 338-1871

Industry: Education

World Wide Web:
http://www.sfsu.edu/

San Francisco Unified School District Classified Jobs
135 Van Ness Avenue
San Francisco, CA 94102
(415) 241-6162

Industry: Teaching and education

World Wide Web:
http://nisus.sfusd.k12.ca.us/

Sierra Club
100 Bush Street
San Francisco, CA 94104
(415) 978-9085

Industry: Environmental

World Wide Web:
http://www.sierraclub.org/

Sybase Inc.
6475 Christie Avenue
Emeryville, CA 94608
(510) 922-8494

Industry: Client/server software

World Wide Web:
http://www.sybase.com

Transamerica Corp.
600 Montgomery Street
San Francisco, CA 94111
(415) 983-4000 (ask operator for job hotline)

Industry: Insurance

Union Bank
350 California Street
San Francisco, CA 94104
(415) 705-7013

Industry: Banking

World Wide Web:
http://www.careermosaic.com/cm/ union_bank/

University of California, San Francisco
1350 7th Avenue
San Francisco, CA 94143
(415) 502-5627

Industry: Education

U.S. Geological Survey
345 Middlefield Road
Menlo Park, CA 94025
(415) 329-4122

Industry: Geology

World Wide Web:
http://www.usgs.gov/

U.S. Postal Service
1300 Evans Avenue
San Francisco, CA 94124
(415) 550-5534 (ext. 1)

Industry: Postal

World Wide Web:
http://www.usps.gov/

VISA
3125 Clearview Way
San Mateo, CA 94402
(415) 432-8299

Industry: Credit card business services

World Wide Web:
http://www.visa.com/

Williams-Sonoma
100 North Point Street
San Francisco, CA 94133
(415) 616-8333

Industry: Retail cookware shops/
catalog

Workforce Solutions
A Division of International Business
Machines (IBM)
425 Market Street
San Francisco, CA 94105
(415) 545-3756

Industry: Computers, business
machines

World Wide Web:
http://www.empl.ibm.com/

Ziff-Davis Publishing Co.
950 Tower Lane
Foster City, CA 94404
(415) 578-7537

Industry: Periodicals, publishing

World Wide Web:
http://www.zdnet.com/home/filters/
maina.html

PROFESSIONAL ORGANIZATIONS/ CAREER DEVELOPMENT SERVICES

The following listing contains the names of various nonprofit career development organizations and professional societies that serve as job-finding resources. Membership rates and services are subject to change.

Alumnae Resources
120 Montgomery Street, Suite 1080
San Francisco, CA 94104
(415) 274-4747
(415) 274-4715 Fax

Description: Alumnae Resources is a unique career development organization offering career planning and job search assistance in a professional and supportive environment. They provide a comprehensive range of services to Bay Area women and men who are seeking to begin, advance, or change their careers.

Fee: $75 membership

What You Get: Quarterly newsletter and calendar; career counseling at a discount; self-assessment workshops at a discount; workshops on exploring career options, self-employment, strategic career planning, professional development, personal and technical skills, and leadership development at a discount. They've also just put in place a telephone career line.

Note: Call or write for a newsletter/calendar and see for yourself what they offer.

Career Action Center
445 Sherman Avenue
Palo Alto, CA 94306
(415) 324-1710
(415) 324-9357 (fax)

World Wide Web: **http://www.gatenet.com/cac/**

Description: The Career Action Center is a nonprofit organization nationally recognized for its leadership and expertise in the development and delivery of career management services. Clients range from recent graduates and those looking for entry-level positions to technical specialists and managers with many years of experience. Currently there are about 200 corporate partners.

Fee: $70 annual membership or $110 membership, which includes a counseling appointment

What You Get: Your membership gets you the quarterly newsletter *Connections* and access to programs, resources, counseling, and workshops. Programs include Career Action Network, Career Management Forums, Employer Forums, and Friday Forums. There are also more than 13,000 job listings monthly from over 1,400 local employers.

Note: Try the Resource Center for a day for a $15 fee.

Chamber of Commerce Job Forum
465 California St., Ninth Floor
San Francisco, CA 94104
(415) 392-4520

Description: The Job Forum is a unique community service aimed at helping people help themselves in their job search. The emphasis is on intelligently planning and conducting a job-finding campaign. The Forum is neither a placement service nor an employment agency.

Fee: None

How It Works: Every Wednesday evening, from 7 P.M. to 9 P.M., a rotating panel of four experts from business, academia, and government volunteer their time to discuss a wide variety of individual job finding problems. Attendees are welcome to discuss their own situation in open session. Attendees are also encouraged to exchange with one another any helpful job information they may have. Typical topics include newcomers to the community, recent graduates, job information sources, voluntary or involuntary termination.

Note: Call or write the Chamber of Commerce for an informational brochure.

International Association of Business Communicators (IABC)
San Francisco Chapter
5 3rd Street, Suite 724
San Francisco, CA 94103
(415) 773-9654 (Infoline)
(415) 433-3400 (membership info)

World Wide Web: **http://www.hooked.net/iabc.com/sanfran.html**

Description: This is an organization of Bay Area communications professionals whose mission is to help members develop professional and ethical excellence and contribute more effectively to their organizations and their communities. It offers valuable contact with other communication professionals through regular meetings, awards competitions, seminars, and other projects.

Fee: $246 includes $40 application fee

What You Get: Membership includes the monthly newsletter *Communiqué*, monthly programs, professional development seminars and roundtables, job referrals through the job listing newsletter *Leads* and the job resource guide *Hot Hints*.

Note: IABC events are open to the public and can be accessed by calling the Infoline above. Also, you can request a sample issue of *Leads,* the twice-monthly job listing newsletter.

LifePlan Center
5 3rd Street, Suite 324
San Francisco, CA 94103
(415) 546-4499

Description: A nonprofit organization dedicated to men and women in their 50s, 60s, and 70s who are in transition as they address change in their work and personal lives.

Fee: $55 membership

at You Get: Quarterly newsletter and calendar, orientation to the center, peer guidance, career exchange network, women's and men's forums, work strategies, access to the resource center including job listings, and discounts on workshops and programs.

Note: This is an independent project of Alumnae Resources. Call or write for a newsletter/calendar.

Media Alliance
814 Mission Street, Suite 205
San Francisco, CA 94103
(415) 546-6334 (general info)
(415) 546-6491 (classes)

Description: This is a nonprofit organization that serves media and communications professionals. It's also an advocacy organization for media issues such as media access and professional responsibility.

Fee: $45 standard membership plus $20 with JobFile Access plus $20 for discount computer access and classes

What You Get: Quarterly class brochure, discounts for classes, and JobFile Access, which is an in-office access to listings of Bay Area media jobs. Many reputable Bay Area companies list their jobs here. Listings fall into categories such as freelance, permanent/full-time, and internships.

Note: Ask about volunteering your services in exchange for free classes.

National Writers Union
Local 3 San Francisco Bay Area
337 17th Street, #101
Oakland, CA 94612
(510) 839-1248
(415) 979-5522 (Technical Writing Job Hotline)

World Wide Web: **http//www.igc.apc.org/nwu/**

e-mail: nwu3@well.sf.ca.us

Description: The National Writers Union (NWU) is an innovative labor union committed to improving the economic and business concerns of freelance writers through the collective strength of its members. Members include journalists, novelists, biographers, historians, poets, commercial writers, and technical writers. Some union activities include handling grievances, working with journalists and their contracts, helping book authors get fair contracts, and operating a Writers Job Hotline with available technical and business writing jobs.

Fee: $75 to $170, based on a sliding scale according to what you earn as a writer

What You Get: Membership in the NWU is open to all qualified writers, published and unpublished. Membership includes *Writer,* a quarterly newsletter; invitations to forums, seminars, and workshops; and in-office access to valuable resource materials like the Internet, discounted health plan, and agent database.

Women in Communications, Inc. (WICI)
120 Village Square, Suite 143
Orinda, CA 94563
(510) 253-1784 (office)
(510) 253-8685 Job Hotline
(members only)

Women in Communications is an international organization with over 11,000 members and 80 chapters. The Bay Area Chapter has a membership of over 400 women representing all areas of the communications industry. WICI is dedicated to professional development through an annual conference and local educational programs and awards. You can become a short-term user of the WICI hotline at a cost of $50 for a four-month period. Job Bank categories include public relations, marketing communications, print media and journalism, advertising and broadcasting, graphics/visual media, and development.

Recommended Reading

Albin, James R. 1994. *Bay Area Employment Agency and Executive Recruiter Directory.* Sausalito: Albin Publications.

Albin, James R. 1988. *Bay Area Employer Directory.* Sausalito: Albin Publications.

Beach, Janet. 1983. *How to Get a Job in the San Francisco Bay Area.* Chicago: Contemporary Books, Inc.

Benjamin, Janice, and Barbara Block. 1992. *How to be Happily Employed in San Francisco: A Step-by-Step Guide to Finding the Job That's Right for You.* New York: Random House.

Bob Adams, Inc. 1996. *San Francisco Bay Area Job Bank.* Boston: Bob Adams, Inc.

Camden, Thomas M., and Donald A. Casella. 1994. *How to Get a Job in San Francisco.* Chicago: Surrey Books.

Reference Press, Inc., The. 1996. *The Bay Area 500: Hoover's Guide to the Top San Francisco Area Companies.* Austin: The Reference Press, Inc.

WORLD WIDE WEB RESOURCES

The following list of World Wide Web job-finding resources for the San Francisco Bay Area is not complete. Some Web sites offer their own specific services, and others link to different resources related to your job search.

Bay Area Multimedia Technology Alliance Job Bank
(http://mlds-www.arc.nasa.gov/BAMTA/)
Bay Area Multimedia Technology Alliance (BAMTA) provides this Web space for posting job openings in multimedia and Web technology. Companies and organizations submit job openings to be posted. Individuals can browse through the opening lists or search interested openings. Furthermore, if an individual has his or her own idea of the perfect job, it can be posted under the job classification of "My Dream Job" for potential employers to browse.

CareerMosaic
(http://www.careermosaic.com/)
offers job listings around the globe as well as in the Bay Area. Includes a Jobs Offered section, which has the search capability that lets you define the type of job you want, along with location and employer. Other features of CareerMosaic are Information Center, which has articles from the *National Business Employment Weekly* and the *International Herald Tribune,* and the College Connection, which lets you know about entry-level openings and how to prepare your resume.

Employment and Housing
(http://www.hyperion.com/ba/emplmt.html)
is a list of Bay Area employment opportunities along with other employment resources. Listings include the previously mentioned CareerMosaic, the San Francisco Symphony, Oracle, Intel, and more.

Employment Outreach Project
(http://www.cpb.org/jobline/jobline.html)
If you're interested in working in public broadcasting, either radio or television, this lists job opportunities locally.

Internet Online Career Center
(http://www.occ.com)
claims to be the most accessed career home page on the Internet. You'll find Bay Area job listings by clicking Search Jobs, Browse Jobs by City, and selecting San Francisco Bay Area. This Web site also offers other resources, such as career assistance and employment events.

JobHunt
(http://rescomp.stanford.edu/jobs.html)
provides a listing of useful Internet-accessible job search resources and services. Those services listed are relatively stable and appear to be useful or relevant to a broad range of job types and geographical locations. Online job listing categories include academia; science, engineering, and medicine; recruiting agencies;

classified ads; newsgroups; and general resources. Different resource
America's Job Bank, California Career and Employment Center, and ~~~
Employment Weekly Jobs Online, are listed and defined for the user.

San Francisco Chronicle *and* Examiner *Job Classifieds* (http://www.sfgate.com/)

is the Web site for San Francisco's two major newspapers. Select Classifieds and
at Job Opportunities (770) you browse by letter of the job you're looking for.
There is also a separate category for temporary job opportunities (771).

San Jose Mercury News *Help Wanted Listings* (http://www.sjmercury.com/class/help/)

When high-tech companies are hiring, they advertise in the newspaper of the
Silicon Valley. The *San Jose Mercury News* lists more jobs than any newspaper or
online service in the country.

San Mateo Times *Help Wanted Listings* (http://www.baynet.com/smtimes/market/classified/clas2210.html)

lists job openings in the area or searches for a job by keyword.

24-Hour Recorded Job Lines (http://www.webcom.com/~rmd/)

When the Index screen appears, click on Bay Area Joblines. This lists job
hotlines for companies in the Bay Area. Use this along with the listing in this
chapter.

Yahoo Job Listings (http://www.yahoo.com/business/employment/)

is a World Wide Web directory. Like JobHunt mentioned above, this directory
lists different job-finding resources on the Internet like Bay Area Job Location
Finder and Electronic Job Guide—Bay Area Jobs.

PART 4

SETTLING IN

PHOTO BY KITTI HOMME

CHAPTER EIGHT

▸ Getting Involved in the City

EVEN THOUGH SAN FRANCISCO is a major metropolitan city, it offers its residents countless activities that are fun, safe, and social. Getting involved in the city by joining a health club or professional organization, by volunteering, or by taking a class will enable you to meet people who share similar interests while doing something you enjoy. Before you know it, your social calendar will be filled seven nights a week. Here are a few things to remember before joining a club or organization, especially if a fee is involved:

Make sure you're doing something you enjoy. If you join Encore (the young professionals group that supports the ballet) but you hate the ballet, then you're not going to click with the true ballet enthusiasts there. You're better off joining the museum club because you love modern art.

Make sure your involvement will help you meet your goals in some way. For example, by joining a gym you'll be able to work toward your goal of losing 10 pounds. By taking a class in personal finance you'll be able to plan for your financial future. Perhaps you've used the services of the Red Cross, and you want to give back to that organization by volunteering your time.

Understand any commitment it may involve. This is especially true if you decide to volunteer or take a class. Nonprofit organizations depend on their volunteers, and many require a once-a-week, six-month commitment to start out. If you're taking a class, make sure your schedule allows you to be there, on time, the once or twice a week it may meet.

So do your research. Contact organizations and clubs and ask for information, visit the facilities, request guest passes, and put your name on a mailing list.

HEALTH AND FITNESS

The city of San Francisco could be considered one big health club. Climbing the hills is as effective as a Stairmaster workout. You can find countless books about the glorious bike trails all around the Bay Area, such as the ride from San Francisco over the Golden Gate Bridge and into Sausalito. And for a funky experience, join a tai chi session at Washington Square Park in North Beach—you'll be balancing on one leg with almost 100 Chinese neighbors.

San Francisco and the Bay Area have many healthy workout opportunities, including quality health clubs and sports clubs. The following lists represent the major health and sports clubs in the Bay Area. Once you get to know the area, you'll discover more opportunities to stay fit and meet friends. Request newsletters from sports clubs to find out what they do. Health clubs will usually let you try the facilities for free and give you a three-day or one-week pass. Note that the prices and services are subject to change.

HEALTH CLUBS IN SAN FRANCISCO

Joining a health club is a good way to interact with others while staying in shape. It can put some routine in your life during a period of uncertainty and change that comes with your move to San Francisco. You may be temping at a different company every week, but you can escape to the same health club and start recognizing familiar faces. The following is a list of health clubs and their offerings.

24 Hour Nautilus
Various locations
800-24-WORKOUT (800-24-967-5688)

24 Hour Nautilus has the most locations throughout San Francisco and the Bay Area. Each location offers different amenities. These fitness centers are the most affordable, and they constantly run membership specials. Ask for free passes.

Initiation fee: $200

Monthly dues: $25 to $45

Amenities: Aerobics, weight machines, free weights, cardio, and more, depending on the site

Advantage Fitness
3741 Buchanan Street
San Francisco, CA 94123
(415) 563-3535

Initiation fee: $120

Monthly dues: $65

Amenities: Aerobics, machine weights, free weights, cardio, sauna, towel service, massage, personal trainers

Bay Club
150 Greenwich Street
San Francisco, CA 94111 or
555 California Street
(Bank of America Center)
San Francisco, CA 94104
(415) 433-2550 (Membership)

Initiation fee: Greenwich Street, $950; Bank of America Center, $400

Monthly dues: Greenwich Street, $99; Bank of America Center, $75

Amenities: Greenwich Street—Pool, racquetball, squash, aerobics, tennis, sundeck, parking, social activities; Bank of America Center—Cardio, free weights, machine weights, aerobics, women's workout area, steam room, sauna, hot tub, massage, spa, personal trainer, laundry, towel service, tanning, parking

Club One

Two Embarcadero Center
San Francisco, CA 94111
(415) 788-1010;
Citicorp Center
One Sansome Street
San Francisco, CA 94104
(415) 399-1010;
Museum Parc
350 Third Street
San Francisco, CA 94107
(415) 512-1010;
Other Locations
(415) 398-1111

Initiation fee: $250

Monthly dues: $72

Amenities: Cardio, aerobics, free
weights, machine weights, personal
trainer, pool, racquetball courts,
tennis courts, laundry, towel service

Cole Valley Fitness

957 Cole Street
San Francisco, CA 94117
(415) 665-3330

Initiation fee: $35

Monthly dues: One-month membership, $65; three-month membership,
$175; etc.

Amenities: Cardio, free weights,
machine weights, personal trainers

Embarcadero YMCA

169 Steuart Street
San Francisco, CA 94105
(415) 957-9622

Initiation fee: $250

Monthly dues: $50

Amenities: Cardio, aerobics, free
weights, machine weights, pool,
racquetball, squash, basketball,
massage, towel service, personal
trainer, volleyball, steam room, sauna,
Jacuzzi, sundeck

Fitness Break

30 Hotaling Place
San Francisco, CA 94111
(415) 788-1681

Initiation fee: $125

Monthly dues: $45

Amenities: Aerobics, free weights,
machine weights, towel service

Golden Gateway Tennis and Swim Club

370 Drumm Street
San Francisco, CA 94111
(415) 616-8800

Initiation fee: $450 to $750

Monthly dues: $86 to $122

Amenities: Tennis, swimming,
massage, personal training, cardio,
machine weights, free weights, towel
service, steam room, sauna, sundeck,
parking, laundry, social activities

Gold's Gym

501 2nd Street Square
San Francisco, CA 94107
(415) 777-4653

Initiation fee: $99

Monthly dues: $39

Amenities: Aerobics, cardio, free weights, machine weights, massage, personal trainer, tanning, towel service, steam room

In Shape
3214 Fillmore Street
San Francisco, CA 94123
(415) 922-3700;
371 Hayes Street
San Francisco, CA 94102
(415) 241-0203

Initiation fee: None

Monthly dues: Pay by the class ($10), or buy an unlimited one-month class card for $110

Amenities: Aerobics

Marina Club
3333 Fillmore Street
(at Lombard Street)
San Francisco, CA 94123
(415) 563-3333

Initiation fee: $120

Monthly dues: $49

Amenities: Aerobics, cardio, machine weights, free weights, sauna, steam room, towel service, personal trainers, sundeck

Pacific Heights Health Club
2358 Pine Street (at Fillmore Street)
San Francisco, CA 94115
(415) 563-6694

Initiation fee: None

Monthly dues: $65

Amenities: Cardio, free weights, machine weights, personal trainers, towel service

Pinnacle Fitness
345 Spear Street
San Francisco, CA 94105
(415) 495-1939;
61 New Montgomery Street
San Francisco, CA 94105
(415) 543-1110

Initiation fee: $250 plus $49 processing fee

Monthly dues: $59

Amenities: Cardio, free weights, machine weights, aerobics, steam room, towel service, personal trainers, circuit training

Physis
One Post Street
San Francisco, CA 94104
(415) 781-6400

Initiation fee: $250 plus $49 processing fee

Monthly dues: $49

Amenities: Aerobics, cardio, free weights, machine weights, pool, towel service, personal trainers, circuit training, massage

Note: Specialists on staff include a cardiologist, sports medicine physician, registered nurse, registered dietitian, and back care specialists

San Francisco Tennis Club
645 Fifth Street
San Francisco, CA 94107
(415) 777-9000

Initiation fee: $750 to $1,000

Monthly dues: $93 to $127

Amenities: Tennis, aerobics, machine weights, free weights, spa, massage, cardio, personal trainer, social activities, towel service, steam room, sauna, hot tub, parking

Notes: A court fee is charged for indoor courts. Tennis lessons are available. This is an upscale club with banquet facilities, restaurant, pro shop, car wash, and other amenities.

HEALTH CLUBS OUTSIDE SAN FRANCISCO

Alameda Athletic Club
1226 Park Street
Alameda, CA 94501
(510) 521-2001

Initiation fee: $250

Monthly dues: $35

Amenities: Cardio, machine weights, free weights, aerobics, private women's gym, personal trainers, sauna, Jacuzzi, tanning

Bay-O-Vista
Swimming and Tennis
1881 Astor Drive
San Leandro, CA 94577
(510) 357-8366

Initiation fee: $250

Monthly dues: $86

Amenities: Pool, tennis, machine weights, free weights, aerobics, social activities, steam room, sauna, basketball, parking

City Beach Volleyball
4701 Doyle Street
Emeryville, CA 94608
(510) 428-1221

Initiation fee: $50

Monthly dues: $30

Amenities: Volleyball, cardio, free weights, parking

City Rock Gym
Indoor Climbing Center
1250 45th Street
Emeryville, CA 94608
(510) 654-2510

Initiation fee: $120

Monthly dues: $46

Amenities: Climbing wall, cardio, free weights, machine weights, personal trainers

Mariner Square Athletic Club
2227 Mariner Square Loop
Alameda, CA 94501
(510) 523-8011

Initiation fee: $115 to $400

Monthly dues: $60 to $80

Amenities: Racquetball, pool, basketball, free parking, aerobics, cardio, free weights, machine weights, steam room, sauna, massage, Jacuzzi, personal trainers, salon services, towel service

Mission Cliffs
2295 Harrison Street
San Francisco, CA 94110
(415) 550-0515

Initiation fee: $100

Monthly dues: $50

Amenities: Climbing wall, cardio, free weights, machine weights, sauna, towel service, personal trainers

Pinnacle/Oakland Athletic Club

1418 Webster Street
Oakland, CA 94612
(510) 893-3421

Initiation fee: Under $100

Monthly dues: $35 to $44

Amenities: Aerobics, pool, cardio, free weights, machine weights, private women's gym, racquetball, basketball, volleyball, personal trainers, towel service, steam room, sauna, whirlpool, sundeck, tanning, massage, parking

Sports Club at City Center

1200 Clay Street
Oakland, CA 94612
(510) 835-2000

Initiation fee: $96

Monthly dues: $72

Amenities: Cardio, free weights, machine weights, aerobics, basketball, pool, racquetball, squash, volleyball, circuit training, personal trainers, massage, towel service, sundeck, sauna, steam Jacuzzi, private women's gym

World Gym

5651 Paradise Drive
Corte Madera, CA 94925
(415) 927-9494

Initiation fee: $150

Monthly dues: $45

Amenities: Cardio, free weights, machine weights, aerobics, steam room, tanning, personal trainers

SPORTS CLUBS

If sports is your game, San Francisco is the place to get involved at any level. There are social sports clubs and competitive sports clubs. All will give the newcomer to San Francisco an opportunity to meet others who share the love of sports. I list below some of the more well-known sports clubs. Participate in a club meeting or event, and if you don't think it's a good fit, use it as a resource to find out about other sports clubs.

Cal Sailing and Windsurfing Club

Across from the Berkeley Marina (foot of University Avenue)
Berkeley, CA 94710
(510) 287-5905

World Wide Web: **http://www.well.com/user/csc/**

This club offers low-cost instruction on sailing and windsurfing. Open houses are on the first weekend of the month and include free lessons and sailboat rides. Memberships are a steal at $45 for three months, which entitles you to unlimited lessons and equipment use.

Dolphin Swim and Boat Club

502 Jefferson Street (foot of Hyde Street)
San Francisco, CA 94109
(415) 441-9329

When you see those crazy people swimming in the San Francisco Bay, you can bet they're members of the Dolphin Club. Membership to this aquatics club is $300, which includes six-month dues and initiation. You get access to clubhouse showers, sauna, and lockers. It's a no-frills organization that doesn't offer instruction or training but sponsors competitive open-water swims and holds parties and swimmer appreciation dinners. Membership also includes use of kayaks, skiffs, and other vessels in the boat club and a quarterly newsletter. For more information, attend a club meeting held the third Wednesday of every month.

Golden Gate Sports and Social Club

1766 Union Street (at Octavia Street)
San Francisco, CA 94123
(415) 921-1233

The Sports and Social Club offers coed football, volleyball, floor hockey, soccer leagues, and even ballroom dancing. There are three levels (recreational, intermediate, and competitive), so anyone can join. Playing the sport is the tough part. Afterward, teams enjoy socializing at the many bars and restaurants that offer club member discounts. Membership is around $30.

Golden Gate Triathlon Club

1500 Sansome Street
San Francisco, CA 94111
(415) 434-4482

World Wide Web: **http://www.slip.net/~leewaya/** (San Francisco Bay Area triathlon training sites); **http://www.cycling.org/mailing.lists/ggtc** (mailing list for the Golden Gate Triathlon Club)

e-mail: majordomo@cycling.org (put "subscribe GGTC" in the message to get on the Internet mailing list)

The club has coached track workouts once a week and long runs on the weekends. There are also bike rides on the weekends, open-water swims, and a masters swim program at the Koret Center at University of San Francisco. Members train for the many different area triathlons.

Mission Bay Golf Club

1200 Sixth Street
San Francisco, CA 94107
(415) 431-PUTT

If golf is your game, this city golf club is a great gathering spot for players of all levels. The $120 membership includes discounts at golf courses, on lessons, and buckets of balls. The club also has many tournaments and events for all levels as well as social events such as a monthly party, which includes a free golf clinic.

San Francisco Recreation and Parks Department Adult Softball
(415) 753-7023

These are city-run adult men, women, or coed softball leagues held in the spring and summer. You can pull together your own team and register it for a $370 fee or, if you're solo, register your name and level of experience so a team manager can contact you. People who play adult softball are from all walks of life, and their ages range from 20s to 40s.

San Francisco Recreation and Parks Department Volleyball
(415) 753-7031

Volleyball season is October through December. There are four levels of play, from entry to advanced. Team fees are about $150, but if you want to join a team instead of putting one together, call toward the end of August to put your name on a list, and team captains will contact you if they're looking for players. The maximum individual fee is about $12. If you are not contacted, then you will be sent a schedule of open volleyball nights at Kezar Stadium. The type of crowd you'll find is a mid-20s to 30s mix of working class and professionals.

San Francisco Recreation and Parks Department Women's Basketball
(415) 753-7031

Basketball season is January to March. Choose from four levels: A, BB, B, C (entry level). The team fee is $365; 12 players maximum per team. Call at the end of October to put your name on a list. A team captain who is looking for players will contact you. If you're not contacted, then you will be sent a schedule of open-play basketball nights. The players are a mix of working-class and professional women in their mid-20s to early 30s.

San Francisco Ski Club
(415) 337-9333 (Hotline)

World Wide Web: **http://www.jaws.com/baski/clubs/sf/sf.html**

This is an organized and active club whose activities aren't limited to skiing. There are tons of social and sports events year-round, such as hikes, barbecues, houseboat tours, gong shows, wine tastings, movie nights, camping, baseball games, and, of course, skiing.

Sierra Club Chapter Activities
Chapter Schedule
5237 College Avenue
Oakland, CA 94618
(510) 653-6127

World Wide Web: **http://www.sierraclub.org/**

You don't have to be a Sierra Club member to enjoy their chapter activities. In fact, Sierra Club membership does not include the activities schedule of the San Francisco Bay Chapter. The 75-page booklet (costs around $5) is filled with hikes, bike rides, backpacking trips, canine hikes, and social events.

Tuesday Night Tennis
(415) 721-1845 (Hotline)

This is a group of single professionals that meets once a week for tennis and dinner. The season is May through September; membership is $150, or pay $12 to try it out once. Call ahead to RSVP, because space is limited to 24 players due to the number of courts available. The format is mixed doubles, and the matches take place at Golden Gate Park.

MASTERS SWIMMING
Masters swimming is a coached, organized workout for triathletes, competitive swimmers, and fitness swimmers. Masters swimming is about personal achievement and self-improvement, and we could all use a little of that. The following is a short list of where to find San Francisco Masters Swimming:

South End Rowing Club, (415) 776-7372

The Olympic Club, (415) 285-3234

Embarcadero YMCA, (415) 957-9622

University of San Francisco, (415) 666-6247

San Francisco Rec and Park, (415) 285-5659

Dolphin Club, (415) 441-9329

For online information, check out a Masters Swimming Internet site at **ftp:// 128.196.64.234/pub/usms_info/clubs.swm** or **http://www.hk.super.net/~kff/ wms.html**

BICYCLING CLUBS
The San Francisco Bay Area has so many wonderful, scenic places to ride your bike. There are also many bicycle clubs for competitive racers, fitness buffs, and

social cyclers. The following is a list of some San Francisco and Bay Area bike clubs. There's also local bicycling information on the Web, at **http://www. cycling.org/** or **http://xenon.stanford.edu/~rsf/mtn-bike.html**.

Berkeley Bicycle Club

P.O. Box 817
Berkeley, CA 94701
(510) 527-3222 (Hotline)

This is a fun yet serious bunch of 10-speed racers that holds group rides and trains for different races. It publishes a funky newsletter called the *Berkeley Bicycle Club Pneusletter* and holds regular meetings and rides.

Fremont Freewheelers

P.O. Box 1868
Fremont, CA 94538
(510) 888-3787 (Hotline)

These are mountain bikers that train for races and ride for fun. They have regular Wednesday night pizza rides and Friday morning training rides. There are also many weekend recreational rides that can have a coffee or ice cream theme. Monthly club meetings give you an opportunity to get more involved with the group. Call for a copy of the club newsletter, the *Spoke'nTruth*.

San Francisco Bicycle Coalition

1095 Market Street, Suite 215
San Francisco, CA 94103
(415) 431-BIKE

World Wide Web: **http://reality.sgi.com/employees/jonim_csd/SFBC.home/**

e-mail: sfbc@igc.apc.org

This is an activist and social group for bike riders in the city. Their most well-known event is Critical Mass, a bike ride with thousands, held the last Friday of the month. The route isn't revealed until the time of the ride, which is 6 P.M. Police escort cyclists and block traffic, making it a safe and fun event. There are also committees that fight for safer roads and better bike lanes. Membership in the group gets you the *Tubular Times* newsletter with a list of all the planned activities, a survival kit with bike maps and safety items, and discounts at area bike shops. Many of the members are bike messenger types and artists.

Single Cyclists

P.O. Box 656
Kentfield, CA 94904
(415) 459-2453 (Hotline)

Single Cyclists is a social club for singles aged 21 and over who participate in a variety of mountain and road bicycle rides, weekend trips, parties, dances, cultural performances, and other events in the San Francisco Bay Area. The over 900 members are about evenly divided between men and women. Members must be single. The monthly newsletter lists a calendar of events, which features some 40 to 80 rides of all levels as well as social events. Annual membership is $27.

Wombats
P.O. Box 757
Fairfield, CA 94978
(415) 459-0980 (Hotline)

World Wide Web: **http://www.wombats.org/wombats.html**

Wombats stands for Women's Mountain Bike and Tea Society, a 1,200-member group of women who enjoy cycling. The group was established to help women overcome obstacles when taking up the sport of cycling. It's for women who want to mountain bike but don't like competition, can't keep up with "the guys," don't know much about the equipment, and want to get better at riding before going out alone. Membership is around $40 per year. For more information, call the hotline or check out the home page address above.

RUNNING CLUBS
If running is your thing, you're not alone. There are many running clubs and races to participate in. A few are listed below, but for an even more comprehensive list, pick up *The California Schedule,* available at sporting goods stores or by calling the magazine at (415) 472-7223 or e-mailing TSchedule@aol.com. The staff is very friendly and can help you find a good group. Also check out the San Francisco Bay Area Running Pages on the World Wide Web at **http://users.aol.com/wferunner/brp/**.

Bay Area Distance Runners
(415) 626-1380

This group offers marathon training for gays/lesbians/friends.

Dolphin South End Runners (DSE)
(415) 978-0837 (Hotline)

San Francisco's largest running club with over 400 members. There's both competitive and recreational running as well as socials, potlucks, and civic volunteer events. Ask to see a copy of their newsletter. There are minimal charges for event participation. Annual dues are $15 and race entry fees are around $3. There are regular weekly track workouts, weekly runs and walks, special club runs, and special events, including Bay to Breakers.

East Bay Striders Workouts

(510) 428-1200 (Hotline)

This group offers weekly workouts in Berkeley along with competitions and weekend runs.

Fleet Feet

2086 Chestnut Street
San Francisco, CA 94123
(415) 921-7188

San Francisco is an athletic town. Because of year-round good weather, any sport can be pursued, from sailing to rollerblading. San Francisco also knows how to host some fun charity foot races that attract the most seasoned runners as well as social strollers. The following is just a few of the many runs and walks you should look out for in the local newspapers:

UNIQUE SAN FRANCISCO RACES

RACE	HELD IN:	DESCRIPTION
First Run	New Year's Eve	This is promoted as the alternative New Year's Eve celebration. The race begins at the stroke of midnight, ringing in the new year. Afterward they have an alcohol-free celebration.
Zoo Run	January	Supports the San Francisco Zoo
Hoolihans to Hoolihans	March	Hoolihans is a popular bar with locations in San Francisco and Sausalito. The run is from the Sausalito location, over the Golden Gate Bridge, to the San Francisco location. This race benefits the Edgewood Children's Center for emotionally disturbed children.
Gimme Shelter	April	This is the biggest corporate-sponsored event in the city benefiting St. Vincent de Paul Society.
Bay to Breakers	May	San Francisco's most famous and popular race sponsored by the local newspaper. Participants can dress in costume, run tied together as a centipede, or just walk and soak it all in.
San Francisco Marathon	July	Every city has one.
Corporate Challenge	September	This race is held in the Financial District where the business crowd shed their suits for a good cause.
Hillstride	October	This is a fun walk over seven of San Francisco's steepest hills. It benefits the Pacificare Foundation.
Race to the Far Side	November	Benefiting the California Academy of Sciences, this is a fun race sponsored by Far Side cartoon creator Gary Larson. This race attracts close to 10,000 participants, many who dress up as their favorite Far Side character.

Fleet Feet is a store that sells running shoes and clothes. If you are able to run five miles, then join them for weekly runs in the Marina District.

Hash Harriers
(415) 334-HASH (Hotline)

This is a running club with the emphasis on drink. Weekly fun runs are followed by gatherings at local watering holes.

Hoy's Sports
1632 Haight Street
San Francisco, CA 94117
(415) 252-5370

Impala Racing Team for women and Hoy's Racing Team for men are competitive running teams with organized workouts. Participants train for trail, marathon, and other types of races.

San Francisco Frontrunners
(415) 978-2429 (Hotline)

This is a social run/walk club for gays, lesbians, and bisexuals, but it is open to all. There are usually two weekly runs, one during the week and one on the weekend. Running distance ranges from one to five miles, and on weekends there's a one-mile walk.

CULTURAL AND SOCIAL ORGANIZATIONS
San Francisco is a cultural mecca with its critically acclaimed symphony, ballet, opera, and world-renowned museums. The various arts organizations are committed to getting young professionals involved and keeping them interested through clubs and activities. The following is a list of some of the many art and social organizations in town.

Act 1
30 Grant Street
San Francisco, CA 94108
(415) 749-2ACT

Membership fee: $50 per year

Description: Act 1, an affiliate of the American Conservatory Theater (A.C.T.), is an organization of young Bay Area professionals who participate in live theater through performance attendance, special events, education, volunteer work, and fund raising. Membership includes discounted ticket prices for all A.C.T. plays, invitations and discounted pricing to all Act 1 special events, a subscription to the *Preview* newsletter, and invitations to various live theater events where you can meet performers, directors, and creative staff.

Bravo!

San Francisco Opera
301 Van Ness Avenue
San Francisco, CA 94102
(415) 565-3261

World Wide Web: **http://www.sfopera.com**

Membership fee: $50 per year

Description: This is an organization of young professionals who support the San Francisco Opera. Bravo! club hosts a variety of events, preperformance receptions, and fund-raising benefits for the San Francisco Opera while educating its membership about the world of opera. Membership includes free admission with a guest to the Trio Series preperformance reception and Opera House tours. Opera tickets are offered to Bravo! members at a discount.

Encore!

San Francisco Ballet
455 Franklin Street
San Francisco, CA 94102
(415) 553-4634

World Wide Web: **http://www-leland.stanford.edu/~rbeal/sfb.html**

Membership fee: $50 per year

Description: This is the young professional's organization that supports the San Francisco Ballet. Members are of the ages between early 20s to late 30s. Membership includes invitations to ballet performances and pre- and post-event socials like cocktail parties or dinners. These events and socials are all an additional but discounted cost.

City Club of San Francisco

155 Sansome Street, Tenth Floor
San Francisco, CA 94104
(415) 362-2480

Membership fee: Initiation fees between $400 to $850 and monthly dues $99 to $152

Description: The City Club of San Francisco offers business, social, and athletic privileges. Membership includes weekly breakfast series lectures, business networking forums, special events such as wine tastings, art tours and progressive dinners, access to the San Francisco Tennis Club and other athletic facilities, and more.

Initiation fee and monthly dues, though not cheap, are comparable to a membership at a health club.

Commonwealth Club
595 Market Street
San Francisco, CA 94105
(415) 597-6700

Membership fee: $110 per year

Description: This is a public affairs speaking forum that holds a variety of meetings (breakfasts, lunches, dinners, receptions) at which speakers discuss issues of the day. Besides formal lectures, the club sponsors a number of special events each month that allows members the opportunity to socialize in a more informal atmosphere. Group visits to cultural and sporting events, tours of local companies and research facilities, wine tastings, and restaurant outings are a few of the activities. Membership includes the publication *The Commonwealth*.

Contemporary Extension
San Francisco Museum of Modern Art
151 Third Street
San Francisco, CA 94103
(415) 357-4086

World Wide Web: **http://www.sfmoma.org/**

Membership fee: $50 per year plus $55 per year regular museum membership

Description: This is a dynamic group of young professionals between the ages of 25 and 40 who share an interest in modern art and have a desire to take an active role in supporting the museum. Membership includes special museum tours; visits to artists' studios, local galleries, and private collections; and cocktail receptions. The only requirement to join is a regular museum membership.

Film Arts Foundation
346 9th Street, Second Floor
San Francisco, CA 94103
(415) 552-8760

Membership fee: $35 per year

Description: This is the largest regional organization of independent filmmakers in California. Services and facilities available to members include a monthly newsletter, use of the editing room, seminars and workshops, a resource library, a viewing room, a group legal plan, and more.

Junior Arts Council

M. H. De Young Memorial Museum
Golden Gate Park
San Francisco, CA 94118-4598
(415) 750-7607

World Wide Web: **http://www.island.com/famsf/famsf_deyoung.html** or **http://www.island.com/famsf/famsf_legion.html**

Membership fee: $60 per year

Description: The Junior Arts Council (JAC) supports two fine arts museums in San Francisco: the M. H. De Young Memorial Museum, which houses the American collection, and the California Palace of the Legion of Honor, which houses the European collection. Membership includes free entry to the museum, exhibit tours, downtown gallery tours, benefits, cocktail parties, dinner parties, and visits to private collections.

San Francisco Chamber of Commerce

465 California Street, Ninth Floor
San Francisco, CA 94104
(415) 392-4520

Membership fee: $225 per year

Description: The Chamber of Commerce is a nonprofit organization representing area businesses. Its mission is to attract, develop, and retain business in San Francisco. Members include over 1,800 companies and individuals. There are monthly business development activities like luncheons, after-hour networking socials, and committees. The $225 individual membership fee is steep, but if you're planning on freelancing, the exposure through this organization is worth it. A budget-minded option is to bypass a formal membership and attend events at a higher nonmember price.

Scholastics

San Francisco School Volunteers
65 Battery Street, Third Floor
San Francisco, CA 94111
(415) 274-0250

World Wide Web: **http://nisus.sfusd.k12.ca.us/sfsv/sfsv.html**

Membership fee: None

Description: The Scholastics is a group of young professionals that supports public education. They hold fund-raisers and are volunteer readers in the classroom.

Symphonix

San Francisco Symphony
Davies Symphony Hall
San Francisco, CA 94102
(415) 552-8000 (ext.500)

World Wide Web: **http://www.hooked.net/sfsymphony/sfshome.html**

Membership fee: $40 per year

Description: Symphonix, one of the San Francisco Symphony's 11 volunteer leagues, is for young professionals interested in supporting the symphony. Membership includes discounts on dinner and concerts planned once a quarter, a quarterly newsletter, quarterly membership meetings with a musical program, and invitations to members-only events.

Toastmasters International

(714) 858-8255

World Wide Web: **http://www.ni.net/toastmasters.org/**

Membership fee: None

Description: Toastmasters is a public speaking group. It's also a good way to meet people and professional contacts. Call the national headquarters number above for a listing of Toastmasters groups in the area.

Tuesdays at Six

Leukemia Society of America
Northern California Chapter
55 Hawthorne Street, Suite 510
San Francisco, CA 94105
(415) 543-9821

Membership fee: None

Description: This is a group of San Francisco-based young professionals who coordinate fund-raising events for the Leukemia Society. The group meets every Tuesday at 6 P.M., and it's a social and professional networking opportunity for predominantly single business people. Events include a golf tournament and Valentine's Day Ball.

The World Affairs Council of Northern California

312 Sutter Street, #500
San Francisco, CA 94108
(415) 982-0430

World Wide Web: **http://205.162.155.2/gaianet/wac**

Membership fee: $55 per year

Description: The council has over 11,000 members and offers over 200 programs a year on current and important foreign policy issues. The general membership includes a subscription to the newsletter *Spotlight,* use of the library, invitations to special members-only events, and reduced admission to all events. Events include dinners with diplomats, lectures from top U.S. CEOs, and forums on important domestic and international issues.

SINGLES ACTIVITIES

Contrary to popular belief, San Francisco is home to plenty of single, heterosexual men and women interested in dating and finding the right partner. I'm not saying being single is easy in this city—it's not easy anywhere. But there are opportunities to meet other singles through safe, fun, nonthreatening groups and socials. The following are some of the more popular ones.

Jewish Community Federation
121 Steuart Street
San Francisco, CA 94105
(415) 777-0411

World Wide Web: **http://www.jewish.com/** (Jewish Bulletin of Northern California)

The Young Adult Division has an active membership of over 400 people plus a mailing list of around 2,000. A quarterly calendar lists weekly events. A popular event is Blue Monday, which is a dinner party held once a month in different restaurants. Also, First Friday Shabbat dinners are held in private homes. Five committees, including a Newcomers Committee, are responsible for the programs. The age range is 21 to 39.

Lafayette Orinda Presbyterian Church
49 Knox Drive
Lafayette, CA 94549
(510) 283-8722

Hotlines:
(510) 284-1425, Islanders (born since 1955)
(510) 283-5699, Shipmates (born between 1940-1955)
(510) 283-2535. Single Ships (people age 50 or over)

This church has one of the most well-known singles clubs in the Bay Area. Singles are grouped according to age range, and you can call the hotlines for the many activities that occur daily. Sunday night is an orientation for prospective members.

Singles Supper Club

P.O. Box 60518
Palo Alto, CA 94306
(415) 327-4645

The Singles Supper Club is a dining and social club serving single professionals between the ages of 25 to 55. Events are planned in upscale restaurants and are designed to help you meet other successful singles. For example, at dinners, guests change tables after each course. Membership is about $125 and dinner events range from $30 to $60. You don't have to be a bona fide member to participate, but event prices will be about $15 more.

Stanford Bachelors

P.O. Box 2345
Stanford, CA 94305

These are Stanford alumae and non-Stanford men that host several events a month all over the Bay Area. These events attract from 100 to 500 people. The crowd age is in the mid-30s to 40s.

St. Vincent De Paul Young Adult Group

2350 Green Street
San Francisco, CA 94123
(415) 522-9242 (Hotline)

A Catholic singles group comprised of young professionals between the ages of 24 and 40. Activities include biweekly meetings, volunteer events, social activities, and choir.

Tennis Matchmakers

2929 Russell Street
Berkeley, CA 94705
(510) 548-6240

The focus of Tennis Matchmakers is social tennis for single, professional people. Events are held at the best private tennis clubs in the Bay Area and include a mixed doubles format followed by a catered dinner party. Membership is free, but an entry fee is charged for each event. All age and skill levels are welcome. Tennis Matchmakers is a member of the United States Tennis Association (USTA).

VOLUNTEER OPPORTUNITIES

Volunteer opportunities are an excellent way to meet people and feel good about what you're doing. You can also learn skills to apply to a professional job by doing volunteer work. The following list has local volunteer organizations as well as some nonprofit organizations in the city to get you started.

American Red Cross
Bay Area Chapter
1550 Sutter Street
San Francisco, CA 94109
(415) 202-0725

World Wide Web: **http://www.crossnet.org/**

Mission: A volunteer-led humanitarian organization that provides relief to victims of disaster and helps people prevent, prepare for, and respond to emergencies.

Volunteer activities: Assistance to disaster victims, emergency relief, special events, and Associate Leadership Cabinet for young professionals

Enterprise for High School Students
3275 Sacramento Street
San Francisco, CA 94115
(415) 921-6554

Mission: Help high school students prepare for job opportunities through career apprenticeships and a job referral program.

Volunteer activities: Volunteer mentors act as adult role models, developing positive one-on-one relationships with students in order to support them throughout the job search and to assist with career exploration.

Hands On San Francisco
350 Bay Street, Suite 100-334
San Francisco, CA 94133
(415) 281-9953

Mission: Hands On San Francisco (HOSF) is a nonprofit volunteer service organization that creates, manages, and leads volunteer projects.

Volunteer activities: You can get involved in the areas of fund raising, marketing, managing projects, and volunteering for projects. Some past projects on the calendar were Special Olympics, Hamilton Family Center Shelter, and Habitat for Humanity. Call to be put on the mailing list and get more information. Every month, new volunteers are required to attend a 30-minute orientation.

Friends of the Urban Forest
512 2nd Street, Fourth Floor
San Francisco, CA 94107
(415) 543-5000

Mission: This is San Francisco's citizen urban forestry organization. They offer financial, technical, and practical assistance to individuals and neighborhood groups who wish to plant and care for trees.

Volunteer activities: Tree plantings occur every weekend and sometimes during the week. This could involve activities like digging and tree maintenance. Train to be a Planting Leader or Tree Tour Guide.

Little Brothers/Friends of the Elderly
481 O'Farrell Street
San Francisco, CA 94102
(415) 771-7957

Mission: To alleviate loneliness and isolation of homebound elders in San Francisco through friendship visits by volunteers and social parties.

Volunteer activities: Visiting the elderly, putting together gift packages

Project Open Hand
2720 17th Street
San Francisco, CA 94110
(415) 558-0600

World Wide Web: **http://www.well.com/user/hbp/poh/openhand.html**

Mission: To provide hot meals and groceries to people with AIDS in San Francisco and the East Bay.

Volunteer activities: Meal delivery, kitchen prep work

Raphael House
1045 Sutter Street
San Francisco, CA 94109
(415) 474-4621

World Wide Web: **http://www.meer.net/users/taylor/raphael.html**

Mission: Work with families to help them overcome the immediate crisis of homelessness and provide a safe, structured environment in which they can work to resolve other difficult problems related to their homelessness.

Volunteer activities: Preparing meals for residents, tutoring children

San Francisco Maritime Park
Building E
Fort Mason Center
San Francisco, CA 94123
(415) 556-1871

World Wide Web: http://www.apl.com/nmma/home.html

If you're a seafarer at heart, then volunteer for the Maritime Park. They are always looking for docents and volunteers who are interested in rigging, living history, woodwork, welding, artifact preservation, and more. You could be doing carpentry work on the *Eureka* or rigging work on the historic *Balclutha*.

San Francisco Society for the Prevention of Cruelty to Animals (SPCA)
2500 16th Street
San Francisco, CA 94103
(415) 554-3000

World Wide Web: http://www.sfspca.org/

Mission: This is a charitable animal-welfare organization dedicated to protecting and providing for animals in need, fostering an awareness of their importance in our lives, and finding a loving home for life for every animal taken into the shelter. If you love animals but your lifestyle or landlord doesn't allow pets, this is a great place to volunteer. It's a very committed bunch that is involved.

Volunteer activities: Adoption counselor, adoption outreach, dog walkers, cat and dog socializers, animal behavior, animal-assisted therapy, humane education

San Francisco Street Project

World Wide Web: http://www.makesense.com/SFSP/

e-mail: SFSP-info@chaos.apple.com

Mission: This is a community service organization that provides a vital link between young professional volunteers and established community service organizations in the San Francisco area. The Street Project committee develops and schedules projects with limited time commitments to meet the needs of the volunteer's schedule. Projects only take place on weekends and evenings.

Volunteer activities: Assisting in many different organizations such as Glide Memorial Soup Kitchen, Habitat for Humanity, San Francisco Food Bank, and Christmas in April.

San Francisco Volunteer Center
1160 Battery Street, Suite 70
San Francisco, CA 94111
(415) 982-8999

World Wide Web: http://meer.net/users/taylor/sfvogen/html

Additional volunteer centers are listed here:

Volunteer Center of Alameda County
1904 Franklin Street, Suite 211
Oakland, CA 94612
(510) 419-3970

World Wide Web: **http://meer.net/users/taylor/volalame.html**

Volunteer Center of Contra Costa County
1820 Bonanza Street, Suite 100
Walnut Creek, CA 94596
(510) 472-5760

World Wide Web: **http://meer.net/users/taylor/volcencc.html**

Volunteer Center of Marin County
70 Skyview Terrace
San Rafael, CA 94903
(415) 479-5660

World Wide Web: **http://meer.net/users/taylor/volmarin.html**

Volunteer Center of San Mateo County
800 South Claremont, Suite 108
San Mateo, CA 94402
(415) 342-0801

World Wide Web: **http://meer.net/users/taylor/volcensm.html**

Mission: The Volunteer Center serves nonprofit organizations, individuals, city agencies, and civic groups by promoting volunteerism throughout the city. The Community Service Program provides a referral service connecting people with a wide variety of volunteer opportunities in San Francisco's diverse nonprofit community.

Volunteer activities: Attend a weekly orientation of the center or request a quarterly Volunteer Opportunities list they publish. Also, a Board Match Plus program matches people with nonprofits in need of new board members.

EDUCATION/CLASSES
The following is a list of places to take classes or pursue a degree.

Academy of Art
79 New Montgomery Street
San Francisco, CA 94105
800-544-ARTS

This is a professional college that offers education in several fields of art and design. Choose from Bachelor of Fine Arts (BFA) programs, certificate programs, and nondegree programs. The course selection is outstanding.

Berkeley Extension
55 Laguna Street
San Francisco, CA 94102
(510) 642-4111

World Wide Web: **http://www.unex.berkeley.edu:4243**

This is an extension of the University of California, Berkeley campus. Quarterly catalogs are chock-full of classes in everything from art and design to travel study. You'll find certificate and study programs in areas like business administration, publishing, and accounting. You're sure to find your interest or a skill you could learn to advance your career.

City College
50 Phelan Avenue
San Francisco, CA 94112
(415) 239-3000

World Wide Web: **http://hills.ccsf.cc.ca.us:9878/**

This community college offers associate degrees and a credit certificate curricula. Noncredit classes are also available for those who want to brush up on a skill or pursue an interest.

Culinary Academy
625 Polk Street
San Francisco, CA 94102
800-BAY-CHEF

World Wide Web: **http://www.baychef.com/**

This is the premier cooking school in San Francisco. Serious foodies train here and go on to work as chefs in some of the Bay Area's finest restaurants. There is a 16-month Professional Chef Training program, Baking and Pastry Arts Certification program, and many consumer programs for those of us that find cooking a great pastime. Call to request a catalog.

Golden Gate University
536 Mission Street
San Francisco, CA 94105
(415) 442-7000 or 442-7800

Degree and nondegree courses of study are offered. The campus is fully equipped with libraries, computer labs, telecommunications lab, student lounge, and bookstore. Undergraduate, graduate, and law school courses are offered.

HomeChef Cooking School

3525 California Street
San Francisco, CA 94118
(415) 668-3191

This school offers cooking classes that teach quick and easy dishes. Attend either lecture/demonstrations or hands-on workshops. The Basic Cooking program is 13 lessons teaching cooking basics, starting with stocks and broths and leading up to menus for entertaining. There are also individual classes, such as cooking for couples, tamale workshop, Spanish tapas, and how to write a cookbook.

Learning Annex

291 Geary Street, #510
San Francisco, CA 94102
(415) 788-5500

The Learning Annex offers the most eclectic mix of classes and hosts some surprising speakers. You'll find classes in everything like the *Celestine Prophecy* Workshop, Feng Shui, How to Become a Private Eye, Comedy Writing, and more. In the past, popular personalities like M. Scott Peck have been featured.

Media Alliance

841 Mission Street, Suite 205
San Francisco, CA 94103
(415) 546-6334

Media Alliance is a nonprofit advocacy organization that serves media professionals. It was started in 1975 by a group of Bay Area journalists to unite local media professionals and the community to change the way media professionals do business. Though their mission statement seems political, their services are very practical. If you're interested in writing, journalism, communications, public relations, advertising, or film, this is a good organization to join. An excellent job file will help you search for jobs in creative fields. They also offer a good selection of writing, editing, publishing, and Macintosh classes. A standard membership is $45; JobFile access is an additional $20. If this leaves you too broke to take classes, then volunteer your time in exchange for class time.

San Francisco Conservatory of Music Extension

1201 Ortega Street
San Francisco, CA 94122
(415) 759-3446

The San Francisco Conservatory Extension Division is dedicated to enhancing adult lives through music. Classes offered include Jazz Harmony and Theory, Singing Handel's *Messiah*, Piano, and Voice.

San Francisco State University
1600 Holloway Avenue
San Francisco, CA 94132
(415) 338-1111

World Wide Web: http://www.sfsu.edu/

The University offers undergraduate, graduate, certificate, academic, and credential programs.

San Francisco State University
College of Extended Learning
425 Market Street
San Francisco, CA 94105
800-987-7700

World Wide Web: http://www.cel.sfsu.edu/

San Francisco State offers continuing professional education in the heart of the Financial District. Over 20 programs such as Multimedia and Global Business are taught on evenings and weekends.

WORLD WIDE WEB RESOURCES

Bay Area Volunteer Information Center
(http://www.meer.net/users/taylor/)
is your online resource of information about volunteer opportunities in the San Francisco Bay Area. It's very thorough and not only does it list local opportunities but it has links to national volunteer information. Check out San Francisco Volunteer Center information.

California Resources
(http://www.contact.org/cali.html)
has California resources such as community service, education, health, and more.

CHAPTER NINE

▶ Something for Nothing

SAN FRANCISCO, one the world's most popular travel destinations, is now your place to call home. Quality entertainment, fabulous restaurants, and countless activities are yours for the taking—if you have the bucks to spend. But fun can still be had even if your wallet tells you otherwise. The following is a list of free things to do in San Francisco.

FREE MUSEUM DAYS

Asian Art Museum
75 Tea Garden Drive
Golden Gate Park
(415) 379-8801

World Wide Web: **http:// www.artdirect.com/california/ san.francisco/museums/sf/asian/**

Each month, the first Wednesday (all day) and the first Saturday (10 A.M. to noon) are free.

Cable Car Museum
1201 Mason Street
(415) 474-1887

All the city's cable car cables run out of this building. It also houses a cable car from 1880. It's always free.

California Academy of Sciences
9th Street and Lincoln Boulevard
Golden Gate Park
(415) 750-7145

World Wide Web:
http://www.calacademy.org/

Each month, the first Wednesday is free.

Center for the Arts
Yerba Buena Gardens
Center for the Arts Galleries
701 Mission Street
(415) 978-ARTS

World Wide Web:
http://www.hia.com/hia/yerbabuena/

Each month, the first Thursday, from 6 P.M. to 8 P.M., is free.

Chinese Historical Society Museum
650 Commercial Street near
Montgomery Street
(415) 391-1188

Artifacts and photos tracing the history of Chinese Americans. Always free.

M. H. De Young Museum
10th and Fulton Streets
Golden Gate Park
(415) 863-3330

World Wide Web:
http://www.island.com/famsf/
famsf_deyoung.html

This museum has a large collection of traditional art by American artists and some European art. Each month, the first Wednesday (all day) and the first Saturday (from 10 A.M. to noon) are free.

Exploratorium
3601 Lyon Street
(415) 563-7337

World Wide Web:
http://www.exploratorium.edu/

Great science fun for kids and adults alike. Each month, the first Wednesday is free.

Federal Reserve Bank
101 Market Street
(415) 974-2000

"The World of Economics" is a block-long exhibit of economic principles and history. Different computers give you the power to raise or lower interest rates and even make presidential decisions while showing how it affects the economy. There is also a free bank tour. Always free.

Fort Mason Center Museums
Intersection of Marina Boulevard and Buchanan Street

Fort Mason Center used to be a military site for over 200 years. Today the former barracks house about 50 resident nonprofit groups. Among these groups are the following four fine museums:

The Mexican Museum, (415) 441-0404

Museo ItaloAmericano, (415) 673-2200

San Francisco African-American Historical and Cultural Society, (415) 441-0640

San Francisco Craft and Folk Art Museum, (415) 775-0990

These museums are free the first Wednesday of the month.

The Jewish Museum
121 Steuart Street
(415) 543-8880

Free the first Monday of each month.

Musée Mechanique
Cliff House
1090 Point Lobus Avenue
(415) 386-1170

This antique mechanical arcade has the largest collection of coin-operated musical instruments in the world. Always free.

Museum of the City of San Francisco
2801 Leavenworth at Beach Streets
The Cannery, Third Level
(415) 928-0289

World Wide Web:
http://www.slip.net/~dfowler/1906/
museum.html

San Francisco earthquake exhibits including the 1989 Loma Prieta earthquake. Always free.

Palace of the Legion of Honor
100-34th Avenue at Clement Street
Lincoln Park
(415) 750-3600

World Wide Web:
http://www.island.com/famsf/
famsf_legion.html

Newly renovated majestic marble building looks like it just dropped in from Paris. The Palace is home to ancient and European art by artists such as El Greco, Rembrandt, Manet, Monet, and Degas. A visit will help satisfy a Louvre craving. Free every second Wednesday of the month.

San Francisco Maritime National Historical Park Museum
Aquatic Park at the foot of Polk Street
(415) 556-3002

Maritime history dating back to the Gold Rush era up to World War II. There are ship models, nautical artifacts, and a maritime bookstore. Always free.

San Francisco Museum of Modern Art
151 Third Street
(415) 357-4000

World Wide Web: http://
199.182.35.123/

Free the first Tuesday of each month.

San Francisco Zoo
1 Zoo Road at Sloat Boulevard and
45th Avenue
(415) 753-7080

Free the first Wednesday of each month.

San Francisco Public Library
200 Larkin Street
(415) 557-4400

World Wide Web: http://sfpl.lib.ca.us/

Free films on travel, art, and classics.

Wells Fargo Historical Museum
420 Montgomery Street
(415) 396-2619

World Wide Web: http://
www.wellsfargo.com

Artifacts from the Old West and authentic stagecoaches. Always free.

FREE CONCERTS
Many public plazas and churches hold free concerts, usually during the summer months when the weather is pleasant.

Old St. Mary's Cathedral
660 California Street
(415) 288-3840

Free noontime concerts featuring soloists, bands, pianists, and other performers.

S.F. Community Music Center
544 Capp Street
(415) 647-6015

Features musical lectures and performances.

Stern Grove Outdoor Concerts
19th Avenue and Sloat Boulevard (park where concerts are held)
(415) 252-6252

Features quality musical entertainment and dance concerts every Sunday afternoon from mid-June until mid-August. Past programs featured the San Francisco Opera, Ballet, and Symphony.

Summer Sound Waves Concert Series
Justin Herman Plaza
Four Embarcadero Center

Wednesdays at noon, July to September. Mostly jazz and blues.

Transamerica Redwood Park Music Series
Foot of Transamerica Pyramid
600 Montgomery Street

Fridays at noon, July-September. Mostly jazz and blues.

FREE TOURS

NEIGHBORHOOD WALKING TOURS

The Friends of the San Francisco Public Library offer free neighborhood walking tours. This is an excellent way to get acquainted with different neighborhoods and their history. The tours take about one-and-a-half hours and only group reservations are needed. Neighborhood tour themes include

- Art Deco Marina

- Cathedral Hill's Churches

- Haight-Ashbury

- Mission Murals

- North Beach

- Pacific Heights Mansions

- Roof Gardens and Open Spaces

- Victorian San Francisco

Call (415) 557-4266 for information, or send a self-addressed, stamped envelope for a schedule to City Guides, Friends of the San Francisco Public Library, Main Library, Civic Center, San Francisco, CA 94102.

GOLDEN GATE PARK TOURS

The Friends of Recreation and Parks is an organization that supports the city's biggest park, Golden Gate Park. Every Saturday and Sunday from May to October, this organization offers free historical walking tours of Golden Gate Park that last about 90 minutes. The West End Tour features park stables and a restored windmill. The Strawberry Hill Tour teaches the history of Stow Lake and offers spectacular views. For more information and a summer schedule, call (415) 750-5105 or send a self-addressed, stamped envelope to Friends of Recreation and Parks, McLaren Lodge, Golden Gate Park, San Francisco, CA 94117. Or visit their Web site at **http://www.wco.com/%7edale/ggnra.html**.

OTHER PARK ACTIVITIES

The Golden Gate National Recreation Area includes 114 square miles of coastal wilderness, city waterfront, and historical landmarks. A quarterly calendar lists dozens of free activities offered in San Francisco and outlying areas. Some city happenings are:

- Pier Crabbing: Learn about equipment, bait, regulations, and other important aspects of crabbing in the bay

- San Francisco National Cemetery Walk

- Presidio Walking Tour: Covers more than 200 years of San Francisco history and architecture

- Alcatraz Fortress Walk: This has a $5.75 ferry fee, but the tour is free

For more information, contact the Golden Gate National Recreation Area at (415) 556-0560, or write to them at Fort Mason, Building 201, San Francisco, CA 94123. Or visit their Web site at **http://www.wco.com/%7edale/ggnra.html**.

MOUNT TAMALPAIS

Mount Tamalpais State Park Hikes
P.O. Box 3318
San Rafael, CA 94912
(415) 388-2070

World Wide Web: **http://marin.org/mcenter/mt.tam.html**

The Mount Tamalpais Interpretive Association leads free Saturday, Sunday, and moonlight hikes through Mount Tamalpais State Park.

FREE ENTERTAINMENT

FAIRS AND FESTIVALS

During the summer, San Francisco neighborhood fairs and festivals happen almost every weekend. The music, entertainment, and people watching are free. Contact the San Francisco Convention and Visitors Bureau for a schedule at (415) 974-6900. Following are four of the most popular San Francisco fairs and festivals.

North Beach Fair

North Beach is San Francisco's Little Italy. The neighborhood main street, Grant Avenue, becomes a street vendor's mall full of handmade crafts like jewelry and pottery. Famed Washington Square Park has a petting zoo, pony rides, and many juggling acts and puppet shows.

Union Street Festival
Union Street is the main artery in Pacific Heights, San Francisco's yuppie neighborhood. This festival is colorful, classy, and civilized. You'll find crafts, great shops, and boutiques along the street.

Haight-Ashbury Fair
The opposite of the Union Street Festival is the Haight-Ashbury Fair. Tie-dye and grunge mix with the scent of incense and ethnic foods. Enjoy loud bands and lots of young energy. If a flashback to the sixties is what you're looking for, this fair is it.

Fillmore Festival
The highlights of the Fillmore Festival are the excellent jazz performances. The crowd is a mix of artsy folks and yuppies. This is a pleasant, mellow affair.

COMEDY IN THE PARK
Once a year on the last Sunday in July, the best local Bay Area comedians gather together at the Polo Field in Golden Gate Park to make the crowds laugh. Many are familiar faces from television's "Evening at the Improv" and "Comic Strip Live." Sometimes a surprise appearance or two by stars such as Robin Williams and Whoopi Goldberg add to the excitement. Located off John F. Kennedy Drive in Golden Gate Park. For information, call (415) 777-7120.

SHAKESPEARE FESTIVAL
If you've never seen a Shakespeare play performed on stage, don't miss out on the Shakespeare Festival in the Park, held every September. It's at Golden Gate Park near Liberty Tree Meadow; call (415) 666-2222.

CARNAVAL
The annual Memorial Day Weekend Carnaval Grand Parade is a celebration of San Francisco's multicultural heritage. This 16-year tradition is held in the Mission District and features exotically dressed paraders, rhythmic marching bands, and colorful floats. The parade is followed by a street fair with ethnic foods, crafts, bands, and exhibits. Call the event planners at (415) 826-1401 for details and directions.

FREE LITERARY EVENTS
Book readings are stimulating, interesting, and free. The following bookstores publish monthly newsletters with calendars of events that go beyond the author simply reading his or her work. You can also enjoy concerts, lectures, and even singles events. Visit the bookstore, get on their mailing list, and ask about any frequent buyer discounts. Also check the book review section of the Sunday *San Francisco Chronicle* and *Examiner* for weekly events.

A Clean Well-Lighted Place for Books
Opera Plaza
601 Van Ness Avenue
San Francisco, CA 94102
(415) 441-6670

World Wide Web:
http://www.well.com/www/jwscott/

e-mail: sfinfo@bookstore.com

Frequent-buyer program. One hour free validated parking

Alexander Book Company
50 Second Street
San Francisco, CA 94105
(415) 495-2992

Alexander Book Company holds lunch-time readings. It also publishes a newsletter with book news and reviews.

Book Passage
51 Tamal Vista Boulevard
Corte Madera, CA 94925
(415) 927-0960 or 800-999-7909

World Wide Web:
http://www.bookpassage.com/

e-mail: bookpass@well.com

They publish a nice, hearty newsletter packed full of readings, events, and classes. Classes and seminars attract such well-known authors as Anne Lamott, Mary Morris, and Peter Mayle. Conferences held include Travel Writing and Mystery Writing.

Booksmith
1644 Haight Street
San Francisco, CA 94117
(415) 863-8688

World Wide Web:
http://www.sirius.com/~books/

They have a reading group anyone can join that meets once a month at the store. They also publish a schedule of free readings held at night. Some past authors include Marianne Faithfull and Brett Easton Ellis.

Borders Books and Music
400 Post Street
San Francisco, CA 94102
(415) 399-1633 (Events hotline)

Not only does this place have book readings, it also holds music events. Past guests have included Bruce Hornsby and Judy Collins.

Stacey's
581 Market Street
San Francisco, CA 94105
(415) 421-4687

World Wide Web:
http://www.staceys.com

Their events are geared to the lunch and after-work business crowd. Past events included speakers on the Internet, business, self-help books, and other nonfiction. Sign up for their free literary license and get a discount on every purchase.

FREE PERFORMING ARTS
Be an usher or volunteer for the performing arts and don't miss great theater, dance, and music events because of the cost. Call the theater way ahead of time and ask if they need ushers or other volunteers for a show. A good resource for local art events is the *San Francisco Arts Monthly,* which is a free newspaper and available at many locations or you can call (415) 543-6110. Here are some local theaters to contact:

Center for the Arts Theater
700 Howard Street
(415) 978-ARTS

Features contemporary dance and performances.

Cowell Theater

Fort Mason Center
Intersection of Marina Boulevard and
Buchanan Street
(415) 441-3400

Features contemporary dance and theater.

Curran Theater

445 Geary Street
(415) 474-3800

Features Broadway-style performances.

Golden Gate Theater

1 Taylor Street
(415) 474-3800

Features Broadway theater.

Herbst Theater

401 Van Ness Avenue
(415) 621-6600

Features concerts and lectures.

Louise Davies Symphony Hall

201 Van Ness Avenue at Grove Street
(415) 864-6000

Features symphony concerts.

Orpheum Theater

1192 Market Street
(at Hyde and 8th Streets)
(415) 474-3800

Features Broadway theater.

Magic Theater

Fort Mason Center
Intersection of Marina Boulevard and
Buchanan Street, Building D
(415) 441-8822

Features plays.

Marines Memorial Theater

609 Sutter Street
(415) 771-6900

Features dance and theater.

Theater on the Square

450 Post Street
(415) 433-9500

Features theater.

War Memorial Opera House

301 Van Ness Avenue
(415) 864-3330

Features ballet and opera.

FREE HAIRCUTS

Be a hair model at San Francisco's better salons and get a great haircut. Check the local phone book for the many salons the city has. Some of the bigger names include Vidal Sassoon, Architects & Heroes, Yosh for Hair, and Henrik + Company. Call them and find out if they need hair models.

CHAPTER TEN

Things to Do on the Weekends

T HE BAY AREA offers many fun things to do on the weekends, both in the city of San Francisco and out of town. The city has theaters, cinemas, museums, shopping, festivals, expos, and more. Just over the Golden Gate and Bay Bridges are wonderful biking and hiking trails, beaches, national parks, and the wine country. Even if you're new to the city, there is no excuse for being bored. Participate in a tree planting with Friends of the Urban Forest, visit the Museum of Modern Art, hang out at the Marina Green and watch a volleyball game, or check the Sunday "pink pages" for a calendar of things going on in the area.

This chapter will highlight activities and attractions in San Francisco and the Bay Area. The first part will list activities around the city that are a little touristy but a lot of fun. The second part will name cool places to visit out of town. You'll soon be running out of weekends before running out of things to do.

AROUND THE CITY

San Francisco is an entertainment playground, with many things happening in and around the city all the time. Many activities have already been mentioned throughout the book. I will now list some popular local attractions, but the more time you spend exploring San Francisco, the more cool things you'll discover.

TOURIST STUFF

Pier 39 at (415) 981-PIER, Fisherman's Wharf, The Cannery at (415) 771-3112, and Ghirardelli Square at (415) 775-5500 are four tourist attractions that San Francisco residents should familiarize themselves with. You never know when friends and family are coming to town and will want the grand tour. When these attractions are not packed with tourists, they can be very fun.

Pier 39 is home to a colony of sea lions that lounge on the marina dock slips. There's also a virtual reality theater and pinball arcade, making this area more interesting than cheesy. It's soon to be the home of a new aquarium. Fisherman's Wharf, a few blocks to the west, has many seafood restaurants, a wax museum, and lots of souvenir T-shirt shops. Both The Cannery and Ghirardelli Square, situated side-by-side, have nicer shops and restaurants. Ghirardelli Square, once a chocolate factory, is now an ice cream parlor and candy store. After you've checked out these tourist attractions, you can grab a cable car to Nob Hill and Union Square.

Alcatraz Island
(415) 546-2805

World Wide Web: http://www.nps.gov/alcatraz

This legendary maximum security prison once held such notorious criminals as Al Capone and "Machine Gun" Kelly. It is now maintained by the park service, and tours are led daily. Accessible only by ferry, this is one of San Francisco's most popular attractions. Advance ticket purchase is recommended.

- San Francisco's tourist industry generates an average of $11 million of business per day in the city.
- Estimated daily spending per visitor is $127.
- Total city revenue derived from visitor spending is more than $231 million annually.

Angel Island State Park
(415) 435-1915 (Information)
(415) 897-0715
(Angel Island Company)

A short ferry ride from San Francisco, this undeveloped 750-acre island in the middle of the bay offers spectacular views of the city. There are many hiking and biking trails as well as campsites and picnic areas with barbecues. Tram tours, bike rentals, and sea kayaking are available.

Coit Tower
Telegraph Hill access via Lombard Street
(415) 362-0808

Built as a memorial to San Francisco's volunteer firefighters, Coit Tower is one of the city's most recognizable landmarks

along with the Transamerica Pyramid building and Golden Gate Bridge. The lobby has an incredible Diego Rivera mural depicting Depression-era California. A climb to the top of the tower is rewarded with fantastic views of the city and bay.

Mission Dolores
Dolores and 16th Streets
(415) 621-8203

Built in 1776, this is the oldest building in San Francisco. The chapel is a well-preserved reminder of the Spanish missionary days in the city. There is a small museum and an old and spooky cemetery.

The Presidio
Enter from Lombard Street, Presidio Boulevard, Arguello Boulevard, or Lincoln Boulevard
(415) 561-4323

A former military base, its 1,480 acres are now under the management and care of the National Park Service. More than 100 scenic miles offer trails for hiking, biking, and jogging; there's even an Arnold Palmer Company-managed golf course.

Golden Gate Park

Bordered by Stanyan Street, The Great Highway, Lincoln Way, and Fulton Street
(415) 666-7200 (Park Info)

World Wide Web: http://www.nps.gov/parklists/index/goga.html

This 1,017-acre park is a one-stop place for culture and recreation. It is the home to such established museums as the De Young, the Academy of Sciences, and the Asian Art Museum. It also has countless outdoor activities for all tastes, including the following:

- Tennis courts, (415) 753-7001 or 753-7100

- Biking paths

- Boating, (415) 752-0347

- Golf, (415) 751-8987

- Horseback riding, (415) 668-7360

- Basketball

- Archery

- Lawn bowling, (415) 753-9298

BEACHES

San Francisco is bordered by the Pacific Ocean, so it naturally has many beaches. Ocean Beach is a viewing beach—swimming is not allowed due

- The most international visitors come from (in order): Germany, Japan, United Kingdom, Canada, and Australia.
- The most U.S. visitors come from the following states: California, New York, Texas, Illinois, Florida, Pennsylvania, New Jersey, Ohio, and Washington.

to volatile currents. The views are exhilarating of the crashing surf and of Seal Rocks, located offshore, with its inhabitants of shorebirds and sea lions. At Baker Beach, off 25th Avenue, swimming is dangerous, but the views of the Golden Gate Bridge are breathtaking. A section of Baker Beach is set aside as a nude beach. One of the few swimming beaches in the city is China Beach, at 28th Avenue and Sea Cliff.

MUSEUMS

San Francisco has its share of quality museums. The new Museum of Modern Art has been recognized around the world. The De Young Museum houses a fine collection of classical art and has hosted such traveling shows as the Monet exhibit. On a smaller scale, there are independent museums such as the Cable Car Museum and Jewish Museum. Chapter 9 lists city museums, big and small.

LOCAL ATTRACTIONS

San Francisco Zoo

45th Avenue at Sloat Boulevard
(415) 753-7080 (Recorded info)
(415) 753-7083

The San Francisco Zoo has exhibits like the Koala Crossing, Penguin Island, and the Feline Conservation Center. There's also a fun Children's Zoo.

San Francisco Giants Baseball
800-SF-GIANTS

World Wide Web:
http://www.sfgiants.com/ or
http://www2.nando.net/SportServer/ baseball/mlb/sfg.html
This is a top-ranked baseball team that makes for a fun afternoon at the 'Stick (Candlestick Park, also known as 3Com Park).

San Francisco 49ers Football
(415) 468-2249

World Wide Web:
http://www.49ers.com/ or **http:// sfgate.com/sports/49ers/**

These are the Super Bowl champs of 1995, their fifth Super Bowl win. The all-star lineup of players, including quarterback Steve Young, is not to be missed.

Movie Theaters
For local movie information, check the newspapers or access it at your finger-tips on the Internet. On the World Wide Web, check out **http://www.movietimes. com/sf6.html.**

Shopping
Two very pleasant and popular shop-ping centers in San Francisco are the Embarcadero Center at (415) 772-0500 and San Francisco Shopping Centre at

San Francisco Visitor Profile:
42 years old
$54,200 median household income
Average length of stay is four nights
Arrived in San Francisco by plane
38% are first-time visitors
26% are frequent visitors who had five or more previous visits
57% are in San Francisco for vacation, 22% for business, and 16% for a convention
64% of visitors are domestic; 36% are international
92% of visitors rate their visit with a Very Satisfied rating
What visitors like best about San Francisco (in order): Weather, people, views, and restaurants

(415) 495-5656. The Embarcadero Cen-ter is located in the Financial District at the base of four consecutive high-rise office buildings. The center is open-air but is sheltered from the rain. It opens up to Justin Herman Plaza, which holds many outdoor concerts and events. The shops include clothing stores such as Talbots and Ann Taylor, bookstores and newsstands, home furnishing stores such as Pottery Barn, and more. The San Francisco Shopping Centre, or Nordstrom Shopping Center as it is sometimes referred to, is located at the foot of Powell Street near the cable-car turnaround. Majestic winding escala-tors lead to shops like J. Crew, Williams-Sonoma, and, of course, Nordstrom.

There are also many neighborhood shopping districts in the city such as the South of Market factory outlets; Union

Square with Neiman-Marcus and Saks Fifth Avenue department stores; the Marina and Union Street neighborhoods with their boutiques and novelty shops; and Haight Street with its vintage clothing stores, incense shops, and other paraphernalia.

PLAYHOUSES
The following are some of the bigger local playhouses in the city. Some Broadway hits that have played include *Phantom of the Opera, Hello Dolly!* and *Jelly's Last Jam.* On the World Wide Web, contact **http://sigmar.artdirect.com/tba/** or **http://www.sfgate.com/chronicle/ pink-section/theater.html**

Curran Theater, 445 Geary Street, (415) 474-3800

Golden Gate Theater, 1 Taylor Street, (415) 474-3800

Orpheum Theater, 1192 Market Street, (415) 474-3800

Geary Theater, 415 Geary Street, (415) 749-2228

Marines Memorial Theater, 609 Sutter Street, (415) 771-6900

Center for the Arts Theater, 701 Mission Street, (415) 978-2787

Club Fugazi (always plays *Beach Blanket Babylon*), 678 Green Street, (415) 421-4222

Theater on the Square, 450 Post Street, (415) 433-9500

COMEDY CLUBS

Cobb's, The Cannery, 2801 Leavenworth Street, (415) 928-4320

The 10 most frequently visited attractions in San Francisco are:
Fisherman's Wharf (87%)
Chinatown (72%)
Golden Gate Bridge (68%)
Union Square (65%)
Cable-car ride (64%)
Golden Gate Park (53%)
Museums/galleries (37%)
Alcatraz (29%)
Union Street (27%)
North Beach (21%)

The three most visited areas outside of San Francisco are:
Sausalito/Tiburon/Muir Woods (40%)
Wine Country (21%)
Carmel/Monterey (18%)

Josie's Cabaret and Juice Joint, 3583 16th Street, (415) 861-7933

Punchline, 444 Battery Street, (415) 397-7573

OUT OF TOWN
Out of town to San Franciscans could mean anything from biking to Marin for the day or driving up to Lake Tahoe for the weekend. The following is a list of some fun things to do and fun places to go outside of the city. On the World Wide Web, look up **http://www.hyperion.com/ ba/beyond.html.**

BERKELEY

Berkeley Convention and Visitors Bureau
(510) 549-7040

World Wide Web:
http://www.ci.berkeley.ca.us/

The sixties are alive and well in Berkeley. This college town is full of funky people, bohemian cafes, and unique boutiques. The main drag of Telegraph Avenue has street vendors, who sell handmade jewelry and tie-dye T-shirts, and some excellent bookstores. It's an easy drive from the city and an even easier commute by BART.

CARMEL AND MONTEREY

Carmel Chamber of Commerce
(408) 624-2522

Monterey County Visitors and Convention Bureau
(408) 649-1770

The drive from San Francisco down Highway 1 to Monterey and Carmel is breathtaking, with ocean views and dramatic cliffs. Monterey is the first stop on this scenic journey. The Monterey Aquarium on 886 Cannery Row, (408) 375-3333, is renowned for its aquatic species and presentation. Carmel is a seaside village with craft stores and cafés tucked behind lush foliage. Not to be missed is 17-Mile Drive, which winds around Pebble Beach Golf Course along the rough northern ocean with its tide pools and sea lions. A great day trip or weekend getaway.

PALO ALTO

Stanford Shopping Center
(415) 617-8585

World Wide Web:
http://wall-street-news.com/ims/ssc/ssc.html

Stanford University
(415) 723-2300

World Wide Web:
http://www.stanford.edu/

This upscale community is home to Stanford University and the posh Stanford Shopping Center. Stanford University campus has a Rodin sculpture garden and outstanding libraries like the Hoover Institution, that are open to the public. Stanford Shopping Center will rate high with shopaholics. The anchor department stores include Neiman Marcus and Macy's; the shops range from Pottery Barn to Ralph Lauren.

SACRAMENTO

Sacramento Convention and Visitors Bureau
1421 K Street
Sacramento, CA 95814
(916) 264-7777

World Wide Web:
http://www.pageweavers.com/sacvisitors.html

This is the state capital of California. Attractions include Olde Towne, the California State Railroad Museum, the Governor's Mansion, a zoo, and the Capitol Building.

SANTA CRUZ

Santa Cruz Convention and Visitors Bureau
701 Front Street
Santa Cruz, CA 95060
(408) 426-7433 (Recorded information)
(408) 425-1234 (Visitor information)

World Wide Web:
http://www.infopoint.com/sc/cvc/ or
http://www.human.com/scruz.html

Santa Cruz is a bustling beach town with a boardwalk that has amusement parks and eateries. It is also home to University of California at Santa Cruz, which you can visit.

SAUSALITO AND TIBURON

Tiburon Chamber of Commerce
(415) 435-5633

Sausalito Chamber of Commerce
(415) 332-0505

These are two bayfront towns across the Golden Gate Bridge that are great places to hang out on a lazy weekend afternoon. Many San Franciscans ride their bikes over the bridge and into Sausalito to browse the shops and art galleries. Further along is Tiburon, which has Sam's, a waterfront bar and restaurant that attracts crowds willing to wait two hours for a table in the sun.

OTHER OUT OF TOWN ATTRACTIONS

Great America
Great America Parkway
San Jose, CA
(408) 988-1776

Disneyland may be in Southern California, but northerners have Great America. About a one-hour drive from the city, this amusement park has concerts, rides, and other entertainment.

Lake Tahoe
Lake Tahoe Visitors Bureau
(916) 583-3494

World Wide Web:
http://www.hyperion.com/ba/
beyond_2.html

Bay Area residents ski at Lake Tahoe in the winter and enjoy mountain biking and water sports in the summer. A four-hour drive from San Francisco, this getaway offers not only outdoor activities but also gambling on the Nevada side of the lake.

Lindsay Museum
1901 1st Avenue at Buena Vista Avenue
Walnut Creek, CA
(510) 935-1978

This natural history museum highlights Contra Costa County wildlife. It has hands-on exhibits, an injured animal rehab center, and a pet lending library.

Marin Headlands
(415) 331-1540

For nearly 100 years this was land used by the Army. There are still remnants of military bunkers and forts that helped defend the Golden Gate from 1870 through World War II. Visitors enjoy many hiking and equestrian trails that have incredible views of San Francisco.

Marine World Africa USA
(707) 643-6722

World Wide Web:
http://www.freerun.com/napavalley/
outdoor/marinewo/marinewo.html

A combination wildlife park and oceanarium. Ride elephants, see performances by killer whales, sea lions, tigers, and chimps.

Mono Lake
(619) 647-6331

Located in the eastern Sierra, this lake is believed to be a million years old. There is much to do here, such as camping, hiking, swimming, or taking a naturalist-guided tour or moonlight tour.

Mount Diablo State Park
(510) 837-2525 or 837-6119

Located in Contra Costa County, this is a 19,000-acre state park. Recreation activities include camping, hiking, rock climbing, and horseback riding.

Mount Tamalpais State Park
Pantoll Ranger Station
(415) 388-2070

World Wide Web:
http://marin.org/mcenter/ mt.tam.html

A short drive from San Francisco, over the Golden Gate Bridge into Marin County, is Mt. Tam, as it's known by locals. The views are breathtaking, and there are many hiking and biking trails. The Sierra Club offers hikes as does the Mount Tamalpais Interpretive Association, (415) 388-2070, which has moonlight hikes through the park.

Muir Woods
(415) 388-2595

World Wide Web:
http://www.nps.gov/parklists/index/ muwo.html

This is a 550-acre coastal redwood forest with some trees reaching almost 200 feet high. Though the park may seem crowded, there are back trails that will offer some peace and solitude.

An estimated 66,000 jobs in San Francisco are directly supported by tourists:

Hotel (27%)
Restaurant/bar (26%)
Entertainment/sightseeing (15%)
Retail (13%)
Airport (12%)
Local transportation (4%)
Convention/other (3%)

Oakland Zoo
(510) 632-9523

World Wide Web:
http://www.fwl.org/seaba/members/ oz/oak.zoo.web.page.html

This zoo across the bay from San Francisco has more than 300 animals, including Bengal tigers, giraffes, and elephants. There is also a petting zoo and picnic areas.

Raging Waters
Lake Cunningham Regional Park
San Jose, CA
(408) 270-8000 (Recorded information)

A great way to escape the cold San Francisco summers is to drive out to sweltering San Jose and play in their premier water park. There are wave pools, the Pirate's Cove, and a seven-story water slide.

Stinson Beach
(415) 868-0942 (Information)
(415) 868-1922 (Weather, surf, parking info)

This is a popular beach sheltered by the cliffs of the Marin Headlands.

Tilden Park
(510) 635-0135

Tilden Park is located 30 minutes from San Francisco over the Bay Bridge. There are many attractions in this 2,000-acre wilderness-type area. There are a variety of hiking trails, Lake Anza for swimming and sunbathing, Tilden Little Farm with farm animals and vegetable gardens, old-fashioned miniature steam railroad trains, and a golf course.

Wine Country
Sonoma Wine and Visitor Center
(707) 586-3795
Napa Valley Conference and
Visitors Bureau
(707) 226-7459

World Wide Web:
http://www.winecoco.com

The Sonoma and Napa wine countries are two attractions considered Northern California highlights. Both are an easy one-and-a-half hour drive from San Francisco. A trip to Napa Valley might include visits and tours of wineries like Robert Mondavi, Beringer, Sutter Home, and Sterling, to name a few of the more popular ones. Traveling further along Route 29 will take you to Calistoga, famous for its mud baths and hot springs. Route 12 takes you to Sonoma, where you can take a bicycle or horseback tour of the local wineries like Kenwood, Benziger and Sebastiani. Town center is quaint and old-fashioned, a nice place to stop and have lunch.

Recommended Reading

Jerry Graham's Complete Bay Area Backroads: The All-New and Definitive Guide, by Jerry and Catherine Graham (HarperPerennial). Based on a popular television program that goes off the beaten path to discover Bay Area locations and sights.

Stairway Walks in San Francisco, by Adah Bakalinsky (Wilderness Press). Features 27 guided neighborhood stair walks.

San Francisco: The Ultimate Guide, by Randolph Delehanty (Chronicle Books). Contains self-guided walking tours organized around neighborhoods, historic sites, and museums.

San Francisco at Your Feet, by Margot Patterson Day (Grove Weidenfeld). A walker's guide to San Francisco with anecdotes and history.

Mountain Biking in the Bay Area: A Nearly Complete Guide, by Michael Hodgson and Mark Lord (Western Tanager Press). The Bay Area's best bike rides from San Francisco to Santa Cruz.

Quick Escapes from San Francisco, by Karen Misuraca (Globe Pequot). There are 30 weekend trips within hours from San Francisco.

Great Outdoor Getaways: To the Bay Area and Beyond, by Tom Stienstra (Foghorn Press). Full of secret, beautiful spots for hiking, biking, boating, and more.

Yosemite National Park
P.O. Box 577
Yosemite, CA 95389
(209) 372-0264
(209)327-0265 (General park information)

World Wide Web:
http://woodstock.rmro.nps.gov/wro/ nps/yosemite/ or **http://www.nps.gov/ parklists/index/yose.html**

If wilderness and the great outdoors is your thing, a five-hour drive from the city will get you to this popular national park. Camping, hiking, and skiing are three of the many activities you can do alone or with a ranger leading you. Expect crowds and even traffic on the weekends, especially in the summer.

WORLD WIDE WEB RESOURCES

Bay Area Places to See Guide
(http://hamilton.netmedia.com/ims/pts/pts.html)
is a database with 150 interesting places to see in the San Francisco Bay Area.

Art Direct San Francisco Home Page
(http://www.artdirect.com/california/san.francisco)
is an artistic home page with listings of city galleries, performing arts, festivals, and more.

Year-Round Calendar of Events

There's a lot of stuff going on in San Francisco all the time. A weekend rarely goes by without sporting events, conventions, conferences, festivals, fairs, shows, and more. The following calendar lists some annual city events that have become almost tradition. If you're interested in events outside of the city, check with each town's visitor and convention bureaus.

JANUARY

MacWorld Expo: 800-645-EXPO

FEBRUARY

Chinese New Year celebration:
(415) 982-3071

San Francisco Ballet season begins:
(415) 865-2000

MARCH

Bay Area Music Awards (BAMMIES):
(415) 388-4000

St. Patrick's Day parade:
(415) 661-2700

San Francisco Chronicle
Great Outdoors Adventure Fair:
(415) 777-8497

Tulipmania: (415) 705-5512

APRIL

Cherry Blossom Festival:
(415) 563-2313

Festival of Animation: (415) 957-1205

Opening Day on the Bay:
(510) 523-2098

San Francisco Giants baseball season
begins: (415) 467-8000

San Francisco International Film
Festival: (415) 929-5000

MAY

Bay to Breakers race: (415) 777-7000

Carnaval celebration and parade: (415)
826-1401

Cinco de Mayo celebration and parade:
(415) 826-1401

JUNE

Black and White Ball (odd numbered
years only): (415) 864-6000

Haight Street Fair: (415) 661-8025

Lesbian and Gay Freedom Day Parade:
(415) 864-3733

North Beach Fair: (415) 403-0666

San Francisco Music Day

Stern Grove concerts: (415) 252-6252

Union Street Fair: (415) 346-4446

JULY

Blues and Art on Polk Festival:
(415) 346-4561

Cable Car Bell Ringing Champion-
ships: (415) 474-1887

Chronicle Fourth of July Waterfront
Festival: (415) 777-8498

Comedy Celebration Day:
(415) 777-7120

Jazz and All That Art on Fillmore
Street Festival: (415) 346-4561

KQED International Beer and Food
Festival: (415) 553-2200

San Francisco Marathon:
(415) 391-2123

AUGUST

Escape from Alcatraz Triathlon:
(415) 924-7500

Festival of the Sea

San Francisco Fair and
International Expo

San Francisco 49ers football season
begins: (408) 562-4949

San Francisco Shakespeare Festival:
(415) 666-2221

SEPTEMBER

Folsom Street Fair

Free Shakespeare in the Park:
(415) 666-2221

Opera in the Park: (415) 864-3330

San Francisco Blues Festival:
(510) 762-BASS

San Francisco Hillstride

San Francisco Opera season begins:
(415) 864-3330

San Francisco Symphony season
begins: (415) 431-5400

Sausalito Arts Festival: (415) 332-3555

OCTOBER

American Conservatory Theater
season begins: (415) 749-2ACT

Autumn Moon Festival Street Fair in
Chinatown: (415) 982-6306

California First Mile Bike Challenge

Castro Street Fair: (415) 467-3354

Columbus Day celebration and parade

Exotic Erotic Halloween Ball:
(415) 864-1500

Festa Italiana Food and Culture:
(415) 673-3782

Fleet Week: (415) 705-5500

German Fest

Great Halloween and Pumpkin
Festival: (415) 346-4561

San Francisco Jazz Festival:
(415) 864-5449

San Francisco Open Studios:
(415) 861-9838

NOVEMBER

Run to the Far Side: (415) 750-7142

San Francisco Bay Area Book Festival:
(415) 908-2833

DECEMBER

First Run

Ice skating rink at Justin Herman Plaza

San Francisco Ballet *Nutcracker*:
(415) 865-2000

Santa Claus parade

Union Square Christmas tree lighting

Numbers to Know

The phone book is always the best reference for phone numbers. But if you need an emergency number or important city number for, say, the phone company, then this quick reference guide will help.

CITY SERVICES

Pacific Bell Telephone
800-773-2355 (To order service)
800-848-8000 (To order directories)

World Wide Web:
http://www.pacbell.com

Pacific Gas and Electric (PG&E)
800-743-5000 (Customer service and 24-hour emergency assistance)

Viacom Cable
800-945-2288 (To order service and for billing questions)

Water Department
(415) 923-2400

GARBAGE AND SANITATION IN SAN FRANCISCO

Golden Gate Disposal
(415) 626-4000

Sunset Scavengers
(415) 330-1300

RECYCLING AND ENVIRON-MENTAL INFORMATION

Recycling Program Hotline
(415) 554-6193

NEWSPAPERS

San Francisco Chronicle
(morning daily newspaper)
(415) 777-7000

San Francisco Examiner
(afternoon daily newspaper)
(415) 777-7800

World Wide Web:
http://www.sfgate.com

EMERGENCY/SECURITY

POLICE
Emergency: 911

Non-emergency dispatch
(415) 553-0123

Central Station
766 Vallejo Street
(415) 553-1532

Ingleside Station
Balboa Park
(415) 553-1603

Mission Station
1240 Valencia Street
(415) 553-1544

Northern Station
1125 Fillmore Street
(415) 553-1563

Park Station
Stanyan and Waller Streets
(415) 753-7280

Potrero Station
2300 3rd Street
(415) 553-1021

Richmond Station
461 6th Avenue
(415) 553-1385

Southern Station
850 Bryant Street
(415) 553-1373

Taraval Station
2345 24th Avenue
(415) 553-1612

Tenderloin Task Force
1 Jones Street
(415) 557-6700

FIRE DEPARTMENT IN SAN FRANCISCO

Emergency: 911

Non-emergency: (415) 861-8020

HOSPITALS IN SAN FRANCISCO

California Pacific Medical Center
3700 California Street
(415) 387-8700
(415) 923-3333 (Emergency services)

Davies Medical Center
Castro and Duboce Streets
(415) 565-6000 (General information)

St. Francis Memorial Hospital
900 Hyde Street
(415) 353-6000

St. Luke's Hospital
Army and Valencia Streets
(415) 647-8600 (General information)

St. Mary's Medical Center
450 Stanyan Street
(415) 668-1000 (General information)

UCSF Medical Center
505 Parnassus Avenue
(415) 476-1000 (General information)
(415) 476-1037 (24-hour emergency service)

UCSF Mount Zion Medical Center
1600 Divisadero Street
(415) 567-6600 (General information)
(415) 885-7520 (24-hour emergency service)

MISCELLANEOUS EMERGENCY INFORMATION

American Red Cross: (415) 202-0600

Poison Control (24-hour service): 800-523-2222

San Francisco Health Department:
(415) 554-2500

TRANSPORTATION INFO

PARKING AND TRAFFIC DEPARTMENT IN SAN FRANCISCO

General parking information:
(415) 554-7275

Residential parking permits:
(415) 554-5000

Bicycle information: (415) 554-2351

Department of Motor Vehicles in San Francisco
1377 Fell Street
(415) 557-1179 (General information and appointments)

World Wide Web:
http://www.ca.gov/dmv/dmv.html

PUBLIC TRANSPORTATION

General travel information:
(510) 817-1717

World Wide Web: **http://server.berkeley.edu/transit/**

MUNI Bus
Information (routes, schedules, and Fast Pass outlets): (415) 673-6864 or 673-MUNI
Complaints: (415) 923-6164

BART (Bay Area Rapid Transit)
(415) 992-2278

Serves San Francisco, Daly City, Alameda, and Contra Costa counties

AC Transit (Alameda-Contra Costa Transit)
(510) 817-1717

Golden Gate Transit
(415) 332-6600

Provides local bus service and ferry service from Marin and Sonoma counties to San Francisco

CalTrain
800-660-4287

Train service runs between San Francisco and San Jose

Alameda-Oakland Ferry
(510) 522-3300

Daily commuter and excursion service between Alameda, Oakland, and San Francisco

Red & White Fleet
(415) 546-2815

Ferry service between Sausalito, Tiburon, and San Francisco

SamTrans
800-660-4287

Bus service to Daly City and Hayward BART stations, San Francisco International Airport, Southern Pacific Cal train stations, San Francisco Greyhound Depot, Stonestown Mall, and Santa Clara County Transit

TAXICAB SERVICE IN SAN FRANCISCO

De Soto: (415) 673-1505

Luxor: (415) 282-4141

Veterans: (415) 552-1300

Yellow Cab: (415) 626-2345

CAR RENTAL COMPANIES

Avis: 800-331-1212

Budget: 800-527-0700

Hertz: 800-654-3131

National: 800-227-7368

AIRPORT SHUTTLES

Marin Airporter: (415) 461-4222

SFO Airporter: (415) 495-8404

SuperShuttle: (415) 558-8500

AIRPORTS

San Francisco International (SFO):
(415) 761-0800

Oakland International Airport:
(510) 577-4000

CHAMBERS OF COMMERCE

Chamber of Commerce, Berkeley
1834 University Avenue
Berkeley, CA 94703
(510) 549-7000

Chamber of Commerce, Concord
2151 Salvio Street
Concord, CA 94520
(510) 685-1181

Chamber of Commerce, Daly City
244 92nd Street
Daly City, CA 94015
(415) 991-5101

Chamber of Commerce, Foster City
1125 East Hillsdale Boulevard, #116
Foster City, CA 94404
(415) 573-7600

Chamber of Commerce, Mill Valley
85 Throckmorton Avenue
Mill Valley, CA 94941
(415) 388-9700

Chamber of Commerce, Oakland
475 14th Street
Oakland, CA 94612
(510) 874-4800

Chamber of Commerce, San Francisco
465 California Street
San Francisco, CA 94104
(415) 392-4520

Chamber of Commerce, Palo Alto
325 Forest Avenue
Palo Alto, CA 94301
(415) 324-3121

Chamber of Commerce, Redwood City
1675 Broadway Street
Redwood City, CA 94063
(415) 364-1722

Chamber of Commerce, San Mateo
1730 South El Camino Real, #200
San Mateo, CA 94402
(415) 341-5679

Chamber of Commerce, San Rafael

818 Fifth Avenue
San Rafael, CA 94901
(415) 454-4163

Chamber of Commerce, Sausalito

333 Caledonia Street
Sausalito, CA 94965
(415) 332-0505

Chamber of Commerce, Tiburon

96 Main Street, #B
Tiburon, CA 94920
(415) 435-5633

Chamber of Commerce, Walnut Creek

1501 North Broadway Street, #110
Walnut Creek, CA 94596
(510) 934-2007

MISCELLANEOUS

Lawyer Referral Service

Sponsored by the San Francisco
Bar Association
(415) 764-1616

San Francisco Convention and Visitors Bureau

900 Market Street
San Francisco, CA 94102
(415) 391-2000
Business Office
201 3rd Street
San Francisco, CA 94103
(415) 974-6900
24-hour events recording:
(415) 391-2001

San Francisco Library

General information: (415) 557-4400

World Wide Web: http://sfpl.lib.ca.us/

General Information

Time: (415) 767-8900

Weather: (415) 936-1212

Highway road conditions:
(415) 557-3755

Local Government

CONTACTS

San Francisco Mayor's Office
(415) 554-6141

San Francisco City Hall General Information
(415) 554-4000

San Francisco Board of Supervisors
(415) 554-5184

Registrar of Voters (register to vote)
(415) 554-4398

World Wide Web: http://sf95.election.digital.com/

SAN FRANCISCO POLITICS

ELECTED OFFICIALS
All San Francisco city and county officials are elected to four-year terms. These elected officials are:

- Mayor
- Board of Supervisors
- Controller
- Treasurer
- Assessor

- Sheriff
- City Attorney
- Public Defender
- District Attorney
- Municipal Court
- Superior Court
- Chief Administrative Officer

To get an overall picture of what San Francisco city government looks like, the organization chart on pages 206–207 shows the different elected officials and departments they oversee.

CITY HALLS

Alameda City Hall
2250 Central Avenue
Alameda, CA 94501
(510) 748-4500

Berkeley City Hall
2180 Milvia Street
Berkeley, CA 94704
(510) 644-6480

Concord City Hall
1950 Parkside Drive
Concord, CA 94519
(510) 671-3000

Assessor | Controller | Sheriff | Treasurer | Mayor

Sheriff's Department

Tax Collector

Housing Authority Commission

Redevelopment Agency

Aging Commission | Airports Commission | Art Commission | Asian Art Commission

Building Inspection Commission | Civil Service Commission | Ethics Commission | Film & Video Arts Commission

Fire Commission | Health Commission | Health Services System Board | Human Rights Commission

Parking & Traffic Commission | Board of Permit Appeals | Planning Commission | Police Commission

Port Commission | Public Library Commission | Public Transportation Commission | Public Utilities Commission

Recreation & Park Commission | Relocation Appeals Board | Residential Rent Board | Retirement System Board

Small Business Commission | Social Services Commission | Southeast Community Commission | Commission on the Status of Women

Fine Arts Museums Board of Trustees* | War Memorial Board of Trustees

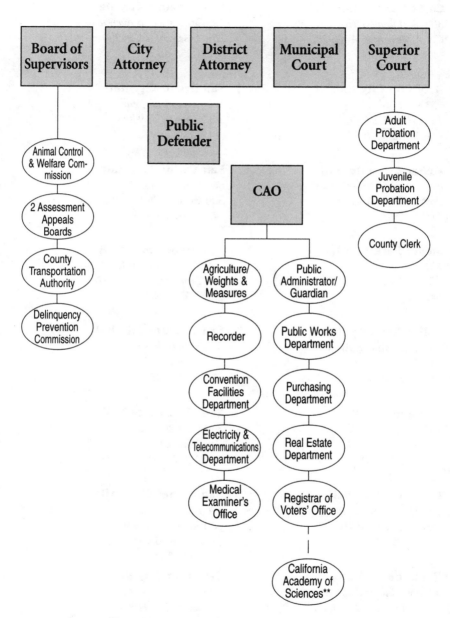

* The mayor is an ex-officio member of the Fine Arts Museums Board of Trustees. Board members are elected through a process of trustee nomination and election.

** The California Academy of Sciences ia a private institution. The CAO has jurisdiction only over city-related functions of the Academy.

Corte Madera City Hall
300 Tamalpais Drive
Corte Madera, CA 94926
(415) 927-5050

Daly City City Hall
333 90th Street
Daly City, CA 94015
(415) 991-8000

Foster City City Hall
610 Foster City Boulevard
Foster City, CA 94404
(415) 349-1200

Menlo Park City Hall
701 Laurel Street
Menlo Park, CA 94025
(415) 858-3380

Mill Valley City Hall
26 Corte Madera Avenue
Mill Valley, CA 94941
(415) 388-4033

Oakland City Hall
1 City Hall Plaza
Oakland, CA 94612
(510) 238-2130

Palo Alto City Hall
250 Hamilton Avenue
Palo Alto, CA 94301
(415) 329-2571

Redwood City City Hall
1020 Middlefield Road
Redwood City, CA 94063
(415) 780-7000

San Anselmo City Hall
525 San Anselmo Avenue
San Anselmo, CA 94960
(415) 258-4600

San Bruno City Hall
567 El Camino Real
San Bruno, CA 94066
(415) 877-8897

San Carlos City Hall
666 Elm Street
San Carlos, CA 94070
(415) 593-8011

San Francisco City Hall
400 Van Ness Avenue
San Francisco, CA 94102
(415) 554-4000

San Leandro City Hall
835 East 14th Street
San Leandro, CA 94577
(510) 577-3351

San Mateo City Hall
330 West 20th Avenue
San Mateo, CA 94403
(415) 377-3300

San Rafael City Hall
1400 5th Avenue
San Rafael, CA 94901
(415) 485-3066

Sausalito City Hall
420 Litho Street
Sausalito, CA 94965
(415) 289-4100

Tiburon City Hall
1155 Tiburon Boulevard
Tiburon, CA 94920
(415) 435-0956

Walnut Creek City Hall
1666 North Main Street
Walnut Creek, CA 94596
(510) 943-5800

WORLD WIDE WEB RESOURCES

Access to Bay Area Governments (ABAG) Online
(http://www.abag.ca.gov/)
is a public information service of the Association of Bay Area Governments.

CityWatch Cable Channel 54
(http://www.well.com/user/ctywatch/)
is CityWatch Cable Channel 54's home page of local government information, including city departments, board of supervisors, city notices, and more.

Information on Bay Area community government, including San Francisco and Oakland, can be found at http://www.hyperion.com/ba/cities.html

Schools

There are approximately 105 K–12 public schools in San Francisco along with 36 private and parochial schools. Bay Area counties also have their share of elementary, middle, and high schools. The following is a listing of school resources for those new to the area.

PUBLIC SCHOOLS

ALAMEDA COUNTY

Alameda Unified School District
2200 Central Avenue
Alameda, CA 94501
(510) 748-4000

Albany Unified School District
904 Talbot Avenue
Berkeley, CA 94706
(510) 559-6500

Berkeley Unified School District
2134 M.L. King Jr. Way
Berkeley, CA 94704
(510) 644-6147

Castro Valley Unified School District
4400 Alma Ave.
CastroValley, CA 94546
(510) 537-3000

Dublin Unified School District
7471 Larkdale Avenue
Dublin, CA 94568
(510) 828-2551

Emeryville Unified School District
4727 San Pablo Avenue
Emeryville, CA 94608
(510) 655-6936

Fremont Unified School District
4210 Technology Drive
Fremont, CA 94538
(510) 657-2350

Hayward Unified School District
24411 Amador Street
Hayward, CA 94544
(510) 784-2600

Livermore Valley Joint Unified School District
685 E. Jack London Blvd.
Livermore, CA 94550
(510) 606-3200

New Haven Unified School District
34200 Alvarado Niles Road
Union City, CA 94587
(510) 471-1100

Newark Unified School District
5715 Musick Avenue
Newark, CA 94560
(510) 794-2141

Oakland Unified School District
1025 Second Avenue
Oakland, CA 94606
(510) 836-8100

**Pleasanton Unified
School District**
4665 Bernal Avenue
Pleasanton, CA 94566
(510) 462-5500

**San Leandro Unified
School District**
14735 Juniper Street
San Leandro, CA 94579
(510) 667-3536

**San Lorenzo Unified
School District**
15510 Usher Street
San Lorenzo, CA 94580
(510) 317-4600

CONTRA COSTA COUNTY

**Acalanes Union High
School District**
1212 Pleasant Hill Road
Lafayette, CA 94549
(510) 935-2800

**Antioch Unified
School District**
510 G Street
Antioch, CA 94509
(510) 706-4100

Brentwood Union School District
255 Guthrie Lane
Brentwood, CA 94513
(510) 634-1168

Moraga School District
1540 School Street
Moraga, CA 94556
(510) 376-5943

**Mt. Diablo Unified
School District**
1936 Carlotta Drive
Concord, CA 94519
(510) 682-8000

Orinda School District
8 Altarinda Road
Orinda, CA 94563
(510) 254-4901

Pittsburg Unified School District
2000 Railroad Avenue
Pittsburg, CA 94565
(510) 473-4000

**West Contra Costa Unified
School District**
1108 Bissell Avenue
Richmond, CA 94802
(510) 234-3825

**San Ramon Valley Unified
School District**
699 Old Orchard Drive
Danville, CA 94526
(510) 837-1511

Walnut Creek School District
960 Ygnacio Valley Road
Walnut Creek, CA 94596
(510) 944-6850

MARIN COUNTY

Bolinas-Stinson School District
Star Route
Bolinas, CA 94924
(415) 868-1603

Dixie School District
380 Nova Albion Way
San Rafael, CA 94903
(415) 492-3700

Kentfield School District
699 Sir Francis Drake
Kentfield, CA 94904
(415) 925-2230

Lagunitas Elementary School District
Sir Francis Drake Blvd.
P.O. Box 308
San Geronimo, CA 94963
(415) 488-9399

Larkspur School District
18 Magnolia Avenue
Larkspur, CA 94939
(415) 927-6960

Mill Valley Elementary School District
411 Sycamore Avenue
Mill Valley, CA 94941
(415) 389-7700

Nicasio Elementary School District
5555 Nicasio Valley Road
Nicasio, CA 94946
(415) 662-2184

Novato Unified School District
1015 Seventh Street
Novato,CA 94945
(415) 897-4201

Reed Union School District
105-A Avenida Miraflores
Tiburon, CA 94920
(415) 435-7844

Ross School District
Lagunitas & Allen Avenue
Ross, CA 94957
(415) 457-2705

Ross Valley School District
46 Green Valley Court
San Anselmo, 94960
(415) 454-2162

San Rafael School District
225 Woodland Avenue
San Rafael, CA 94901
(415) 485-2300

Sausalito School District
630 Nevada Street
Sausalito, CA 94965
(415) 332-3190

Tamalpais Union High School District
395 Doherty Drive
Larkspur, CA 94939
(415) 945-3737

SAN FRANCISCO COUNTY

San Francisco Unified School District
135 Van Ness Avenue
San Francisco, CA 94102
(415) 241-6000

SAN MATEO COUNTY

Bayshore School District
1 Martin Street
Daly City, CA 94014
(415) 467-5444

Belmont School District
2960 Hallmark Drive
Belmont, CA 94002
(415) 593-8203

Brisbane School District
1 Solano Street
Brisbane, CA 94005
(415) 467-0550

Burlingame School District
2303 Trousedale Drive
Burlingame, CA 94010
(415) 259-3800

Cabrillo Unified School District
498 Kelly Avenue
Half Moon Bay, CA 94019
(415) 712-7100

Hillsborough School District
300 El Cerrito Avenue
Hillsborough, CA 94010
(415) 342-5193

Jefferson Elementary School District
101 Lincoln Avenue
Daly City, CA 94015
(415) 991-1000

Jefferson Union High School District
699 Serramonte Boulevard
Daly City, CA 94015
(415) 756-0300

La Honda-Pescadero Unified School District
620 North Street
Pescadero, CA 94060
(415) 879-0286

Laguna Salada School District
375 Reina Del Mar
Pacifica, CA 94044
(415) 359-1641

La Lomitas School District
1011 Altschul Avenue
Menlo Park, CA 94025
(415) 854-2880

Menlo Park City School District
181 Encinal Avenue
Atherton, CA 94027
(415) 321-7140

Millbrae School District
555 Richmond Drive
Millbrae, CA 94030
(415) 697-5694

Portola Valley School District
4575 Alpine Road
Portola Valley, CA 94028
(415) 851-1777

Ravenswood City School District
2160 Euclid Avenue
East Palo Alto, CA 94303
(415) 329-2800

Redwood City School District
815 Allerton Street
Redwood City, CA 94063
(415) 365-1550

San Bruno Park School District
500 Acacia Avenue
San Bruno, CA 94066
(415) 244-0133

San Carlos School District
826 Chestnut Street
San Carlos, CA 94070
(415) 508-7333

San Mateo/Foster City School District
300 West 28th Avenue
San Mateo, CA 94402
(415) 312-7700

San Mateo Union High School District
650 North Delaware Street
San Mateo, CA 94401
(415) 348-8834

Sequoia Union High School District
480 James Avenue
Redwood City, CA 94062
(415) 369-1411

South San Francisco Unified School District
398 B Street
South San Francisco, CA 94080
(415) 877-8700

Woodside School District
3195 Woodside Road
Woodside, CA 94062
(415) 851-1571

NONPUBLIC SCHOOLS

The following is resource information for those interested in private and Catholic schools:

California Department of Education
P.O. Box 271
Sacramento, CA, 95812
(800) 995-4099

They have a Bay Area private school directory for sale for $17.50 plus tax and $4.95 shipping. This directory is also available at public libraries.

Archdiocese of San Francisco
Office of Catholic Schools
443 Church Street
San Francisco, CA 94114
(415) 565-3660

The Archdiocese of San Francisco Office of Catholic Schools has information about Catholic schools in the San Francisco, Marin, and San Mateo counties.

Archdiocese of Oakland
Office of Catholic Schools
2900 Lakeshore Avenue
Oakland, CA 94610
(510) 893-4711

The Archdiocese of Oakland Office of Catholic Schools has information about Catholic schools in Alameda and Contra Costa counties.

WORLD WIDE WEB RESOURCES

Bay Area School Districts
(www.abag.ca.gov/abag/local_gov/schools.html)
A partial list of web sites for Bay Area schools.

AC Transit (Alameda-Contra Costa Transit), 201. *See also* transportation

activities. *See* balls/parties; fairs/festivals; free things to do; museums; music; parades; weekend activities

African-American influence. *See* Western Addition

age. *See* demographics; *various neighborhoods: statistics*

airports/shuttles, telephone numbers, 202

Alameda County, xiv, 120
   Alameda-Oakland ferry, 201
   City Hall, 205
   rental guide, 42
   School Districts, 211–212
   Volunteer Center, 173

Alcatraz Island, 186

Alumnae Resources, 141–142

American Conservatory Theater (A.C.T.)
   Act 1, social organization, 163
   season opening, 196

American Red Cross, 170

amusement parks. *See* Great America

Angel Island State Park, 186

Animation, Festival of, 195.
   See also film

apartment, setting up costs, 4

apartments and housing, xvi, 17–38.
   See also various neighborhoods: statistics
   apartment/roommate finding agencies, 43–46
   Apartments for Rent, 42
   Bay Area Rental Guide, 36
   budget-minded options, 17, 33–36

comparison chart, short-term housing, 37

furnished apartments, 17–23

methods of searching, 42–43

questions to ask landlord, 49

questions to ask yourself, 41–42

real estate/property management companies, 46–48

residence hotels, 23–32

short-term housing, 17–38

tenant rights/*California Tenants, Your Rights and Responsibilities,* 49

tips on apartment hunting, 48–49

University of San Francisco (USF), (summer only), 35–36

what you will need with you, 48–49

WWW resources, 36, 38, 50

YMCA, 35

youth hostels, 33–35

Art, Academy of, 56, 173–174

arts. *See also* cultural and social organizations; free things to do: museums

Art Direct San Francisco Home Page (WWW site), 194

Arts Council, Junior, 166

modern art, Contemporary Extension club, 165

San Francisco Open Studios, 196

Sausalito Arts Festival, 196

Asian Art Museum, 14, 177

attractions
   Bay Area Places to See Guide (WWW site), 194
   most visited sites, 189
   outside of San Francisco, 189–194
   recommended reading, 193

auto. *See* car; car repair; parking

bakeries. *See various neighborhoods: resources*

ballet, xvi. *See also* dance
   Encore!, San Francisco Ballet social organization, 164
   Nutcracker, 197
   season opening, 195

balls/parties. *See also* fairs/festivals; free things to do; music; parades; special events
   Black and White Ball, 196
   Exotic Erotic Halloween Ball, 196

BAMMIES (Bay Area Music Awards), 195

banks. *See various neighborhoods: resources*

barber shops. *See various neighborhoods: resources*

bargains. *See* free things to do

BART (Bay Area Rapid Transit), 201. *See also* transportation

baseball. *See* Giants, San Francisco

basketball. *See* health and fitness: sports clubs

Bay to Breakers race, 195

Bayview, 52

Berkeley, 120
   Chamber of Commerce, 202
   City Hall, 205
   Convention and Visitors Bureau, 189–190

Bernal Heights, 52, 53–56
   resources, 53–55
   statistics, 55–56

bicycling/mountain biking. *See also* health and fitness: bicycling clubs
   California First Mile Bike Challenge, 196
   recommended reading, 193

books and bookstores. *See various neighborhoods: resources*

book readings, 182–183

San Francisco Bay Area Book Festival, 197

Buena Vista Park, 63

Burlingame, 121

bus lines. *See various neighborhoods*

cable cars
   bell ringing championship, 196
   Cable Car Museum, 177

calendar of events, year-round, 195–197

California Department of Food and Agriculture, 10

CalTrain, 201. *See also* transportation

camping. *See also* parks
   recommended reading, 193

Cannery, The, 185–186

car. *See also* car repair; parking; transportation
   car rental companies, telephone numbers, 202
   Department of Motor Vehicles (DMV), telephone number, 201
   registration, 4

car repair. *See various neighborhoods: resources*

Career Action Center, 142

Carmel, 190

Castro. *See* Upper Market/Eureka Valley

central San Francisco, 52

Chamber of Commerce, San Francisco, 166, 202

Chamber of Commerce Job Forum, 142–143

Chambers of Commerce, address and telephone, 202–203. *See also* tourist bureaus

Chinese heritage
   Autumn Moon Festival in Chinatown, 196
   Chinese Historical Society Museum, 177
   Chinese New Year celebration, 195

Christmas tree lighting, Union
    Square, 197
churches. *See various neighborhoods:
    resources*
City Club of San Francisco, social
    organization, 164–165
city halls, address and telephone, 205,
    208–209
city services, telephone numbers, 199
Civic Center. *See* Downtown/Union
    Square/Civic Center
cleaners/laundromats. *See various
    neighborhoods: resources*
Coit Tower, 186
Cole Valley. *See* Haight-Ashbury/
    Cole Valley
comedy
    clubs, 189
    Comedy in the Park, 182
    Comedy Celebration Day, 196
Commonwealth Club, public affairs
    forum, 165
community organizations. *See various
    neighborhoods: resources*
Concord, 120–121
    Chamber of Commerce, 202
    City Hall, 205
Contra Costa County, xiv, 120–121
    School Districts, 212
    Volunteer Center, 173
Convention and Visitors Bureau, San
    Francisco, 181, 203
cooking. *See* education/classes
copy shops. *See various neighborhoods:
    resources*
Corte Madera, City Hall, 208
Craft and Folk Art Museum,
    San Francisco, 178
credit reporting agencies, 9, 48
crime, 52–53. *See also various
    neighborhoods: statistics*
Crocker Amazon, 52

cultural and social organizations,
    163–168. *See also* singles activities;
    volunteer opportunities

Daly City
    Chamber of Commerce, 202
    City Hall, 208
dance. *See also* ballet
    Center for the Arts Theater, 177,
        183, 189
    Cowell Theater, 184
    Marines Memorial Theater, 184
    War Memorial Opera House, 184
demographics. See *UPCLOSE San
    Francisco Bay Area 1991; various
    neighborhoods: statistics*
Department of Motor Vehicles (DMV),
    telephone number, 201
De Young Museum, 178, 187
Downtown/Union Square/Civic
    Center, 52, 56–60
    resources, 58–60
    statistics, 60

East Bay, 120–121
education/classes, 173–176
    Academy of Art, 56, 173–174
    Berkeley Extension, 174
    City College, 174
    Culinary Academy, 174
    Golden Gate University, 174–175
    HomeChef Cooking School, 175
    Learning Annex, 175
    Media Alliance, 175
    San Francisco Conservatory of Music
        Extension, 175–176
    San Francisco State University, 52, 176
Embarcadero
    waterfront, xiii
    shopping, 188
emergency, miscellaneous, telephone
    numbers, 199–201

employment. *See also* job hunting
  Alumnae Resources, 141–142
  Career Action Center, 142
  Chamber of Commerce Job Forum,
    142–143
  executive recruiters, 135–136
  International Association of Business
    Communicators (IABC), 143
  job lines, various companies, 136–141
  LifePlan Center, 143–144
  Local Talk, phone company tips
    (temping), 133
  Media Alliance, 143–144
  National Writers Union, 144–145
  *1995 Book of Lists, San Francisco
    Business Times,* 128, 135
  nonprofit agencies, career
    development, 141–145
  personnel agencies, xvi, 128–133
  recommended reading, 145
  specialized temporary employment
    agencies, 132–133
  temporary job wages, 127
  temporary, 125–128
  Women in Communications, Inc.
    (WICI), 145
  WWW resources, 146–147
Enterprise for High School
  Students, 170
ethnicity. *See* demographics; *various
  neighborhoods: statistics*
Excelsior, 52
extension courses. *See* education/classes

Fairmont Hotel, 78
fairs/festivals. *See also* balls/parties;
  music; parades; special events
  Autumn Moon Festival in
    Chinatown, 196
  Carnaval, 182, 195
  Cherry Blossom Festival, 195
  Chinese New Year celebration, 195

Cinco de Mayo, 195
Columbus Day parade, 196
Comedy Celebration Day, 196
Festa Italiana Food and Culture, 196
  Festival of Animation, 195
Festival of the Sea, 196
Fillmore Festival, 182
Fleet Week, 196
Folsom Street Fair, 196
Fourth of July Waterfront Festival, 196
Great Halloween and Pumpkin
  Festival, 196
Great Outdoors Adventure Fair *(San
  Francisco Chronicle),* 195
Haight Street Fair, 182, 195
Jazz and All That Art on Fillmore, 196
KQED International Beer and Food
  Festival, 196
Lesbian and Gay Freedom Day
  Parade, 195
MacWorld Expo, 195
North Beach Fair, 181, 195
San Francisco Bay Area Book
  Festival, 197
San Francisco Blues Festival, 196
San Francisco Jazz Festival, 196
San Francisco Fair and International
  Expo, 196
Sausalito Arts Festival, 196
Shakespeare Festival, 182
Union Street Festival, 182, 195
ferry service(s), 201
film. *See also* Animation, Festival of
  Film Arts Foundation, 165
  Film Festival, San Francisco
    International, 195
fire department, telephone number, 200
Fisherman's Wharf, 185–186
football. *See* 49ers, San Francisco
Fort Mason, 71
  Fort Mason Center Museums, 178
  Marina Green, 71

49ers, San Francisco,
  season opening, 196
  WWW site, 188
Foster City, 121
  Chamber of Commerce, 202
  City Hall, 208
free things to do, 177–184. *See also*
  weekend activities
  African-American Historical and
    Cultural Society, 178
  Asian Art Museum, 177
  Cable Car Museum, 177
  California Academy of Sciences, 177
  Carnaval, 182, 195
  Center for the Arts, 177, 183–184, 189
  Chinese Historical Society
    Museum, 177
  Craft and Folk Art Museum, SF, 178
  De Young Museum (art), 178, 187
  Exploratorium (science), 178
  Federal Reserve Bank, 178
  Fort Mason Center Museums, 178
  free concerts, 179–180
  free entertainment (fairs/festivals),
    181–182
  free literary events, 182–183
  free theater, 183–184
  free tours (park/neighborhood),
    180–181
  Jewish Museum, 178
  Maritime National Historical Park
    Museum, SF, 179
  Mexican Museum, 178
  Museé Mechanique, 178
  Museo ItaloAmericano, 178
  Museum of Modern Art, SF, 179, 187
  Museum of the City of San
    Francisco, 178
  Palace of the Legion of Honor
    (art), 179
  Public Library, San Francisco, 56, 179
  Shakespeare in the Park, 196
  Wells Fargo Historical Museum, 179
  Zoo, San Francisco, 179, 187–188
Friends of the Urban Forest, 170–171

garbage/sanitation, telephone
  numbers, 199
gay communities, 102, 112. *See also*
  Upper Market/Eureka Valley;
  Women's Building, The
  gay newspaper, 115
  Lesbian and Gay Freedom Day
    Parade, 195
Ghirardelli Square, 185–186
Giants, San Francisco
  season opening, 195
  WWW site, 188
Glen Park, 52, 60–63
  resources, 61–63
  statistics, 63
Golden Gate Park, 52, 63
  free tours and activities, 180–181
  phone numbers/WWW site, 187
Golden Gate Transit, 201. *See also*
  transportation
golf. *See* health and fitness: sports clubs
Grace Cathedral, 78
Great America, 191
gyms. *See* health and fitness
Haight-Ashbury/Cole Valley, 52, 63–67
  Haight Street Fair, 182, 195
  resources, 64–66
  statistics, 67
hairdressing. *See also various*
  neighborhoods: resources
  free cuts, 184
Hands On San Francisco, volunteer
  organization, 170
hardware stores. *See various*
  neighborhoods: resources
health and fitness, 151–162
  bicycling clubs, 159–161
  health clubs in San Francisco, 152–155

health and fitness *(continued)*
  health clubs outside San Francisco,
    155–156
  Masters Swimming, 159
  running clubs, 161–163
  sports clubs, 156–159
health clubs. *See various neighborhoods:*
  resources
highway road conditions (phone
  number for), 203
hiking. *See also* parks
  recommended reading, 193
Hispanic/Spanish influence and
  heritage. *See also* Mission District
  Carnaval, 182, 195
  Cinco de Mayo, 195
hospitals, telephone numbers, 200
housing. *See* apartments and housing

ice skating rink, Justin Herman
  Plaza, 197
International Association of Business
  Communicators (IABC), 143
Italian influence and heritage. *See also*
  North Beach/Telegraph Hill
  Festa Italiana Food and Culture, 196

Japanese influence. *See* Western
  Addition
Jewish heritage
  Jewish Community Federation, 168
  Jewish Museum, 178
job hunting. *See also* employment;
  World Wide Web (WWW)
  resources
  Job Forum, Chamber of Commerce,
    142–143
  job hot lines, various companies,
    136–141
Lafayette Orinda Presbyterian Church
  singles club, 168
Lake Merced, 52, 67

Lake Tahoe, Visitors Bureau, 191
Lakeshore, 52, 67–70
  resources, 67–70
  statistics, 70
Larkspur, 119
Lawyer Referral Service, 203
Lesbian and Gay Freedom Day Parade,
  195. *See also* gay communities
libraries. *See various neighborhoods:*
  resources
Library (Public), San Francisco, xvi, 56,
  179, 203
LifePlan Center, 143–144
Lindsay Museum (wildlife), 191
Little Brothers/Friends of the
  Elderly, 171
live/work areas. *See* SoMa (south of
  Market) area
living expenses, daily, 5
Local Talk, phone company tips, 15, 133
Louise Davies Symphony Hall, 56, 184

mail services. *See* post office; *various
  neighborhoods: resources*
Marin County, xiv, 119–120
  Marin Headlands, 191
  School Districts, 213
  Volunteer Center, 173
Marina, 51, 71–74
  Marina Green, 71
  resources, 72–74
  statistics, 74
Marine World Africa USA, 191
maritime sites/events, historical
  Fleet Week, 196
  Maritime National Historical Park
    Museum, 179
  Maritime Park, San Francisco,
    171–172
Market Street. See SoMa (south of
  Market) area; Upper Market/
  Eureka Valley

massage. *See* health and fitness
Media Alliance, 144
meeting people. *See* cultural and social
    organizations; singles activities
Menlo Park, 121–122
    City Hall, 208
Mexican Museum, 178
military sites, historical
    Marin Headlands, 191
    Presidio, The, 186–187
Mill Valley, 119
    Chamber of Commerce, 202
    City Hall, 208
Mission District, 52, 74–77
    resources, 76–77
    statistics, 77
Mission Dolores, 186
money-saving tips, 5–6. *See also* costs
    ways to obtain quick cash, 5–6
Mono Lake, 192
Monterey, 190
Mount Davidson/Diamond Heights, 52
Mount Diablo State Park, 192
Mount Tamalpais, 181
        Interpretive Association weekend
        hikes, 192
movie theaters. *See also various*
    neighborhoods: resources
    WWW resources, 188
moving
    costs of, 3–7
    planning for, 9–15
    WWW resources, 7, 15
Muir Woods, 192
MUNI bus system, 201. *See also*
    transportation
museums, 177–179, 187. *See also* free
    things to do *and individual listings*
    Asian Art Museum, xiv, 177
    Cable Car Museum, 177
    Chinese Historical Society
        Museum, 177

Craft and Folk Art Museum, SF, 178
De Young Museum (art), 178, 187
Fort Mason Center Museums, 178
Jewish Museum, 178
Lindsay Museum (wildlife), 191
Maritime National Historical Park
    Museum, SF, 179
Mexican Museum, 178
Museé Mechanique, 178
Museo ItaloAmericano, 178
Museum of Modern Art, San
    Francisco, xiii, xvi, 179, 187
Museum of the City of San
    Francisco, 178
Palace of the Legion of Honor (art),
    xvi, 179
Wells Fargo Historical Museum, 179
music, xvi. *See also* BAMMIES (Bay
    Area Music Awards); free things to
    do: free concerts; opera; symphony
Jazz and All That Art on Fillmore
    Street Festival, 196
San Francisco Blues Festival, 196
San Francisco Jazz Festival, 196
San Francisco Music Day, 195
Stern Grove concerts, 195

Napa County, xiv
Napa Valley, Conference and Visitors
    Bureau, 193
National Writers Union, 144–145
neighborhoods, xvi
    Bernal Heights, 53–56
    Downtown/Union Square/Civic
        Center, 56–60
    Glen Park, 60–67
    Haight-Ashbury/Cole Valley, 63–67
    Lakeshore, 67–70
    Marina, 71–74
    Mission District, 74–77
    Nob Hill, 78–81
    Noe Valley, 81–84

neighborhoods (continued)
  North Beach/Telegraph Hill, 84–87
  Pacific Heights/Lower Pacific
    Heights, 87–92
  Portrero Hill, 92–94
  Presidio Heights/Laurel Heights,
    95–97
  Richmond District, 98–102
  Russian Hill, 102–105
  South of Market, xiii, 106–109
  Sunset (Inner), 109–112
  Upper Market/Eureka Valley, 112
newspapers. See also various
    neighborhoods: statistics (for local
    newspapers)
  San Francisco Chronicle and San
    Francisco Examiner, 9, 199
  WWW resources, 7, 15, 146–147
Nob Hill, 52, 78–81
  resources, 79–80
  statistics, 80–81
Noe Valley, 52, 81–84
  resources, 81–84
  statistics, 84
nonprofit organizations, xvi
  Alumnae Resources, 141
  American Red Cross, 170
  Career Action Center, 142
  Enterprise for High School
    Students, 170
  Friends of the Urban Forest, 170–171
  Hands On San Francisco, 170
  LifePlan Center, 143–144
  Little Brothers/Friends of the
    Elderly, 171
  Media Alliance, 144
  Project Open Hand, 171
  Raphael House, 171
  San Francisco Maritime Park,
    171–172
  San Francisco Street Project, 172
  San Francisco Volunteer Center, 172
  Society for the Prevention of Cruelty
    to Animals (SPCA), 172
  volunteer centers (by county), 173
North Bay, 119–120
North Beach/Telegraph Hill, 52, 84–87
  North Beach Fair, 181, 195
  resources, 85–87
  statistics, 87
northern San Francisco, 51–52

Oakland, 120
  Chamber of Commerce, 202
  City Hall, 208
  Oakland-Alameda ferry service, 201
Ocean View, 52
office supplies. See various
    neighborhoods: resources
Opening Day on the Bay, 195
opera, xvi See also music
  Bravo!, San Francisco Opera social
    organization, 164
  Opera in the Park, 196
  season opening, 196

Pacific Bell, telephone company, 199
Pacific Gas and Electric (PG&E), 199
Pacific Heights/Lower Pacific Heights,
    52, 87–92
  resources, 88–92
  statistics, 92
packing tips, 11–12
Palo Alto
  Chamber of Commerce, 202
  City Hall, 208
Panhandle, 63
parades. See also balls/parties; fairs/
    festivals; free things to do; special
    events
  Columbus Day parade, 196
  Lesbian and Gay Freedom Day
    Parade, 195
  Santa Claus parade, 197

St. Patrick's Day Parade, 195
parking, 53. *See also the individual neighborhoods: resources*
parks. *See also various neighborhoods: resources*
  Angel Island State Park, 186
  Buena Vista Park, 63
  free tours (park/neighborhood), 180–181
  Golden Gate Park, 52, 63, 180–181, 187
  Harding Park, 67
  Maritime Park, 171–172
  Mono Lake, 192
  Mount Diablo State Park, 192
  Mount Tamalpais State Park, 192
  Muir Woods, 192
  Presidio, The, xiii, 186–187
  recommended reading, 193
  Tilden Park, 193
  Yosemite National Park, 193–194
Parkside, 52
Peninsula, 121–122
pharmacies. *See various neighborhoods: resources*
photocopying. *See* copy shops
Pier 39, 185–186
pizza. *See various neighborhoods: resources*
plants, 10, 12
poison control, telephone number, 200
police, telephone numbers, 199–200
Portrero Hill, 52, 92–94
  resources, 92–94
  statistics, 94
post office. *See also various neighborhoods: resources*
P.O. Box application, 10
Presidio, The, xiii, 186–187. *See also* parks
Presidio Heights/Laurel Heights, 52, 95–97

Presidio, The, xiii, 186–187
  resources, 96–97
  statistics, 97
Project Open Hand, 171

races, 162, 195–197. *See also* health and fitness
  Bay to Breakers race, 195
  San Francisco Marathon, 196
Raging Waters, 192
Raphael House, 171
rates, employment (hourly), 127
real estate/property management companies, 46–48. *See also various neighborhoods: resources*
recreation centers. *See various neighborhoods: resources*
recycling, telephone number, 199
Redwood City, 122
  Chamber of Commerce, 202
  City Hall, 208
references needed for apartment hunting, 48–49
renting vs. owning. *See* demographics; *various neighborhoods: statistics*
Richmond District, 52, 98–102
  resources, 98–102
  statistics, 102
running. *See* health and fitness: running clubs
Russian Hill, 52, 102–105
  resources, 103–105
  statistics, 105

Sacramento, Convention and Visitors Bureau, 190
sailing. *See* health and fitness: sports clubs
SamTrans, 201. *See also* transportation
San Anselmo, City Hall, 208
San Bruno, City Hall, 208
San Carlos, City Hall, 208

San Francisco, basic areas, 52
  county, xiv
  school districts, 213
  volunteer centers, 172
San Francisco Chronicle. See
  newspapers
San Francisco city timeline, xiii–xix
San Francisco discovery, xvi
San Francisco Hillstride, 196
San Francisco, local government
  Board of Supervisors, 205
  City Hall, general info, 205, 208–209
  elected officials, 205
  Mayor's office, 205
  organization charts, 206–207
  Voters Registrar, 205
  WWW resources, 209
San Francisco, Museum of the City
  of, 178
San Francisco Museum of Modern Art,
  xiii, xvi, 179, 187
San Francisco State University, 52, 176
San Francisco statistics, xiv–xv
San Francisco Street Project, 172
San Francisco Unified School
  District, 213
San Francisco Volunteer Center, 172
San Leandro, City Hall, 208
San Mateo County, 14, 121–122
  Chamber of Commerce, 202
  City Hall, 208
  rental guide, 42
  Volunteer Center, 173
San Rafael, 119
  Chamber of Commerce, 203
  City Hall, 208
Santa Clara County, xiv
  rental guide, 42
Santa Cruz, Convention and Visitors
  Bureau, 190–191
Sausalito, 119
  Chamber of Commerce, 191, 203

City Hall, 208
  ferry service, 201
  Sausalito Arts Festival, 196
Scholastics, school volunteers, 166
schools
  nonpublic schools, 215
  public schools, 211–216
  WWW resources, 216
sex. *See* demographics; *various*
  neighboods: resources
shoe repair. *See various neighborhoods:*
  resources
shopping centers, 188–189
  Embarcadero, 188
  factory outlets, south of Market, 188
  San Francisco Shopping Center, 188
  Stanford, 190
  Stonestown Galleria, 67
short-term housing. *See* apartments
  and housing
Sierra Club, and WWW site, 159
singles activities, 168–169.
  See also cultural and social
  organizations
Singles Supper Club, 169
skiing. *See* health and fitness: sports
  clubs; Yosemite National Park
social clubs, xvi, 163–168. *See also*
  singles activities
Society for the Prevention of Cruelty to
  Animals (SPCA), SF, 172
softball. *See* health and fitness:
  sports clubs
software, recommended programs for
  obtaining employment, 126, 128
SoMa (south of Market) area, xiii, 52,
  106–109
  resources, 106–108
  statistics, 108–109
Solano County, xiv
Sonoma County, xiv
Sonoma, Wine and Visitors Center, 193

south of Market. *See* SoMa (south of Market) area
southern San Francisco, 52
special events, year-round calendar, 195–197. *See also* balls/parties; fairs/festivals; free things to do; music; weekend activities
sports. *See* health and fitness
St. Patrick's Day Parade, 195
St. Vincent De Paul Young Adult Group, 169
Stanford Bachelors, 169
Stanford, Shopping Center and University, 190
Stinson Beach, 192–193
storage facilities. *See also* moving, costs of Bay Area companies, 12–15
Local Talk, phone company tips, 15
WWW info on, 7, 15
suburban areas, 118–122
Sunset District(s)/Inner Sunset, 52, 109–112
resources, 109–111
statistics, 112
supermarkets/groceries. *See various neighborhoods: resources*
swimming. *See* health and fitness: Masters Swimming *and* sports clubs
Symphony, San Francisco, xvi. *See also* opera
season opening, 196
Symphonix association, 167

taxi services, telephone numbers, 201–202
Telegraph Hill. *See* North Beach/Telegraph Hill
telephone numbers
airports/shuttles, 202
car rental companies, 202
central stations, 199–200
Chambers of Commerce, 202–203
city services, 199
Department of Motor Vehicles, 201
emergency, miscellaneous, 200–201
fire department, 200
garbage/sanitation, 199
hospitals, 200
miscellaneous, 203
newspapers, 199
Pacific Bell phone company, 199
Pacific Gas and Electric (PG&E), 199
poison control, 200
police stations, 199–200
recycling, 199
taxi services, 201–202
transportation info, 201
transportation public (bus and train), 201
Viacom Cable, 199
Water Department, 199
Tenderloin, 56
Tennis Matchmakers, 169
tennis. *See* health and fitness
theater. *See also* ballet; comedy; opera
American Conservatory Theater (A.C.T.) and Act 1, 163, 196
Center for the Arts Theater, 177, 183–184, 189
Club Fugazi, 189
Cowell Theater, 184
Curran Theater, 184, 189
free performances, 182
Geary Theater, 189
Golden Gate Theater, 184, 189
Herbst Theater, 56, 184
Magic Theater, 184
Marines Memorial Theater, 184, 189
Orpheum Theater, 184, 189
Shakespeare Festival, 196
Shakespeare in the Park, 182, 196
Theater on the Square, 184, 189
ushering, 183–184
WWW resources, 189

Tiburon, 119–120, 191
  Chamber of Commerce, 191, 203
  City Hall, 209
  ferry service, 201
Tilden Park, 193
time (phone number for), 203
Toastmasters International, 167
tourism
  international and U.S. visitors, 187
  most visited attractions, 189
  number of jobs supported by, 192
  spending, 186
  visitor profile, 188
tourist bureaus. *See also* Chambers of
    Commerce
  Berkeley Convention and Visitors
    Bureau, 189–190
  Lake Tahoe Visitors Bureau, 191
  Monterey County Visitors and
    Convention Bureau, 190
  Napa Valley Conference and Visitors
    Bureau, 193
  Sacramento Convention and Visitors
    Bureau, 190
  San Francisco Convention and
    Visitors Bureau, 181, 203
  Santa Cruz Convention and Visitors
    Bureau, 190–191
  Sonoma Wine and Visitor Center, 193
tours. *See* free things to do, free tours
transportation. *See also* car; parking;
    various neighborhoods (includes
    location, main street, and bus lines)
  information, telephone numbers, 201
  public (bus and train), telephone
    numbers, 201
triathlons, 157
  Escape from Alcatraz Triathlon, 196
Tuesdays at Six, 167
Tulipmania, 195
Twin Peaks, 52

Union Square. *See* Downtown/Union
    Square/Civic Center
  Christmas tree lighting, Union
    Square, 197
UPCLOSE San Francisco Bay Area
  1991, 52
Upper Market/Eureka Valley, 52,
    112–115
  Castro Street Fair, 196
  resources, 112–115
  statistics, 115

Viacom Cable, telephone numbers, 199
video rentals. *See various*
    neighborhoods: resources
Visitation Valley, 52
volleyball. *See* health and fitness:
    sports clubs
volunteer opportunities, 169–173. *See*
    also Scholastics, school volunteers;
    Tuesdays at Six
  Volunteer Center(s), by region,
    172–173
  WWW resources, 176

Walnut Creek, 121
  Chamber of Commerce, 203
  City Hall, 209
wardrobe, for job interviews, 126
Water Department, telephone
    number, 199
weather (phone number for), 203
weekend activities, 185–194
  around San Francisco, 185–189
  out of town, 189–194
  weekend escapes, recommended
    reading, 193
Wells Fargo Historical Museum, 179
Western Addition, 52, 116–118
  resources, 117–118
    statistics, 118

wildlife and natural history.
   See also parks
   Lindsay Museum (wildlife), 191
   Sierra Club, and WWW site, 159
windsurfing. *See* health and fitness:
   sports clubs
Wine Country, 193
Women in Communications, Inc.
   (WICI), 145
Women's Building, The, 74
work. *See* employment agencies; job
   hunting
World Affairs Council of Northern
   California, 167–168
World Wide Web (WWW) resources.
   See individual topics of interest
   apartment hunting, 36, 38
   art events, 194
   job hot lines, 136–141
   job hunting, 146–147

local government, 209
moving (estimate/sharing costs of), 7
places to see, 194
San Francisco WWW resources and
   information, xvii–xviii
short-term housing, 38
storage, 7, 15
theaters, 189
volunteer opportunities, 176
WWW. *See* World Wide Web (WWW)
   resources

Yerba Buena
   Gardens, xiii
   Center for the Arts, 177, 183–184, 189
Yosemite National Park, 193–194

Zoos
   Oakland, 192
   San Francisco, 179, 187–188

The Wealthy Barber,
Updated 2nd Edition

by David Chilton

U.S. $12.95

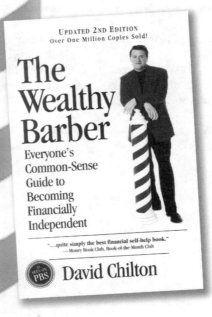

The Wealthy Barber is a fastpaced story set in Hometown, USA. Roy, a quiet, wealthy small-town barber, combines simple concepts, common sense, and an insight into human nature to reshape the shaggy financial affairs of his barbershop patrons. He does this not by badgering them about budgeting, but by throwing them practical, easy-to-implement guidelines that anyone can use.

Small Business Today Guide to Beating the Odds
by Hattie Bryant

U.S. $16.95
Can. $22.95

Based on the popular public television series, this timely book shows readers how to assess their strengths, decide on a business to start, find funding, and set up a business plan. Hattie Bryant is the producer of the successful public television series "Small Business 2000." She lives in Fort Worth, Texas.

The Twentysomething Guide to Creative Self-Employment
by Jeff Porten

U.S. $14.95
Can. $22.95

Ideal for college students, recent grads, and all those eager to build a career on their own terms, this book helps the young and potentially self-employed discover the best way to make a living without compromising themselves. Including step-by-step instructions for starting a successful new business, this book is tailored to meet the needs of the twentysomething crowd. Jeff Porten is the founder of Millennium Consulting, a firm specializing in the innovative use of the Internet, new media technologies, and Mac computers. He lives in Washington, D.C.

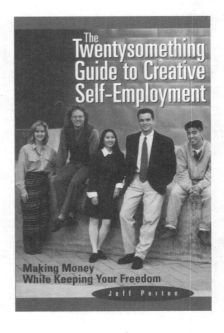

The Healing Mind

by Eileen F. Oster

U.S. $14.00
Can. $18.95

The strong connection between spiritual, physical, and mental health is widely acknowledged, but few books offer the kind of practical, reader-focused approach provided by Eileen Oster. Her book is designed to help people suffering from long-term illness or facing life-threatening diseases. With guided meditations, suggested prayer formats, and visualizations, *The Healing Mind* evolves into the perfect tool for readers hoping to explore the spirit-mind-body connection for overall health and well-being.

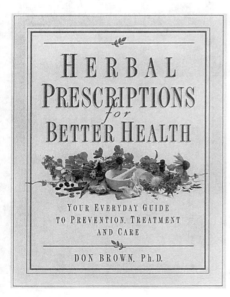

Herbal Prescriptions for Better Health

by Donald J. Brown

U.S. $22.95
Can. $29.95

Herbs such as aloe vera, cayenne, *dong quai,* feverfew, garlic, ginseng, goldenseal, hawthorn, and senna have been used for centuries to cure or control a wide range of medical conditions, but few people know exactly how to administer them. Comprehensive, easy to follow, and organized according to the medical diagnosis, this is a definite must-have book for your reference library.

Camping with Kids in California

by Bill McMillon

U.S. $15.00
Can. $19.95

In *Camping with Kids in California,* Bill McMillon has compiled a comprehensive resource of classic sites and off-the-beaten trail delights ideal for both avid campers and first-timers. Written by a family camping expert, this book covers campgrounds throughout the state and focuses on family-oriented features. Bill McMillon is the author of *Best Hikes with Children in the San Francisco Bay Area* and other books.

Natural Places of the Southwest & Natural Places of the Northwest

by Fraser Bridges

U.S. $17.95 each
Can. $24.95 each

The essential guides for all who love the outdoors, the *Natural Places* series invites thoughtful travelers to immerse themselves in the particular spirit of an extraordinary landscape. The resonance of a lush canyon or desert plateau come to life as Fraser Bridges describes the local history, native peoples, indigenous flora and fauna, and legends of a place. Fraser Bridges is a writer and broadcaster who has been exploring the small towns, national parks, and backroads of America for almost 35 years. He is also the author of Prima's *Road Trip Adventures* series.

To Order Books

Please send me the following items:

Quantity	Title	Unit Price	Total
_____	_____	$ _____	$ _____
_____	_____	$ _____	$ _____
_____	_____	$ _____	$ _____
_____	_____	$ _____	$ _____
_____	_____	$ _____	$ _____

Shipping and Handling depend on Subtotal.

Subtotal	Shipping/Handling
$0.00–$14.99	$3.00
$15.00–$29.99	$4.00
$30.00–$49.99	$6.00
$50.00–$99.99	$10.00
$100.00–$199.99	$13.50
$200.00+	Call for Quote

Foreign and all Priority Request orders:
Call Order Entry department
for price quote at 916/632-4400

This chart represents the total retail price of books only
(before applicable discounts are taken).

Subtotal $ _____
Deduct 10% when ordering 3-5 books $ _____
7.25% Sales Tax (CA only) $ _____
8.25% Sales Tax (TN only) $ _____
5.0% Sales Tax (MD and IN only) $ _____
Shipping and Handling* $ _____
Total Order $ _____

By Telephone: With MC or Visa, call 800-632-8676, 916-632-4400. Mon-Fri, 8:30-4:30.
WWW {http://www.primapublishing.com}

Orders Placed Via Internet E-mail {sales@primapub.com}
By Mail: Just fill out the information below and send with your remittance to:

**Prima Publishing
P.O. Box 1260BK
Rocklin, CA 95677**

My name is _____

I live at _____

City _____ State _____ Zip _____

MC/Visa# _____ Exp. _____

Check/Money Order enclosed for $ _____ Payable to Prima Publishing

Daytime Telephone _____

Signature _____